# Signs

## and

# WONDERS

## The Spectacular Marketing of America

*Also by Tama Starr*

The "Natural Inferiority" of Women:
Outrageous Pronouncements by Misguided Males

Eve's Revenge: Saints, Sinners, and Stand-up Sisters
on the Ultimate Extinction of Men

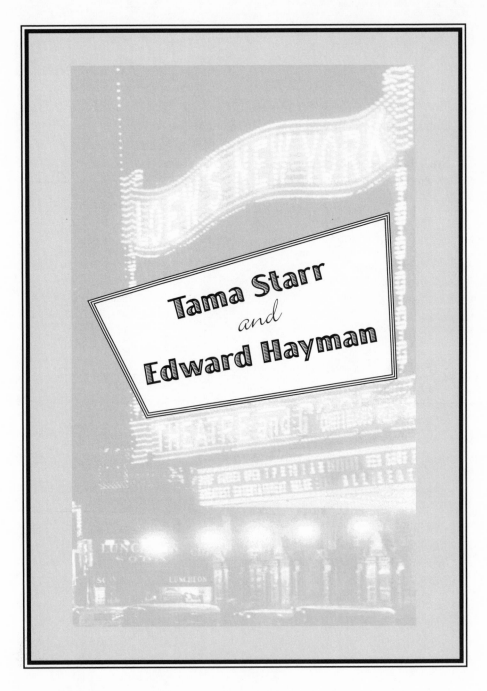

Tama Starr

*and*

Edward Hayman

new york london toronto
sydney auckland

# Signs and

# Wonders

A CURRENCY BOOK
PUBLISHED BY DOUBLEDAY
*a division of Bantam Doubleday Dell Publishing Group, Inc.*
*1540 Broadway, New York, New York 10036*

CURRENCY AND DOUBLEDAY *are trademarks of Doubleday, a division of Bantam Doubleday Dell Publishing Group, Inc.*

BOOK DESIGN BY TERRY KARYDES
PHOTO INSERT BY VERTIGO DESIGN

*Library of Congress Cataloging-in-Publication Data*
*Starr, Tama.*
*Signs and wonders : the spectacular marketing of America /*
*Tama Starr and Ed Hayman. — 1st ed.      p.      cm.*
*1. Outdoor advertising—United States—History—20th century.*
*2. Electric signs—United States—History—20th century.*
*3. Signs and signage—United States—History—20th century.*
*I. Hayman, Ed.      II. Title.      HF5843.S73   1998*
*659.13' 42' 0973—dc21            97-51466*      CIP

*ISBN 0-385-48602-2*

*Printed in the United States of America*

*May 1998*

*1   2   3   4   5   6   7   8   9   10*

FIRST EDITION

*For Jacob Starr*
*And All the Others Who Lit the Way*

# Contents

# List of Chapter-Opening Illustrations

*Acknowledgments*

This book, like a big electric sign, reflects the behind-the-scenes work of a small army of supporters.

At Artkraft Strauss, Bob Jackowitz read and commented on technical sections of the manuscript with the same meticulous attention he applies to the "Scope of Work" for a spectacular display. Bobby Dianuzzo provided an education into the mysteries of electricity. Tony Calvano, Al Miller, and chief of operations Jim Manfredi supplied engineering and construction details. And Gene Kornberg provided insights and memories.

Other sign companies across America generously provided help, information, and encouragement. These include AD-ART of California, Cummings of Tennessee, Everbrite of Wisconsin, Federal of Chicago, Heath of Texas, the Jim Pattison Sign Group of Canada, Nordquist of Minneapolis, YESCO of Salt Lake City and its chairman, Thomas Young, Jr.—and many others, including other members and directors, as well as staff, of the International Sign Association.

*Signs of the Times* magazine was an indispensable resource.

Additional information and historical insights were provided by sculptor and sign collector Gary Bates of Manhattan, Montana; structural engineer Eugene Avallone; neon historian and artist Rudi Stern; Lili Lakich, director of the Museum of Neon Art in Los Angeles; Philadelphia neon artist Len Davidson; author Charles F. Barnard, the nation's leading expert on Las Vegas sign history; Mrs. Florence Strauss Benedict, the daughter of Benjamin Strauss; Charles Portney; and Jonathan Starr.

At Doubleday, editor Harriet Rubin encouraged us with her vision and enthusiasm. Editor Frances Jones and publisher Michael Palgon saw the production through to completion. Senior book designer Terry Karydes and art director Calvin Chu, who designed the book's cover, completed the vision by creating the beautiful final product you now hold in your hand.

There is no product unless it's sold; and once again, tip-top literary agents Glen Hartley and Lynn Chu placed this book in its proper home.

Minda Novek and Lori Andreozzi deserve special mention. Minda combed archives throughout the Northeast, locating remarkable troves of rare and unpublished photographs and little-known facts and stories. Lori spent countless hours fact-checking at the library and on the Internet, and read through mountains of trade publications, locating gems.

Our gratitude is extended to all these people for all their help. Any errors of fact or interpretation, however, are our own.

— *Tama Starr and Edward Hayman*

O ur signs tell us who we are.

From Hollywood Boulevard to Glitter Gulch to the Chicago Loop to Times Square, the ever-changing commercial face of America is portrayed in gloriously illuminated spectacular signs.

These signs do more than advertise products, provide information, and identify locations. They dramatize America's self-image in messages with many layers of meaning. We are the biggest and the best, say our signs, and we are here to stay. And the seeming effortlessness and balletic precision with which our spectaculars operate suggest the confidence and sense of order we like to believe are the defining qualities of our national character.

Our imagination is boundless, say our signs. And our capacity to express that imagination is limited only by our technology at any given moment. From the earliest applications of movable type to the latest advances in computerized robotics, every new technique in the engineer's repertoire has been applied to advertising signs virtually from the moment of its invention. Long before electric light was put to domestic use, it was animating giant images in the cityscape.

But the great illuminated signatures are more than color and lights and images and technology. They are even more wondrous behind their surface than they are in front. Beyond their components—behind the metal and plastic and paint, the lamps, wiring, and tubing, the switches, connections, and relays—is their animating spirit. What a spectacular is *really* about is Image in the Landscape: myth, idea, presence, and context.

"We don't sell lightbulbs and metal and wires," one Lamplighter of Broadway used to say. "The customer can buy those at the hardware store. What he's buying here is a priceless piece of real estate: a place in people's dreams."

Every enterprise, however large or small, takes its stand in the landscape. Whether a sign says "Lemonade 5¢" in crayon on cardboard or "Suntory Whisky" in 25,000 animated golden lightbulbs, it tells the viewer not only about the product but about the product's provider as well.

Like a person, a company proclaims its self-image in the face it presents to the public. Whether a modest shop or a global corporation, its sign is its signature—as individual as handwriting.

Graphic representations of corporate character take innumerable forms. Some emblems—such as the giant neon cowboy Vegas Vic, welcoming pleasure-seekers to Las Vegas with a knowing wink and a jaunty jiggle of his cigarette—whimsically symbolize an entire culture. Some—the huge high-tech video screens and dazzling animated logos that shine down nightly on Times Square—are potent symbols of corporate presence. Others—such as the clusters of familiar trademarks that brand the exits of our superhighways, guiding us to sources of food and fuel and places to rest—are more utilitarian. All are integral parts of our environment, mechanical inventions that have personality and presence, hardware that embodies a life force.

Of all the landscape-sized statements a company can make, the commissioning of a spectacular display in Times Square is arguably the most powerful. It costs more than other displays, is seen by a worldwide audience, and symbolizes a commitment to the latest in technology. On many levels—artistic, financial, social, and technological—it is a company's expression of its place in history.

As an art form, Times Square spectaculars occupy a singular nexus between America's commercial life and its emotional life. In this brightly illuminated intersection we can read, in images writ large, the story of who we are as a people and where we have been—and even catch a glimpse of where we are going.

## What Is a Sign?

*A sign is not merely a slab* of wood, stone, or metal with symbols on it. It is a fundamental unit of intelligence.

Signs convey safety and information. Without signs and their counterparts, canopies and marquees, everybody would be standing around in the dark, in the rain, not knowing where to go or what to do. We would constantly be opening the wrong door.

Not only does a sign represent a reality, it also conveys a *feeling* about that reality. The familiar bright red octagon with its simple command in unadorned white letters not only tells us what to do at the intersection, it also conveys a sense of arrest.

Symbol making is the most characteristically human activity. It predates every other occupation. In Genesis, the first thing Man does—even before he is separated into male and female—is to "name the animals": that is, to attach symbols to them. Naming, or symbol making, is the only activity Adam engages in that the animals do not. Once he gives them names, they became constructs of his mind. He can tell stories about them, transform them into haute cuisine, paint pictures of them on his walls. Paleoanthropologists point to wall art, the earliest advertisements, as the origin of both art and writing, the fundamentals of civilization.

If symbol making goes back to the origin of history, the manufacture of light goes back to the origin of time.

Ancient scribes and modern cosmologists agree that the universe was once an anarchist's dream: chaos everywhere. Then, says the Bible, God "spoke," or, in scientific language, emitted a wave of electromagnetic radiation. And contained within that wave was—surprise!—Light. Then things could be distinguished from one another. Time existed. No wonder that, according to the Special Theory of Relativity, the speed of light, or light as a function of time, is an absolute, representing the maximum boundary of the physical universe.

No wonder either that people have always reacted positively to light embellished with the techniques of time: flashing, blinking, sequenced, rising, and fading. This is as true of our reaction to electric signs as it is of our reaction to dawn, lightning, and campfires. We respond to light because we are programmed to do so at the subatomic level. Every atom that we're made of, as Carl Sagan said, "was once part of the stars." We—or at least our atoms—were present at the Big Bang. And every charged particle oscillates in harmony with the light-containing proto-wave that created it. This is why plants are not the only beings that are phototropic. With few exceptions, mainly microbes, everything that lives turns toward light. We are all sunflowers at heart—a universe of photophiles.

## "But Is It Art?"

*Light has always been* a vital element in the arts because of the feelings it evokes and the meaning it brings. In the theater, the play begins when the house lights dim and the stage lights brighten, directing the audience's awareness to the reality outside themselves— a spectacle intended to transform them inwardly—that is about to be enacted behind the proscenium or upon the platform. The history of painting, especially since the Renaissance, can be seen as a continual reinterpretation of light and a re-viewing of how light defines the world. Architecture and sculpture, both of which define space, depend on the play between light and mass to evoke emotion. Photography, film, video, and even computer-generated graphics employ light almost directly, with only the slimmest of electrochemical intermediaries between the manipulated light and the viewer.

The taming of electricity at the end of the nineteenth century added direct light to the artist's repertoire. The new medium, with its switchability, also offered the rhythmic power of music, which uses the contrast of silence (darkness) to create mystery, texture, and depth. It was put to use almost immediately in the creation of giant, kinetic, commercially financed light sculptures: the same advertising spectaculars we see in the landscape today. And they evoked the same awe.

"Pity the sky with nothing but stars!" rhapsodized a European visitor to Times Square at the beginning of the twentieth century. If only the displays' messages were written in Sanskrit or Chinese, he observed, nobody would doubt their pure artistry.

Like other works of art, a successful display is ultimately "completed" in the mind of the viewer. Its dynamic, like that of radio or poetry, is in the interplay between the content and rhythm of the medium and the heart and imagination of the audience.

We bring a lot of ourselves to the 1936 Wrigley's classic atop the Bond building, depicting a cheery little figure in a boat surrounded by placid, multicolored fish calmly cruising the deep, blowing gentle neon bubbles in rainbow hues. This sign, with its illusion of an immense aquarium, was orchestrated to create a soothing, swaying fish cadence and a sense of the rhythmic, chewy contentment you will feel, just like the carefree little fellow in the boat, if only you will try a delicious, refreshing stick of Wrigley's gum.

A different illusion was created in 1995 by Morgan Stanley at its world headquarters at 1585 Broadway, where a half acre of glittering LED matrices transforms the entire building into a real-time information display. As complex and technologically sophisticated as this presentation is, its effect is simple. It makes you feel good by making you feel smart. The building seems to assume that you are capable of simultaneously processing financial news headlines, stock and bond price fluctuations, currency exchange rates, and the time in twenty-four time zones. And if not, it doesn't matter. It is information as pure kinesthetic experience. The world-beat visual rhythm of pulsing global commerce is pleasing and somehow comforting. Life goes on, the display seems to say. Macroeconomics is big, entertaining, inclusive, and bright enough to care for us all. And about its sponsor, whose name appears only in palely glowing eight-inch letters at the bottom, the display is subliminally saying "MORGAN STANLEY . . . IS . . . INFORMATION."

That something so large and imposing can do its work subliminally is not the only paradox the spectaculars employ.

As students of charisma understand, image can overpower reality—and even outlive it. Some of the great displays of the past continue to work their magic even after they are gone, and even after the companies sponsoring them are gone. The Corticelli Yarn Company has long been forgotten, but the Corticelli rooftop kitten of 1912 continues to frolic with its giant spool of lightbulb thread in the minds of people who have seen it—or have seen even a photo of it. The first neon sign in America, made in 1922 for a Los Angeles Packard dealership, still glows in myth and memory (and probably in someone's garage), long after the last Packard drove off into history. And people constantly claim to remember the famous "smoking" Camel sign who cannot possibly have seen it. That sign came down in 1966.

The peculiar perseverance of these images says as much about the way we perceive the world as it does about the medium itself. The displays that live on in our memories do so because of the way they "play" with us. They create a sense of wonder. They make us feel alive. We know we are alive, not because reasoning tells us so (after all, computers can reason), but because we have the capacity to *feel*. The impulse driving these memorable signs is the same as that behind Mount Rushmore or any other monumental totem. It expresses, larger than life, an essence, an emotion, a sense of being.

The art of the advertising spectacular makes myths come alive. Even today, the Anheuser-Busch neon eagle in flight—our national icon, the image of soaring power wrought in light, surreally large—invigorates and stirs us, touching the same heart in us that responds to music we love.

At the same time, by depicting everyday objects at many times normal size, the signs appeal to the child in us. We love to contemplate a steaming coffee cup bigger than six hot tubs, and savor the sight of the heroic Johnnie Walker, as tall as a skyscraper, striding endlessly across the night sky. In December of 1996, round-the-clock crowds gathered for three days in bone-chilling cold to cuddle up to a 102-foot replica of a Concorde jet while it was parked on Seventh Avenue, before it was hoisted onto the roof of a nearby building—just to feel the power and excitement of this giant toy. This peculiar combination of grandeur and whimsy has an undeniable, if ultimately inexplicable, magnetic attraction.

## GLOBAL IMAGES IN AMERICA'S TOWN SQUARE

*A commercial landscape,* like a newspaper's editorial page, is an expression of the way people think things ought to be. It embodies an ethic and a cultural ideal; it presents a worldview, a set of principles, a context in which novelty can be interpreted. This was as true in Maoist China, with its screaming red posters exhorting Communist obedience, as in medieval London, bedecked with the emblems of merchant guilds, the newly influential class.

Today, from metropolis to prairie, from the desert to the mountains, and from sea to sea, Americans of all ages and origins share a common commercial culture. And this culture—more than even the sum of its artifacts—is our largest global export.

Throughout the world, the McDonald's Arches, the red Coca-Cola logo, and the Marlboro Man are universally recognized symbols. Traveling off the beaten track? Take along some Levi's, Nikes, or Calvins to share with the locals, and make new friends. But don't try any off-brand substitutes. People know the difference. These globally sought-after products promise and deliver quality, variety, and immediate satisfaction. They symbolize the sense of confidence, optimism, and ease that defines American charisma. To acquire these products is to acquire the magnetism they represent.

The world depicted by advertising is a happy world, replete with joy and fulfillment. Everything is okay in the world of Donna Karan, Met Life, and Joe Camel. Everybody is beautiful, secure, and cool.

The point of advertising is not only to create desire but also to make you feel good about participating in something larger than yourself, a universe that, unlike the real world, is defined by satisfaction and contentment.

Times Square is a paradigm of these values. Every town square, marketplace, or other public venue is a microcosm of the larger community and its history. But Times Square offers a multilayered text that is spectacularly easy to read—perhaps because the letters are so large, clear, and brightly lit.

Like other historic venues that have served as "Crossroads of the World"—Jerusalem, Athens, Constantinople, or Thebes—Times Square is a time portal. Walter Winchell said, "If you stand on the corner of 42nd Street and Broadway, you will eventually meet everyone you know." And he was right. Stand in the middle of any one of those places, and watch history unfold.

Times Square is inclusionary. It always has been. A subway token gets you here. If you haven't a theater ticket, you can watch the show on the street. You see rich people, poor people, ordinary people of every race and nationality. You hear end-of-the-world preachers, street musicians, commentary in myriad languages passing by. Or perhaps you arrive via TV or the movies, or by postcard or the Internet. In one way or another, if you are like most people on the planet, you have been here. Times Square is a place that people everywhere enjoy claiming as their own.

This tiny corner of the universe has traditionally been a celebration of free enterprise—the opposite of the joyless, hulking, Soviet architecture of Red Square or Tiananmen Square, which reduce individuals to the size of ants. Central Planning could never have created Times Square. It is the natural expression of a free market in a free society: capitalist exuberance in microcosm.

But if the signs spell opportunity and promise, they have also, inevitably, spelled frustration and defeat. Everything doesn't always work out as intended. Freedom to succeed is also freedom to fail. Therefore this story has a plot. Over the past century, America's commercial landscape has followed a singular trajectory. Using Times Square as the focus, and visiting other venues as well, this book charts the rise and fall and rise again of the American advertising spectacular and its evolving role in the drama of American marketing.

# *Notes from the Authors*

## WALKING ON BROADWAY:
## A NOTE FROM TAMA

**T**imes Square is my village, the place where I grew up and where I now live and work. Like my father, Mel, and my grandfather, Jake, before me, I'm the president of Artkraft

Strauss, the company that for more than a century has sold, designed, and built Times Square's signature spectacular signs.

Artkraft Strauss is one of the few constants in the Square's ever-changing landscape. We have been making signs here ever since my grandfather crafted gaslit theater marquees by hand, delivered them with a horse and wagon, and installed them with a ginpole. And now that signs are sophisticated communications and information devices, with the promise of three-dimensional interactive displays carrying data spanning the globe at the speed of light, the signs have lost none of their allure—either for me or for the millions of people who come from around the world to see and photograph them.

When I was a child, Times Square's neon-lit fantasyland was a world of wonders that felt all-embracing and miles high. When the sun went down and the lights came on, the air seemed to electrify and magically change color, and the frantic flow of life in the street was modulated by the graceful and confident tempo of the giant animated images.

Who wouldn't be soothed by a block-long mini-Niagara pouring between two mammoth Pepsi-Cola bottles? Or fascinated by the giant smoke rings that floated out of the mouth of the great placid Camel smoker? Or beguiled by the so-cool Kool penguin, perched on an ice floe and winking conspiratorially thousands of times a day? Or tantalized by the flying saucer-sized cup of A&P Green 'n' Gold coffee, emitting real steam and the aroma of roasting coffee into the carnival-colored air as it emptied and refilled every fifteen seconds? Or buoyed by the sight of the 50-foot Anheuser-Busch Flying Eagle, its wings flapping majestically as the company's team of powerful neon Clydesdale horses clomped beneath? Or amused by Little Lulu skipping across an immense sheet of multicolored Kleenex woven of light?

Like the other one and a half million people who passed through Times Square every day, I viewed this uniquely American cityscape with awe. But unlike them, I felt an additional, personal attachment to these images. On Saturdays and during school vacations I accompanied my father and grandfather to the factory and watched as craftsmen formed sheets of metal and steel beams and mazes of wiring and neon tubing and countless lamps into the enormous creations that would ultimately take on a life of their own. Thus the other girls and boys whose parents brought them to Times Square could never see it quite the way I did—from behind the scenes as well as from the street.

It seemed to me that we were foremost among the writers of the Times Square drama. Where, I wondered, would all those people get the time and news headlines, and those vague but encouraging weather forecasts like "Fair and Warmer," if it weren't for us? How would they know that, every hour, 3,490 customers buy at Bond's? Or that fun-filled Atlantic City is only two and a half hours away? Or that a bag of Planters peanuts a day guarantees more pep?

Perhaps most important of all, how would anyone know when the New Year arrived without the descent of our great white ball of light atop the Times Tower?

I didn't know then that there was a rich and flourishing world of steel and neon and technological innovation that stretched far beyond the Hudson River. All over America, men like my father and grandfather were erecting glowingly imaginative expressions of America's commercial ebullience in drained swamps and blooming deserts, on frozen prairies and parched mountainsides, and in agricultural and industrial centers that were still just place names in a geography textbook to me.

Las Vegas mushroomed in the Nevada desert after World War II. Those who made the trek by automobile in the 1950s were welcomed to Fremont Street by a neon cowboy 80 feet tall, towering over the glittering beginnings of what would soon become a neon-encrusted concentration of hotels and casinos that, in terms of numbers of light-bulbs, surpassed even Times Square.

In Cleveland, an animated character named Reddy Kilowatt, symbol of the Cleveland Electric Illuminating Company, winked down on Public Square from a sign a half block wide and just as high, assuring customers that they lived in "The Best Location in the Nation."

In the industrial heart of Pittsburgh, a cascade of golden lights poured in sequence from the mouth of a monster bottle of Iron City Beer, filling and refilling a glass large enough to slake the thirst of a hundred thousand steelworkers.

In South St. Louis, at the Hampton and Gravois bus loop, a colossal, revolving, neon-embellished soda bottle urged a parched populace to "Think, Buy, Drink Vess."

In California, visitors looking for the Movie Capital of the World were guided by the world's largest place name sign—the huge HOL-LYWOOD erected on a hillside.

And in Dallas, pride radiated from the stack of letters, each encased in a lone star, that simply proclaimed "Texas" from the side of a building.

As I learned about the wider world, I began to realize that the signs tell a much bigger story than even their surrealistic size and technical razzle-dazzle might suggest. Written in the signs is the history of the electric century, from the first flickering lightbulb to the microchip and beyond. And more: the signs provide a window into America's collective personality.

For as long as I can remember, I have been watching people watch our signs and reflecting on their delight. And knowing the stories behind the signs only enhances their magic. I have conducted numerous tours of both signscape and factory, both physically and via slide show. And people are invariably moved as well as entertained. But a book, like a sign, has to wait for its moment.

That moment is here, created by a driving combination of forces converging at the end of the electric century. There is a general recognition of the importance of preserving and understanding the past. There is a growing appreciation of commercial art, graphic art, and popular icons as "real" art. There is a futuristic fascination with the electronic communications revolution—pioneered by the electric sign, the original advertising broadcast medium. And in my own back yard, the happy rebirth of Times Square, coincident with the 100th Anniversary of Artkraft Strauss. This unique conjunction made this book inevitable.

I've been a published author for twenty-five years—longer, in fact, than I've been in the sign business—but I knew better than to undertake this project single-handed. I'm too immersed in the daily traffic of customers and suppliers, unions and advertisers, landlords and city agencies. It would be like a fish trying to describe the lake she's swimming in.

So I put out the word on Broadway, where, as in any other village, word quickly gets around. I was looking for a collaborator, I said, a professional journalist from outside Times Square and outside the sign business who might bring a fresh perspective to both. And in short order Ed Hayman appeared, introduced to me by Susan Lee, the publicist for the League of American Theaters and Producers.

Writing is a famously solitary occupation. One is generally alone with a blank sheet of paper or a blank computer screen—and frequently a blank mind. "How do you write with someone else?" people ask.

Collaboration is like good conversation, where the ideas build spontaneously. And rereading what we've written, I can no longer tell who researched each section, who drafted, who critiqued, who edited, who polished. In the end, the enthusiasm we shared and the many pleasant surprises we experienced found their way into what we wrote.

Allow me to introduce my partner, Ed Hayman, who came from the big world beyond the Hudson River to help guide our journey through a century of signs.

## THE SHOW STARTS ON THE SIDEWALK: A NOTE FROM ED

*To the out-of-town* theater critic, New York is both Mecca and home away from home. He flies in to the city four or five times a year and launches into a weeklong marathon of playgoing and interviewing. By the time he's in a cab heading back to La Guardia, he's seen as many as a dozen plays and conducted twice as many interviews, and his head is full of echoes—snatches of dialogue, bits of stage business, the lingering glow of lights that illuminate the heart as well as the stage. If he's lucky, he's carrying home with him indelible memories of one or two transcendent experiences, the kind that remind him why he was called to the theater in the first place.

For the ten years I was theater critic for the *Detroit News,* this was my New York life. I logged many miles among the city's playhouses, usually starting and ending in Times Square—the great illuminated commercial art gallery that serves as entry point to America's signature theater district.

It often occurred to me that setting foot in the Square is just like stepping into a theater lobby. And what a lobby! Open to the sky and filled with giant, jumping, jazzy light sculptures. There's a sense of syncopated anticipation: something is about to happen, a transformation about to occur—but what? It scarcely matters. The lobby doesn't require analysis. It's simply *there*, to put the audience in a receptive mood for whatever magic might be in store.

Walking through the Square with the pre-theater throng, I would bathe in the red-and-white glow of the 50-foot-high Coca-Cola sign—the predecessor of the computer-driven high-tech giant that is there now—its familiar logo riding on wave upon wave of animated ruby and pearly-white neon, flooding the street with a rhythmic wash of compelling and oddly comforting light. It had the consonance of a steady heartbeat, the same neon life force that animated all the signs in the Square—the ebb and flow of Fuji's vast sweeping field of emerald green and cool white, the descending diagonal waterfall of brilliant neon-gold that climaxed Goldstar's sublime sequence, the helix of alternating raspberry red and creamy white that filled the five-story expanse of the Canon sign as if stirred by a giant invisible spoon. The play of light on the pavement—especially in rainy weather, when it forms dazzling, multicolored, wet geometrics—turns pedestrians into dancers.

This is Broadway's longest-running show, and I never tired of it. Times Square's neon world embraced me again every time I stepped out of a theater lobby onto the street. This multisensory surround was exhilaratingly different from the theatergoing experience in many other cities, my own foremost among them, where a theater and its gleaming marquee might stand alone in a mostly deserted business district, the dark night spreading coldly from the warm oasis of light beneath the canopy.

In Times Square, there is a synergy between the show inside the theater and the show on the street. The light on the stage—the fearless light of art and ideas, so proudly independent of commercial sponsorship—would fade quickly if the great advertising signs that light these streets went dark. (It has happened before, during the wartime dimouts and the 1970s' energy crunch.) At the same time, the theaters give the signs a ready-made audience and a sense of place, a performance center to be the combination lobby and art gallery for.

I never imagined then that one day the magic of the signs, and the stories behind them, would become as compelling to me as the magic of the theater and its behind-the-scenes dramas.

I met Tama Starr shortly after I moved to New York in 1992. I'd heard that she had an interesting project to discuss, and I, early in the first act of my own new life drama, was ready to hear about it.

The office walls of her aging factory beside the Hudson River are lined with historic photographs of the Square and its classic spectaculars, most built by Artkraft Strauss. Battered file cabinets and scrapbooks are stuffed with many more. They were tickets to time travel, my favorite daydream. I was hooked.

Through the photographs, I proudly became one of those Times Square "denizens" excoriated by Mayor Koch in 1984, as well as a time traveler. And now I have a new after-theater routine. When I step into the great bowl of light to take a spin around the Square, I look at the giant computer-printed fashion models on the Bond building and see the 60-foot-tall Gordon's gin bottle that preceded them. And its predecessor, the massive Bond waterfall, flanked by a pair of giant nude statues. And their predecessor, the Wrigley's gum spectacular, with its school of multicolored neon bubble-blowing fish.

I look at the Coca-Cola extravaganza and see the softly changing pastel face of the White Rock clock flanked by cascading waterfalls of golden light that sparkled on that site before World War I. I look at the black glass expanse of 1500 Broadway and see the Claridge Hotel with its great Camel smoker, puffing perfectly formed steam-vapor O's toward the huge replica of the Statue of Liberty that stood guard over the Square during World War II.

A new "show" is continuously opening on Broadway. And as Tama and I journeyed through the century, we found the commercial face of America depicted in the amazing signs built by her family and their predecessors, and their counterparts across America. I began to think of the signs collectively as cousins of the murals of Thomas Hart Benton and Diego Rivera, teeming with the life of America in the making.

We originally thought this would be a simple, though dazzling, picture book. But the more we saw of the subject, the more our vision expanded. What finally evolved is this illustrated history/memoir—the story of America's electric century told through its signs. And while the story takes us the length and breadth of the North American continent, Times Square is the epicenter of the tale. We decided to use one voice to tell the story—Tama's, because she grew up in this wonderful village, eventually to become a major player in it.

This is a story that has never been told. And I personally guarantee that once you hear it, you will never look at signs in the same way again. Join us on this unique journey through American history. The signs, as always, point the way.

Early in the twentieth century, my grandfather, Jacob Starr, then just a teenager, built one of the first electric signs in Eastern Europe. It identified a fashionable riverfront restaurant in the Ukrainian city of Ekaterinoslav, now Dneprope-trovsk.

Young Jake was an apprentice metalworker—in Yiddish, a *blecher,* related to the English word "blacksmith." It was a traditional trade, and Jake dutifully mastered it. But on his own time he was a talented amateur electrician, a precocious, self-taught whiz kid whose mod-ern-day counterpart would be the adolescent computerphile. By all accounts, his sign proved to be a beacon that drew the curious from towns for miles around—diners as well as those who couldn't afford even a glass of tea in such a place. Young Jake was hooked. Surely America was just waiting for his electric signs.

At the same time, an American-born German-Jewish sign painter named Benjamin Strauss presided over Strauss & Co. Signs, the flour-ishing New York sign and outdoor advertising company he had founded in 1897. A meticulous sign painter and hand-letterer who could perform calligraphy in any style, in any size, Strauss was a con-summate nineteenth-century craftsman. In his second-floor shop at the north end of what was soon to be known as Times Square, he and his crew of artists and artisans turned out hand-painted price tags for retail stores, menus and show cards for restaurants and dinner clubs, gold leafing for the windows of banks and offices, and—Strauss & Co.'s specialties—bright and fanciful theatrical posters and theater marquees illuminated by gaslight.

Modern movie marquees, with their familiar "chasing" lights, are an unconscious imitation of nineteenth century theater marquees, with their twinkling gaslights. And the way we build them today is re-markably similar to the way Strauss built them then.

The light sources—banks of gas jets then—were caged in a metal frame. For each production, a new face was made—painted, enameled, or sometimes wrought of copper, tin, or bronze—with holes punched out to form the names of the production and the performers, and per-haps the show's logo. Colored glass lenses were fitted into the holes. The flickering, multicolored flames shining through the lenses con-veyed the sense of "Welcome! Come on in!" that is still the hallmark of theater. This innovative use of multicolored lenses helped build Strauss. It was a big step up from price tags for department stores—and early vaudeville and the flourishing Yiddish theater made exten-sive use of it.

But Strauss could see that a new, electrical day was about to dawn.

Jake did come to America, and in due course presented himself to Strauss in the second-floor shop, seeking employment as a metal-man and electrician. Strauss hired him on the spot, and within a short time Strauss & Co. was in the electric sign business.

The meeting of the two young men was symbolic of a convergence of two eras. Jake represented the brash new age of electricity, Strauss the dignified age of nineteenth-century handcraftsmanship and dimly glowing gaslight. Strauss' world was waiting for Jake's—hungry for it, dreaming about its mystical power, ready to use that power to write messages in the sky so large they could be read from horizon to horizon.

This convergence was happening everywhere. In sign shops set up in lofts and barns and garages and stores, in burgeoning cities and small towns, the man with the Paint and the man with the Power met and created, in the name of American business, images of mythological proportions—images that marketed dreams as well as products.

It is here that the story of the American spectacular begins—in a world waiting for the Light.

## From Cave Artists to Wall Dogs

*The story of outdoor advertising* traditionally begins with the first symbolic marketers, the cave dwellers during the Upper Paleolithic period, starting about 40,000 years ago. At Lascaux, France, and elsewhere, elaborate action murals depicting a variety of animals and lively hunting scenes portray the dynamic relationship between hunters and the migratory beasts who represented fundamental economic forces: food and clothing, the entire constellation of blessings that Nature could either bestow or withhold.

Anthropologists identify these Stone Age renderings—the first wall-mounted messages—as the earliest examples of both art and writing. They speculate that, like modern media, the messages were intended to influence as well as reflect the viewer's life. Like advertisements, they depict dreams fulfilled—the animals rushing into the hunters' traps—and urge specific, concrete action—Hunt! Be hunted!—on both parties to the economic transaction.

All known cultures use signs, in one form or another, to convey straightforward messages with immediacy. Anthropologist Ashley Montagu defines a sign as a "concrete denoter" with an inherent, specific meaning: "This is it; do something about it!" He points out the essentially human character of signs by noting that while many types of animals respond to signals—interruptions in an energy field for the purpose of communicating—only a few intelligent and highly trained animals can understand even the simplest signs.

History's first known poster bulletin was a notice of a reward for a runaway slave posted on a wall in the Egyptian city of Thebes more than 3,000 years ago. Egyptian merchants of the same period chiseled sales messages into tall, square stone obelisks and roadside stone tablets called stelae, and painted them in bright colors to attract the attention of passersby.

In Pompeii, billboard-like walls covered with advertisements were preserved in the lava that engulfed them when Mount Vesuvius erupted in A.D. 79. Excavations there have revealed wall messages on the shady side of the marketplace too, offering enticing invitations along the lines of "For a Good Time, See Cora." And even earlier, in ancient Greece, innovative practitioners of what may arguably be the world's second-oldest profession (symbol-making being necessarily precedent) expanded their out-of-home client base by carving the message "ΕΠΟΥ ΜΟΙ," "Follow Me," in the bottoms of their leather sandals, leaving an impression in the clay pavement as well as in the imaginations of potential customers. The connection between the two ancient occupations was not limited to amateurs, however. Modern visitors to Kuşadasi in Turkey are shown magnificent Byzantine mosaics that once served as on-premise business signs for houses of pleasure.

The Romans brought the use of whitewashed walls with painted ads on them on their conquests throughout Europe. They also developed artful on-premise business signs specially designed for the illiterate, such as a friendly-looking bush denoting a tavern. Some ancient trade symbols—such as the three golden balls of the pawnshop, the giant key of the locksmith, the big shoe of the shoemaker, and the red and white stripes of the barber—have remained in use for a thousand years and more.

Medieval English merchants were *required* to label their premises with trade signs (no anti-sign ordinances then!), and by the sixteenth century such devices were required in France as well. But shabby installation must have limited the use of the trade sign: in the seventeenth century, what we would now call safety standards came into effect. Signs were no longer allowed to swing haphazardly above the street; they had to be mounted flat to the wall. This devaluation of the symbol—as outdoor advertising people will immediately recognize—as well as a general increase in numeracy, brought about the numbering of buildings and doorways—the system we still use today.

Meanwhile, the art of advertising progressed, and with the advent of the printing press, posting became the out-of-home medium of choice. In Europe by the fifteenth century mechanically printed posters had gained popularity, not only as an advertising medium but also as a popular art form.

The invention of lithography in the mid-1800s led to even greater sophistication and the convergence of art and commerce in an unprecedentedly elegant manner. Posters were then regarded as serious art, engaging the efforts of such important French artists as Manet, Daumier, and Toulouse-Lautrec, eager to place their work before a larger audience. In England, the medium thrived under Beardsley, Walker, Hardy, and a design team known as the Beggarstaff Brothers, who created magnificent and stylish artwork for the theater and publishing industries as well as for a huge variety of retail products and services. Their American counterparts included such artists as Maxfield Parrish, Edward Penfield, and Will H. Bradley.

Out-of-home media have always played an important role in U.S. history. Handbills—political advertisements and sometimes subversive essays printed off-hours on newspaper presses and passed from hand to hand—were instrumental in promoting the American Revolution, both sides of the Civil War, and social causes including abolition, temperance, and universal suffrage.

Itinerant gold-leafers, artisans with a fine hand and supplies of molecule-thin gold leaf that they guarded with their lives, traveled with America's westward migration, inscribing the names of attorneys, doctors, dentists, and other professionals on doors and storefront windows, establishing, for all to see, the good-as-gold bona fides of these practitioners. And wall dogs, itinerant sign painters with a raffish reputation and an eye for underexploited opportunities, traveled the country during its early years, transforming barns and brick walls into rococo ads for soft drinks, patent medicines, and tobacco products.

The billposter of the nineteenth century, however, went beyond these historic forebears. He was the John the Baptist of American outdoor advertising. Like the Biblical prophet who went forth throughout the land preaching the coming of the Messiah, the billposter blanketed city, village, and countryside with signs of the great commercial century that was about to dawn.

The bulletins, as they were called, were elaborately illustrated paper signs that brought, to a largely homebound society, news of novelty in the changing world of trade beyond the horizon—from newly available household products, patent medicines, and tasty packaged edibles to the coming of circuses, operettas, and other traveling wonders.

The citizens of Akron and Hannibal and Knoxville learned from the bulletins that the fine ladies of London, England, and Paris, France, used Pears' Soap and Williams Talcum Powder ("Makes the Skin Feel Like Velvet"); that quality gentlemen smoked Virginia Leaf Tobacco and stepped out smartly with the help of durable and shiny 2 in 1 Shoe Polish; that C&G Corsets could be worn during those long humid summers without fear of rust; that mysterious vapors and failures of energy too private to mention need no longer be endured in silent resignation, thanks to Dr. Pierce's Golden Medical Discovery.

A symphony orchestra might be coming all the way from Seattle for a concert. Or a theater troupe from San Francisco might perform a tear-drenched drama about a beautiful French demoiselle tragically expiring from consumption. Or, better yet, Buffalo Bill's Wild West Show or the Barnum & Bailey Circus might be coming to town!

Before radio and movies, live touring shows of all kinds were the staple of American popular entertainment. To accommodate traveling troupes, even small towns like Cheboygan, Michigan, and Athens, Georgia, had opera houses, many of them little jewel boxes modeled after the show palaces of the big cities. And every hamlet in the country, however remote, was visited several times a year by a circus, of which there were hundreds crisscrossing the country during the warmer weather. By the mid-1880s, competition for small-town America's entertainment coins was growing fierce.

Historians trace the specific origin of the American outdoor advertising industry to a ravenous demand for posters on the part of entertainment providers—especially circus promoters. And no impresario made more extensive use of poster advertising than P. T. Barnum, who teamed up with James A. Bailey and later with the Ringling Brothers to create "The Greatest Show on Earth."

Some of the leading illustrators of the day designed richly colored and detailed posters depicting the myriad exotic wonders assured to a thrill-hungry public by the Barnum name. He promised spectacle on an unprecedented scale, and titillation tinged with danger. His customers needed only to gaze upon the lush renderings of bearded ladies, clowns, jugglers, acrobats, and trumpeting elephants, and the voluptuously exaggerated hourglass figures of trapeze artists in tights and sequins, and eager anticipation would guarantee a sold-out house.

Not to be outdone, his competitors commissioned equally provocative visual promises of astounding sights awaiting just beyond the flap of the Big Top. For just a few cents, myths and wild imaginings would come alive before one's very eyes.

Distortions of scale that are laughable to us were overlooked by all but the most hardheaded patrons. In the posters, tigers were the size of motorcars and mighty stallions so huge they could carry bevies of shapely-limbed maidens in tutus on their muscular backs with room to spare.

Who had the biggest elephant? In the 1880s, Lemen Brothers/World's Best Shows offered Rajah, "the largest elephant that walks the earth," claiming it was two inches taller than Barnum & Bailey's Jumbo. B & B denied this, of course, and the debate raged for several years, with both animals depicted as immense as five-story buildings.

As the poster war escalated and Barnum and other promoters required larger and larger ads, advertising companies learned to assemble blocs of single posters into giant multisheet displays. Bulletins grew from simple two-, three-, and four-sheet assemblages to building-size displays 50 feet wide and more.

Just as big shows demanded big advertising, so did manufacturers with big dreams. The zealous walking stick company that wanted to tell the whole city about its fine product needed a huge image incarnate in the cityscape. So did the maker of flatirons offered as the best money can buy. And so did the maker of footwear for the discerning high-stepper. Advertising companies attempted to meet this need by building giant three-dimensional models of the products—a jumbo cow, for example, to promote a dairy, or a huge shiny top hat for a men's haberdasher. These were mounted on wagons and the tops of buses and pulled through city streets by teams of horses. Sometimes large illustrated banners were draped over the horses themselves, swaying as the animals clip-clopped down the street.

But these early attempts to create surreal advertising icons never really caught on. While the need to make a big statement was keen and growing stronger, without independent light and animation there could be no illusion, and the objects remained just large, inert, horse-drawn objects: no mystery there.

So the bulletin—the bigger and more arresting, the better—remained the principal method of outdoor advertising. Bulletins papered America, and every imaginable empty space was fair game.

Old-timers like Atlantic City adman Jack Tavlin remember the flavor of that world, even after man-made lightning electrified America almost overnight. Tavlin, who was born in Emporia, Kansas, in 1900, ran away to join the circus as a roustabout at thirteen. He says he was lured by the posters—not to become a circus performer, but to sell advertising.

"Everywhere I saw these posters: 'Circus Coming to Town! Come to the Circus!'" he recalls, his huckster's charm undiminished by the years. "Beoo-tiful posters. And everybody came. So I thought to myself, 'Advertising! That's where the money is at!'

"So I made a deal with the guy who owned the elephants in the circus. I rented the rear ends of the elephants to paint ads on them when they marched in the parades. And that's how I started in the outdoor business."

0

Who advertised on the backsides of elephants?

"Goodyear Tires!" Jack proclaims. "U.S. Rubber! Lumber and building materials! Anything that's tough, you just put it on an elephant's ass and everybody will buy it, I guarantee you!"

Connecting the message with the medium in this way placed Jack light-years ahead of Marshall ("the medium is the message") McLuhan.

Most billposters, however, simply slapped up their sheets wherever they could. And the entrepreneurial drive that propelled this legion of pre-electric Willie Lomans was nothing less than ferocious.

## "Post No Bills"

Bulletins were often "sniped"—pasted or tacked to surfaces without bothering to ask the owner—by fleet-footed billposters who stayed one jump ahead of the law. Ragged bills hawking everything from Tutts Pills and St. Jacob's Oil to Battle Ax Plug, Hood's Sarsaparilla, and Official Five Cent Cigars fluttered from every wall, fence, lamppost, and curb, and often even every large rock and tree—a blight that threatened to consume entire cities.

Even nature was not immune. Rock outcroppings provided an irresistible opportunity, and painted advertisements lined the New Jersey Palisades along the Hudson, as well as other major rivers and thoroughfares. Daredevils like "Hote" Houghteling of Bradbury and Houghteling, the leading national outdoor advertising company in the 1870s, gained a reputation for reaching and painting rocks regarded as inaccessible. Soon snipers and billposting "hot-doggers" were provoking the same outrage in most communities that graffiti vandals do today.

Complaints were loud and widespread, like this one from the *New York Times* in 1902 about the state of Broadway from City Hall to Union Square: "...a frightful spectacle, made so more by the wilderness of discordant and shrieking signs than even by the ordinary architecture of the thoroughfare—trying as that also is." But to use the instrument of government to do something about it—and thus interfere with someone's business—was a concept which, in that free-wheeling, laissez-faire era, gave most people pause.

Billposters who paid for space were a cut above the sniper. Dispatched across the country by big-city advertising companies, they sweet-talked farmers, store owners, and householders into giving up their roof and wall space, and rarely paid for its use in cash. Instead, they carried valises full of "premiums" like cheap watches, fountain pens, and safety razors. Because much of the advertising they posted was for patent medicines, as well as for new products like prepackaged coffee, cocoa, condensed milk, and porous cement, they sometimes paid for the space with the commodity being advertised—as well as with jackknives, buttonhooks, shoehorns, and Chinese back scratchers.

Some novelty-hungry property owners were known to sell "exclusive advertising rights" to every successive pitchman who came down the pike. The industry, like most industries, was entirely unregulated. Private property was sacrosanct, and the widely held belief that an owner could do whatever he wanted with his property was an article of faith.

Such unrestrained free enterprise inevitably brought down the wrath of the civic-minded on sniper and legitimate billposter alike. As someone complained in *Street Types of Great American Cities,* an 1896 publication: "The bill poster is an unmitigated nuisance, and his existence ought be forgiven him only for the occasional delight he furnishes the children."

Many years before Lady Bird Johnson declared war on highway billboards, citizen groups and municipal authorities often followed in the billposter's footsteps, tearing down or painting over his work. Postelection celebrations in many towns centered on bonfires fueled by mountains of torn-down campaign posters. Anti-outdoor advertising campaigns were waged all over the country by groups like the American Civic Association, armed with such weapons as the widely distributed 1908 booklet *The Billboard Nuisance.*

This was a global phenomenon. In 1900, *A Beautiful World,* the organ of the British Society for Checking the Abuses of Public Advertising, quoted travelers to Europe, South Africa, Ceylon, Bermuda, the Sudan, and elsewhere. "I know to what lengths this hideous disfigurement may go," runs one testimony, "for I have sailed along the

Lake of a Thousand Islands, where every rock yells at you with advertisements in letters of twenty feet high." Apparently no place was safe. "I was in my garden," declares another witness, "and I heard sudden reports of artillery; presently from the sky fell masses of green and red paper, advertising a tooth powder."

There was some precedent for prohibiting outdoor advertising. The first U.S. regulation dates back to the late 1860s, when some brave sniper painted the name of the mysteriously named patent medicine "ST 1860X" on a rock overlooking Niagara Falls. The response was a local law against "abuse of scenery."

The fledgling outdoor industry realized, from a defensive point of view, that it needed to start to make its product more palatable and police its business methods—before the opposition grew any more organized and brought the law down on their heads. The International Bill Posters Association, formed in 1872, was strong enough by the 1890s to establish a new practice: the standardization of billboards mounted in permanent steel structures, secured by leases and safely maintained. This set the stage for outdoor advertising as we know it today—and for the imminent birth of the electric sign.

It was obviously easier to stick a poster on a fence or the pillar of an elevated railroad track and disappear than it was to negotiate a deal with a property owner, build an expensive sign frame, and market, defend, and maintain the space. But advertisers like Coca-Cola, Anheuser-Busch, and the National Biscuit Company, already understanding the importance of public image to their corporate strategy, demanded the dignity and security of a permanent structure in a well-chosen site—a way to properly display their product and their identity in the landscape.

Such advertisers ultimately bridged the amazingly quick transition from paper posters to electric displays. And as America applied the tenets and technology of the Industrial Revolution to the pursuit of its own expansive vision of itself, outdoor advertising matured into a legitimate industry.

Its foes, however, did not give up easily. In New York before the turn of the century, the formidible Municipal Art Society (MAS), ever the champion of civic art, was the sworn enemy of all outdoor advertising—in the Municipalians' view "the weed of art forms," according to the MAS's chronicler, Gregory F. Gilmartin, in his valuable history

*Shaping the City: New York and the Municipal Art Society*. It was sublimely ironic when, a mere century later, the MAS was instrumental in the fight to Save Times Square and its spectacular electrical advertisements.

The MAS was dedicated to an idea that was a bit of a hard sell in America at the close of the nineteenth century: the idea that a city can and should be beautiful. Paris and the other capitals of Europe were role models. But what would emulating these historic centers of art and culture contribute to the conduct of commerce—to what we now call "the bottom line"?

Proponents of civic beautification wouldn't lower themselves to address such a question. But visionary outdoor leaders knew they must address it—and did.

## GUDE NEWS

*Foremost among these leaders was* O. J. Gude, the owner of New York's leading outdoor advertising company and the first to wear the mantle of "Lamplighter of Broadway." Born in 1862, Gude apprenticed as a sign hanger and billposter, and started his own company in 1889.

For the next three decades, he exercised an extraordinary blend of aggressive sales tactics and a sense of spiritual mission. More than the majority of his contemporaries, he grasped the importance of marketing psychology and the power of public image—and more than most of his followers, he used his instinctive understanding of public relations not merely to aggrandize himself but to promote the industry as a whole.

Early on, Gude saw the long-term value of negotiating advertising deals that made everybody happy by emphasizing the positive, promoting aesthetics, and putting money into the pockets of all concerned. He was the first, for example, to post workmanlike advertising bulletins on the elevated railways, in highly visible permanent locations sanctioned by both the railroad company and the city. His pride in the artistic standard of his work is evident in an early group photo taken on the roof of his Hudson Street shop: he and his staff of neatly mustachioed young men in ties and white lab coats are flanked by large beautifully painted posters for cultural attractions.

His company dominated New York's electric sign business almost from the beginning, and built most of Times Square's earliest great spectaculars—a story that will be told more fully in the next chapter—until the company was sold to the newly created General Outdoor Advertising Company in 1925, the year Gude died.

By 1906, he was routinely credited by the press as the "Creator of the Great White Way"—a title that some later entrepreneurs inaccurately pinned on themselves. Trade publications, writing for a more specialized audience of industry insiders, sometimes saluted Gude as the "Napoleon of Publicity."

Gude was a hearty blend of turn-of-the-century entrepreneur and Edwardian gentleman who believed outdoor advertising men should take their place alongside other dignified professionals and civic leaders of the first rank—because it was the right thing to do, and also because it was better for business in the long run. To the new all-American businessman, practitioner of the American religion of "doing well by doing good," these two impulses were inseparable.

In *Artists, Advertising, and the Borders of Art,* Michele H. Bogart describes Gude as an avowed patron of the arts who nurtured his own notion of civic beautification. He saw art and commerce literally converging in outdoor advertising, resulting in the validation of commercial art in public places as both aesthetically enriching and spiritually instructive. Toward that end, he joined the Municipal Art Society and even got himself appointed in 1913 to its Committee on Advertising.

By then, the outdoor industry had started to recognize the necessity for self-regulation and artistic standards. Staving off the beautification extremists and the sign wreckers who wouldn't be far behind, the industry was beginning to draw from the ranks of leading artists and magazine illustrators like N. C. Wyeth and Edwin Blashfield to create artistically realized expressions of the glories of their customers' products.

Gude took this convergence a step further. He proposed, under the aegis of the MAS, to edify the public by turning selected billboard locations into inspirational outdoor art galleries. These temporary displays would consist of reproductions of "famous paintings and great masterpieces," Gude told the MAS, "which would illustrate the history of the country, and tend to inculcate lessons of patriotism, and thus make the billboards a magnificent auxiliary to the work in the public schools and a power for good in the land."

The MAS was spectacularly unimpressed, and passed on the idea. Undaunted, Gude proposed that his company and the MAS become partners in a sign design competition, to be juried by a panel of "distinguished artists." Again, the MAS passed.

Gude would not be dissuaded. He invited fellow MAS committee member Edwin Blashfield to conduct seminars for employees of the Gude Company's art, sales, and promotion departments. It was to be the first in a series, he told the MAS, "by artists of standing in New York City, on the possibilities of making advertising displays less offensive and more artistic."

The theme of Blashfield's lecture, according to MAS records, was "the possible co-relating of art with publicity" in order to foster "the engendering of an art spirit between the man that spends the money for an Advertising Campaign and those who execute the work."

If Gude liked the concept of an "art spirit" guiding the eyes and hands of his artisans and the words of his salesmen, he worshipped the idea that outdoor advertising could provide moral uplift to the masses. Testifying before the mayor's commission on the regulation of billboards, Gude unfurled from the chamber balcony a large poster showing children being taken to church, beneath the caption "Take your children to church, give them the right start." Gude told the hearing that the advertising men were "doing a little 'uplift' work of their own even while they were being attacked by uplifters."

Gude resigned from the MAS Committee on Advertising after his stint in 1913. He realized he was deep in the enemy camp and unlikely to make real headway in that forum. Outdoor advertising might seize the cultural high ground for a moment; holding it longer than that was another matter. The permanent public synergy he sought between art and commerce hadn't transpired exactly as he had dreamed it would. But a relationship had been forged nonetheless.

By 1913, in any event, the world had changed completely. Urban skies were ablaze in the light of great electric spectaculars. Times Square was Gude's gallery, and his love of art was never more apparent than in the light sculptures he sold and built. The billposter, like

Johnny Appleseed, had been relegated to history, and—in the minds of electric advertising men like Gude who dreamed in operatic proportions—to the realm of myth.

It is here that we leave the story of the American billboard, which has been told so capably elsewhere, and begin the story of the electric advertising spectacular.

## "Do You Need a Strong Man?"

*My grandfather arrived at* Ellis Island with only a couple of kopecks—hundredths of a ruble—in his pocket. "The clothes I wore from Russia, I wore here more than a year," he told me in 1974, nearly three-quarters of a century later. "I lived on a herring a day. A herring and a loaf." A loaf of bread cost only a penny. "I came to America, I was fifteen years old. I came here all alone. Nobody met me at Ellis Island. It was October, nineteen-seven, a Friday."

Work was scarce. "It was Depression, very bad times," he said. "People were jumping out of windows, they lost everything. Nobody could find work.

"They were building the Panama Canal in those days. They would auction off men to go down there for a dollar a week, and I enlisted myself to go. The auction was in a church on Second Avenue, I'll never forget it. I went up there with a sign around my neck, to go; but when I saw it, the men were in the boxcars like animals, I shook to run away. I was so scared they would catch me and I would have to go. But they didn't catch me, I ran away home. Not ran away, but I got out of there. I was so happy to get out of there."

After a few weeks of odd jobs, he landed at Frank & Weiss, a major wrought-iron company, where he was quickly promoted to foreman. Frank & Weiss made decorative staircases, balconies, and fire escapes, ornamental railings and window grilles, indoor and outdoor furniture, and other elaborate wrought-iron specialties. He left F&W when his co-workers elected to go on strike. "Why should I go on strike?" he asked me rhetorically. "I was the highest-paid man there. I was making seven and a half dollars a week. Everybody else was making three dollars."

Rather than transfer his skills and experience to another iron shop, where he would have been more than welcome, Jake followed his drive to become an entrepreneur—trading an employee's security for an artist's freedom. Business was his art, his means of self-expression. And more than that, it kept him always where the action was.

He had spent his early childhood where the action was—at least by local standards. His grandparents' general store seems to have defined the central business district of a tiny village called Staroe Selo in the Ukraine.

"It was a very big store," he told me. "It was two blocks long. They never used money in that store. It was all barter. Someone would bring in some chickens, they would get a pair of shoes; or some eggs, they would get vodka; for a cow or a horse they could buy an overcoat; I don't remember what was exactly. In the back of the store were always fifteen or twenty cows. And sheeps."

Jake's grandmother ran the store. "My grandfather was all the time studying, always learning Torah, so she ran the store. She was a very good businesslady, my grandmother." This was not an uncommon arrangement in the Old Country, where full-time scholarship and piety—for men only, of course—were prized, but someone had to deal with day-to-day reality.

Little Jake learned business math and negotiations from his grandmother, who kept the entire inventory of livestock, cloth goods, building materials, tools, produce, and sundries—as well as the accounts receivable and accounts payable—in her head, and bartered all day long. Before he was old enough to go to school, he arranged goods on the shelves, swept the floor, and even dealt with customers while his grandmother was busy supervising the loading and unloading of wagons, dealing with vendors, and keeping an eye on the mill, which occupied a large outbuilding. The mill was operated by waterpower in summer, and in winter, when the river was frozen, by horsepower. The mill was the scene of his earliest specific memory. This memory, interestingly enough, centered on his first coin.

"Once she gave me a kopki [kopeck], I'll never forget it. A kopki, that was like a penny. There was also a coin, a half a kopki. For a half a kopki you could get a half a glass of kvass, that was like Coca-Cola we had there—like cider, apple cider. For a kopki you could get a whole glass. When my grandmother gave me that kopki, I was so excited! Never before did I have so much money.

"I must have been five years old. I know it was winter, because the horses were walking around, turning the stones. My grandmother was standing by the mill, her apron was white, her black hair was white, everything was white from all the flour flying in the air. She gave me the kopki, and she told me, 'Here, buy yourself a glass of kvass.' I was so excited! A whole kopki! I ran and bought some candy."

Leaving aside the irony of Grandma reclaiming the kopki—her store, after all, was the only store in town—it's easy to see this youth weighing the lives of his grandparents, the scholar and the businessperson, and choosing the business life.

His parents moved to town—to Ekaterinoslav—when Jake was old enough for middle school. He was already demonstrating a gift of invention and a flair for mechanics. When he was fourteen he walked into Ekaterinoslav's best eatery and told the owner he would build him an electric sign. "If it works, pay me," he offered. "If it doesn't, don't pay." He built the sign out of German-made lightbulbs that were constantly burning out (I'd like to believe he negotiated a good maintenance contract, too), and fashioned a waterwheel and immersed it in the Dnieper River to generate DC power. It worked. The restaurant instantly became the most popular nightspot in Ekaterinoslav—which did not yet even have electric streetlights, much less domestic electric lighting.

Teenaged Jake had done something quite remarkable, giving Ekaterinoslav an early taste of the lights that were beginning to come on all over the world. For, by the mid-1880s, the Edison Company had built more than 300 electric generating plants, some even in Russia.

Edison mains, however, were always located near centers of commerce and culture, where Edison's Direct Current, which can't travel over long distances, could be delivered to well-heeled customers. Consequently, Kiev, the major city in Jake's part of the world, had electricity by the early years of the century, but it was 250 miles from Ekaterinoslav. Thus Jake did more than build an electric sign. He built, from scratch, a power source, a crude but effective electric generating plant.

How could a fourteen-year-old manage such an engineering feat? The same way young computer and radio hobbyists in Third World countries today teach themselves the skills they need to build working sets out of found parts. Electricity hovered over the world like a great dawn about to break. Jake read, listened, tinkered, imagined, and somehow pieced it all together, and created not only a small technological marvel but a paying business as well—his own tiny share of the convergence of science and commerce that was transforming the world.

Meanwhile, the Cossacks were riding again. "In nineteen-five, that was the year I graduate school, there was a revolution, and pogroms," Jake told me. "You know what is a pogrom? They come and slaughter the Jews. We were saved because we lived on the same street as the governor. On October 21 there was a terrible pogrom. They burned my father's lumber business, his horses and wagons, everything, to the ground."

It was clearly time for the family to seek new horizons. A great-uncle paved the way. "It was my mother's mother's sister's husband. He had a big store in Russia—until the Cossacks burned it. His father had a big factory, they made tallises [prayer shawls] there. He used to go to China to buy the silk. The looms were worked by Yeshiva men. They would pray, and work the looms. He gave the money to my uncle to come to America. He came with his daughter, my aunt. Then they sent me a ticket. Later his wife came." The immigrant selection process was clearly based on potential earning power. Jake's mission was to accumulate enough money to bring over his parents and kid brother Max, plus another teenaged wage earner to repeat the process.

Jake moved in with his uncle and cousin in their nine-dollar-a-month fifth-floor walk-up on the Lower East Side. "My uncle was a Talmudist. He had a beautiful voice, like a cantor. He became a *bigler*. You know what is a *bigler?* A presser by pants. He made three dollars a week. His daughter sewed piecework, she also made three dollars a week. They were so happy I gave them money for rent. Everybody worked hard. Got up every morning five-thirty, kept going till eight, nine at night. This is not unusual. It is not a story." He meant that there was no romance to it.

After his stint at Frank & Weiss, Jake scavenged and sold scrap metal, eventually earning enough to buy a pushcart and later a horse-drawn wagon. He collected burned-out lightbulbs and rebuilt them—

an enterprise that was so successful he hired teams of immigrant girls to do the work. This drew the attention of the Edison Company, which was in the business of selling *new* lightbulbs, and was not about to let a recycling immigrant upstart cut into their market. "Edison bought me out of the business," Jake said. "That's how I came to get the money to bring over my father" in 1909.

Like Edison, Jake was an inventor, but unlike the "Genius of Menlo Park," he was not yet a businessman. "I had a lot of patents, inventions," he said. The self-starter for the automobile, an electric reclining chair, a high-power-factor transformer. "But I didn't know anything. I gave it all to a lawyer who was a crook, and he stole everything. The self-starter, it was sold to Pierce-Arrow, I got five hundred dollars!"

Jake was ambitious, but impatient. None of his forays into the sphere of business had satisfied him, much less put any real money in his pocket. Here he was, in the Land of Opportunity, and his greatest hit was still the electric restaurant sign he had built back in Ekaterinoslav.

No doubt Jake was thinking about his restaurant sign when he presented himself to Ben Strauss in the new Strauss factory at 47th Street and Broadway—on the second floor of what is now Two Times Square—in 1909. Toting an immense John Brown hammer over his shoulder—strictly an attention-getting prop; nobody needed to drive any railroad spikes—Jake addressed Strauss in Yiddish: *"Kenst usen a starker mann?"* ("Do you need a strong man?")

Strauss laughed. The huge sledgehammer almost dwarfed the elfin, ninety-seven-pound Jake. But Strauss, who was fifteen years Jake's senior, admired the young man's spunk, and after listening to his pitch, he hired him at the then-exorbitant salary of thirteen and a half dollars a week.

What Strauss had actually hired was more than a fine electrician, crackerjack foreman, and insightful salesman. He had welcomed the twentieth century into his shop.

It was essential for Strauss to make this move. His billposting competitors, foremost among them O. J. Gude, had moved quickly into the exciting new business of electric signs, and evidence of their work was beginning to add a new glow to the gaslit nights.

By then, Longacre Square had become Times Square—named for

the newspaper. The Times Tower, outlined in Edison incandescent lightbulbs for frequent special promotions, was a monument to the future. The Square no longer looked like a frontier town. The low wooden buildings covered with tattered posters had given way to new theaters, restaurants, commercial buildings, and hotels, many of which were starting to be adorned with the blazing electrical advertisements that we now call "spectaculars." Rector's, with its fashionable roof garden and famous Dragon sign, brought in the carriage trade. "The Great White Way"—a phrase already in common use by 1909—stretched along Broadway from 23rd to 59th Street, a distance six times the length of the present Times Square.

The first spectacular Jake built for Strauss, that same year, featured the famous Floradora Girls, vaudeville cuties who predated the Ziegfeld Girls, displaying their stuff around the curved corner of the Casino Theater. The Casino, on Broadway and 39th Street, was an eight-story confection resembling a Moorish palace, surmounted by a copper-clad onion dome. Employing pink-gelled spotlights and animated lightbulbs as well as an interconnected set of electric motor-driven mechanisms, the display depicted the Girls wearing their signature feathered leghorn hats, riding in their trademark pony cart. The cart wheels turned, the pony trotted on spinning feet, the wagon rocked, the feathers swayed. And the sweetly grinning Floradoras, lovingly painted by Ben Strauss himself, undulated from side to side, their palms coyly placed beside their roseate cheeks. Hubba hubba! Folks gathered nightly to admire this vision.

The wait for the light was over. The electrical century had begun.

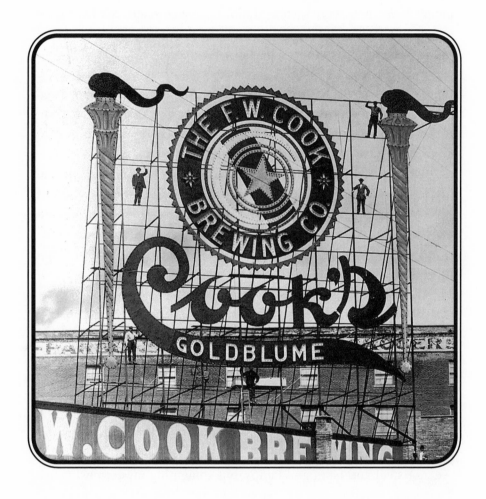

ountains sculpted in electric light gush sparkling water into

urns that never overflow. A colossal kitten, drawn in fine

lines of electric lamps, attacks a spool of thread big enough to squash a horse. A great glowing tire spins through an endless electric downpour, and, as promised, never skids. A strong wind—the same eternal storm, perhaps—whips a giant electric girl's petticoat around her ankles and pelts her umbrella with rain. A drill team of peppy little men with spears—doubtless invigorated by their savvy choice of chewing gum—goes through its paces in a block-long electric fantasia of fountains and peacock feathers.

Welcome to Times Square in the teens, already the Crossroads of the World, already a great gallery of electric advertising art. Surprised, so early in the century, by the delightful variety, immense size, and technical sophistication of the displays? So was I, and I thought I knew Times Square history.

I was even more surprised to learn that every American city had huge, glorious electric displays of its own during this rich period—advertising spectaculars for cars, laxatives, and beer; glittering theater marquees for a soon-to-boom movie industry; the names of businesses proudly ablaze on rooftops; even "talking" signs that predated those I grew up with.

All of this happened with remarkable speed. Almost as soon as electricity was available, and long before most people had it in their homes, the first generation of "sky-signs" appeared, filling the nightscape with stupendous images that both reflected and fed their constituency's dreams.

A population brought up on the promise of romance, contentment, prosperity, and exotic thrills offered by magazine illustration, billboard art, and circus posters was fully prepared to make the metaphysical leap required by lighted animated electric spectaculars—to see, not steel and paint and lamps, but something mysteriously alive.

## AMERICA'S REACH FOR THE SKY

*"Up" was America's direction of* choice in the early years of the electric century. Thanks to the twin inventions of the lightweight steel superstructure and Mr. Otis's electric elevator, skyscrapers—eight, ten, twenty, and even twenty-five stories tall—were springing up in cities across the continent.

The Reach for the Sky was as much psychic as it was physical. The century was young and so was the thinking. Nobody knew what could not be done, and the sky seemed to be literally the limit. A glittering three-story theater marquee was as much an achievement in Shawnee, Oklahoma, as the magnificent Tribune Tower was in Chicago. And these achievements were all the more remarkable because they were stretching the limits of a technology that, despite its great age, had by no means matured.

Today we use derricks—named for John Derrick, the seventeenth-century hangman at Tyburn, London, who invented the device to hoist condemned criminals to their doom—and cranes, named, of course, for the long-legged, long-necked birds the machines resemble. The cranes' venerable ancestor, used exclusively in the early days of the spectacular and still in use where motor power is not available, is the ginpole.

The ginpole's origins, like those of the other five fundamental machines—the lever, the pulley, the wheel, the screw, and the inclined plane—are lost in the mists of antiquity. Ginpoles may have been used to build the pyramids in Egypt and Central America, and to erect Stonehenge. Nobody knows for sure. We do know that the ginpole was the uniquely indispensable tool in the turn-of-the-century's Reach for the Sky.

A ginpole is basically a pulley on a stick. A pulley, or a block—a universally rotating wheel with a groove that a rope runs through—creates a mechanical advantage for moving heavy objects. The genius of the ginpole is that not only does it multiply force, it also moves it in any direction. A ginpole generally has four blocks: one to lift the load, one on either side to move the pole laterally, and one going back from the pole for vertical movement. An operator weighing a hundred pounds (turn-of-the-century workers were small) could lift, turn, position, and lower into place objects many times his size. The simplest components imaginable—a pole, a wheel, and a rope—when animated by brainpower, permit the achievement of amazing feats.

Smaller ginpoles were used to raise larger ginpoles into place, so lifts could be done in apparently impossible circumstances. This was at a time when imagination reigned, and nothing was beyond reach. "Those old-timers could put anything anywhere," says Tony Calvano,

Artkraft's chief of installation—who can also put anything anywhere, but today he uses 450-ton cranes to do it.

The sign erectors' work is often underappreciated in contrast to the flashier evocations of the painters, electricians, and metal-men. But even the greatest creations would languish, as invisible as if they had never existed, unless they could be hoisted into view. As one New York sign man likes to quip: "If you can't get it up, it's a bad sign."

## "LET THERE BE LIGHT!"

*To Americans of the late* nineteenth century, electricity was the miracle of the coming new age. Its invisible power, everyone believed, would one day run machines without horses, heat homes, grow enormous crops, cure illnesses, perhaps even, à la Dr. Frankenstein—Mary Shelley's mad scientist of 1818—create life itself. But most of all, in the dim world of kerosene lanterns and gaslight, the taming of electricity represented a new and almost supernatural light.

People had known about electricity since ancient times in the form of lightning, electric eels, and the way amber rubbed on a cat made its fur stand up. The Greek philosopher Thales of Miletus described the phenomenon in about 600 B.C., and in A.D. 70 the Roman author Pliny the Elder wrote about his own electrical experiments. The modern word "electricity"—from the Greek *elektron,* meaning amber—was coined in 1600 by William Gilbert, physician to Queen Elizabeth I. In his treatise *De Magnete (About Magnets),* he proved that the attraction of bits of fluff to amber is not magnetic, but a different phenomenon—leading to a new way of seeing the world.

The first electrical generator was built by a German physicist, Otto von Guericke, in 1672. The machine consisted of a ball of sulfur mounted on a hand crank. Von Guericke turned the crank with one hand, rotating the ball against his other hand, producing sparks. But electricity could not be properly studied until it was captured by an Italian physicist, Count Alessandro Volta, who built the first battery in 1800.

But while the taming of electricity and the possibility of reliable electric light enthralled the imaginations of scientists and poets, for most people until the 1880s electric light was the light that had been seen only instantaneously in the heavens—crashing across the night sky during storms, flooding the landscape with awesomely brilliant illumination that lasted for but a twinkling of an eye. Suddenly, that wondrous flash of light could be held steadily, indefinitely, merely by turning a switch. The night itself could now be conquered. And messages could be written in the sky.

It's difficult for us, looking back across a century of technological wizardry, to appreciate the emotional impact of electric light on the people of the time. The equivalent invention in our own day is the networked computer, but we're too jaded by our own history of brilliantly applied science to be as impressed as we should be. Not even an alien spacecraft landing in Times Square would get such a rise out of us today. But America in the late nineteenth century was a deeply religious nation where the label "God-fearing" was taken literally—and considered a compliment.

God-fearing citizens gathered, wide-eyed and worshipful, often traveling long distances to witness each new public demonstration of electric lighting. Extra trains brought 10,000 spectators and a horde of reporters to Wabash, Indiana, in 1880, when arc street lighting was turned on there. The scene, as described in *Electrifying America*, David E. Nye's definitive study of the period, was repeated all over the country. Four 3,000-candle arc lights installed on the dome of the courthouse by the Brush Company blazed on, flooding the crowd with the new bright light. The local newspaper reported:

"No shout...or token of joy disturbed the deep silence which suddenly enveloped the onlookers. People stood overwhelmed with awe, as if in the presence of the supernatural. The strange weird light exceeded in power only by the sun, rendered the square as light as midday.... Men fell on their knees, groans were uttered at the sight, and many were dumb with amazement."

As amazing as arc lighting was, Nye says, it was hot and flickering, and therefore less confounding to the population than Thomas Edison's incandescent lamp, with its glowing orange filament inside a clear glass dome. Unveiled in Menlo Park the same year as the

Wabash courthouse lighting, the Edison lamp seemed to defy Nature. "Light by definition had always implied consumption of oxygen, smoke, flickering, heat and danger of fire," says Nye. "For all of human experience light and fire had been synonymous.... The enclosed light bulb seemed an impossible paradox. Fire and light would never again be identical."

Though arc lighting continued to be the street lighting of choice late in the century (New York City had thirty miles of arc-lighted streets by 1886), the incandescent lamp clearly had a different destiny. Because it was smokeless and relatively cool, it was ideal for home and factory lighting. But that rather obvious development had to wait. It simply wasn't yet where the money was. And Thomas Edison, the consummate inventor-businessman who developed, among other things, the earliest electrical power distribution system, always went where the money was. By the mid-1880s, he had built more than 300 generating plants all over the world, most to serve high-profile users—big hotels like Chicago's Palmer House, world-famous theaters like Milan's La Scala, fashionable commercial and residential districts in New York and San Francisco.

Edison and his competitors were in business to sell electricity. That meant selling a means to generate the power and creating a demand for it. The new electricity industry discovered a wonderful pretelevision method of stimulating its potential markets: designing fabulous displays for the world's fairs and expositions that were so popular then. These lavish, sprawling, self-contained complexes of exhibits and demonstrations were all organized around the same theme. They celebrated glorious visions of the modern world. And they all made extensive, spectacular use of electric light.

Fairs and expositions like those in Chicago (1894), Buffalo (1901), St. Louis (1904), and San Francisco (1915) were laid out like elegant little cities. Every thoroughfare was lined with streetlights, an impressive sight from a centrally located tower. Entire buildings, like Buffalo's Electricity Tower and San Francisco's Tower of Jewels, were outlined and decorated in electric light. Designers missed no opportunity to create a lighted canopy between buildings or shine lights on or around the many pools and fountains that burbled in the open public spaces.

Great halls filled with everything under the sun manufactured in an industrializing America were similarly outlined and flooded with light. In the technology exhibits, visitors were shown that modern science and electricity were synonymous. (Steam, of course, was scorned as hopelessly out of date.) And elaborate light shows were staples of after-dark entertainment.

Exhibitors and electric companies poured their resources and products into these fairs as if they were building new worlds from scratch—and, in a sense, they were. The Chicago World's Fair of 1894, the largest and most ambitious of the period, had more electric lights than any city in the country—even New York. Among its many wonders were two gigantic electrical fountains in a vast lighted basin that blasted 22,000 gallons of colored water per minute into the air; a huge lighted Ferris wheel; a moving sidewalk; battery-driven boats gliding among a network of lagoons; and searchlights so powerful they could be seen in Milwaukee, almost a hundred miles away.

Attendance was overwhelming. According to Nye, a total of 55 million people went to the great lighted expositions in Chicago, Buffalo, and St. Louis—a third of the population of the United States. That means it is a virtual certainty that everyone living in the United States between 1894 and 1904 either attended an exposition or had a friend or relative who did. Even the Super Bowl can't claim that degree of penetration.

These highly theatrical events sent their audiences home with an appetite for electrical spectacularity—a term that has a specific meaning to those of us who build outdoor displays. A typical fair, on a grand scale, met perfectly the requirements of spectacularity: it had immense size, plentiful and glittering light, animation, and three-dimensionality. And it was designed to be seen in a dominant, commanding position in the context of its environment—in this case, in the still-dark, workaday world of the late nineteenth century. And if the homes the attendees returned to were still equipped with gas jets, an inspiring dose of spectacularity was as close as downtown—where giant electric advertising signs were redrawing the skyline.

Within twenty years after the first streetlights were turned on in the 1880s, outdoor electric signs, many of staggering size, were being built in large numbers all over the country. The tidal wave of these displays swept the nation far ahead of domestic, factory, and even street lighting. In nineteenth-century America, this was the natural order of things. The juice was simply following the money.

## THE POLITICS OF POWER

*With so much at stake,* power battles raged. And no clash emitted more sparks than that between Thomas Edison, the darling of the elite establishment and defender of Direct Current, and Nikola Tesla, the immigrant Serbian visionary who championed the new Alternating Current that promised power to the masses.

To this day many continue to be electrified by this controversy. Electrical history buffs line up on the side of either Tesla or Edison. There is no middle ground. Their two worldviews are as incompatible as the Alternating Current and Direct Current systems over which they battled.

The difference between the two forms of electrical transmission contains social implications as significant as the technological. DC power can travel only for short distances. After that, line losses reach unacceptable levels: the power just dribbles away. So the user has to be close to the source. Alternating Current, by contrast, is the people's power. Easily manufactured and distributed over wide grids, it is the most democratic of media. But the main business of Edison and the General Electric Company was the sale and installation of DC generating plants wherever the affluent users were. So the difference between the approaches of the two scientists, the pragmatist and the dreamer, was more than philosophical.

Tesla is widely believed to be the greatest inventive genius of the industrial age. He was certainly the most influential. His discovery of the principle of the rotating magnetic field led to his invention of the polyphase AC system, the induction motor, AC power transmission, and the coil transformer. His more than 700 worldwide patents included fundamental discoveries in wireless communications, radio, telephony, high-voltage circuitry, bladeless turbines and pumps, optics and photography, fluorescent light, X-rays, logic circuits, robotics, aeronautics, electrotherapeutics, and much more—including many inventions still unexplored and others for which later developers received credit.

Tesla's inventions permeate the modern world. This is as true today as it was in 1917, when physicist B. A. Behrend told the annual meeting of the American Institute of Electrical Engineers, "Were we to seize and eliminate from our industrial world the results of Mr. Tesla's work, the wheels of industry would cease to turn, our electric cars and trains would stop, our towns would be dark, our mills would be dead and idle." Behrend finished his peroration with an original poem:

> *"Nature and nature's laws lay hid in night!*
> *God said: 'Let Tesla be' and all was light."*

But Tesla's main distinction—the grand insight that places him in the ranks of Thales, Faraday, and Einstein—is his vision of the essence of the universe—a force uniting all phenomena in harmonic resonance—that as a scientist he was determined not only to describe but also to tame and use.

He was literally a grasper of lightning. One of his most famous experiments was the "fireball" with which he amazed visitors to his laboratory, including Mark Twain and other notables. One witness reported: "Imagine yourself seated in a large, well-lighted room, with mountains of curious-looking machinery on all sides. A tall, thin young man walks up to you, and by merely snapping his fingers creates instantaneously a ball of leaping red flame, and holds it calmly in his hands. As you gaze you are surprised to see it does not burn his fingers. He lets it fall upon his clothing, on his hair, into your lap, and, finally, puts the ball of flame into a wooden box. You are amazed to see that nowhere does the flame leave the slightest trace, and you rub your eyes to make sure you are not asleep."

Tesla routinely worked with voltages in the millions. The famous photograph of him in his laboratory shows the elegant young physicist peacefully reading in his chair, surrounded by a nimbus of sparks that would have impressed Thor.

In Colorado Springs, where Tesla lived from 1899 to 1900, he pursued his interests both in high voltage and in transmitting power over long distances. He succeeded in lighting a bank of 200 lamps from a distance of 25 miles, and manufactured flashes of lightning nearly 150 miles in diameter. His claim to have received signals from other planets, and his later boast that he had created a death ray capable of vaporizing 10,000 airplanes at a distance of 250 miles, attracted interest as well as derision. This may help to explain why upon his death in New York in 1943 his papers were confiscated by the U.S. government and still have never been published in their entirety.

Edison, by contrast, was a hardheaded businessman. He was also the more famous of the two, his genius at politics and self-promotion being on a par with his inventiveness.

Born in 1847, Edison by the time of his death in 1931 held more than 1,000 patents. His first, an improved stock ticker, financed the construction of his Newark laboratory in 1871. (In 1876 he moved to his most famous location, Menlo Park.) His other important innovations include a long-lasting filament lightbulb, an improved telephone transmitter, the phonograph, the first motion picture camera, the mimeograph machine, the fluoroscope, an improved battery—and scores of other useful devices that he manufactured and sold, with impressive success. In 1889 the Edison Electric Light Company became the General Electric Company.

To the world, Edison was the "Genius of Menlo Park." But to Tesla, Edison, for all his commercial achievements, was a bit of a dullard. "If Edison had a needle to find in a haystack," Tesla told the *New York Times* in 1931, "he would proceed at once with the diligence of the bee to examine straw after straw until he found the object of his search. . . . I was a sorry witness of such doings, knowing that a little theory and calculation would have saved him ninety per cent of his labor."

Tesla was born in Croatia of Serbian parents in 1856. He sailed for America in 1884, arriving in New York with nothing in his pockets but four cents, a sheaf of poems, and detailed plans and calculations for a flying machine. He presented himself to his hero, Thomas Edison, who immediately put him to work in his New York laboratory. Edison, a hail-fellow-well-met—self-important, obstinate, and somewhat deaf, especially to others' insights—made merciless fun of the refined, courtly European. It wasn't long before the two fell into dispute—not least about the relative viability of Tesla's Alternating Current vs. the Direct Current which Edison was by then wedded to with a passion that in retrospect seems more emotional than scientific.

Within a year after leaving Edison, Tesla was starting to make friends in high places. The most important of these was George Westinghouse, head of the Westinghouse Electric Company, who bought the rights to Tesla's polyphase system of AC dynamos, transformers, and motors—and the services of their inventor. This financed the construction of Tesla's first laboratory. The traveling lecture circuit was the medium of dissemination of scientific knowledge in those days, and Tesla was also taking his show, with its flashy demonstrations and futuristic discourse, on the road, to international acclaim.

Not about to let this Serbian upstart upstage him, Edison threw himself wholeheartedly into discrediting Tesla and his AC power. Throughout the late 1880s Edison traveled the country conducting demonstrations in which he electrocuted dogs and cats by wiring them to metal plates connected to AC and then frying them with volts. By no means the last demagogue to invoke the specter of Our Endangered Children to resist novelty and promote an agenda, Edison announced to a shocked public that the same horrible fate awaited their own offspring, should this dangerous newfangled current be allowed into their homes.

Tesla countered his rival's claims by giving exhibitions in which he lighted lamps without wires by allowing electricity—at massive voltages but minuscule amps—to flow through his body. Tesla identified electricity with the fundamental life force, extolled its health-giving properties, and claimed it was dangerous only when improperly handled.

One of Edison's more interesting schemes was an effort to persuade the New York State legislature to make electric power in voltages above 800 illegal. This would have effectively criminalized Tesla's experiments and ended the use of Alternating Current in New York. Edison's theory was that the rest of the nation would soon follow suit, and Tesla's high-voltage transformers and polyphase motors would land in the dustbin of history. The scheme nearly succeeded. It was foiled only by an impassioned last-minute address to the legislature by George Westinghouse—including threats to sue everyone in sight for conspiracy.

Edison's next attempt was even more ingenious. Through a confederate, Professor Harold P. Brown, he persuaded the warden of Sing Sing prison to install an electric chair for the execution of criminals. He even supplied the device at no charge. Edison reasoned that the efficiency of the electrocution would prove his point to the safety-minded public.

The Edison public relations machine made certain that the model execution was lavishly ballyhooed and well attended by the press. But, alas, the script failed to go as planned. Every newspaper in the country carried the story on its front page on August 7, 1890. Instead of promptly frying the criminal, the chair merely scorched him. In total, four attempts had to be made before the unfortunate felon, a hatchet murderer named William Kemmler, finally gave up the ghost—and even then, it was not before his spine caught fire and his eyeballs exploded. The press, after recovering from the mass fit of vomiting this revolting spectacle induced, reported that electrocution by AC current—or "Westinghousing," as Edison termed it—was undoubtedly the most inefficient means of execution that could possibly be devised.

This fiasco prompted much gnashing of teeth in the Edison camp. Edison, when he heard about it, smashed the contents of his desk, including a brand-new Kodak camera that had just been presented to him by its inventor, George Eastman. He also gave orders to kill Professor Brown on sight. But he forgave him a few days later and sent him back on the road, where he successfully "Westing-housed" more animals, including pigs, calves, and large dogs. It would be twenty years before Edison admitted that his hostility to AC power had been his greatest career blunder. "I don't care so much for a fortune," he was fond of saying, "as I do for getting ahead of the other fellow."

Ultimately, Tesla's AC power triumphed. The Westinghouse group won the contract to build the first power-generating system at Niagara Falls. The project, which still provides the juice that lights up a large part of New York State, bore Tesla's name and patent numbers when the turbines started turning in 1896.

"If there ever was a man who created so much and whose praises were sung so little—it was Nikola Tesla," recalled Gardner H. Dales of the Niagara Mohawk Power Corporation in a 1956 address to the American Institute of Electrical Engineers. "It was his invention, the polyphase system, and its first use by the Niagara Falls Power Company that laid the foundation for the power system used in this country and throughout the entire world today."

## MR. HAMMER'S FLASHER

*The first electric sign* flickered on at one of the most prestigious of the late nineteenth century's world's fairs—the London International Electrical Exposition of 1882. It spelled the name the world would forever connect with the "invention" of electricity—EDISON.

Edison didn't invent the electric sign, but one of his key lieutenants did. He was William J. Hammer, arguably one of the greatest electrical engineers of all time. Hammer's inventions and developments, notably the automatic flasher that enabled electric lamps to turn on and off without human intervention, formed the basis for modern sign technology.

Hammer, who was only twenty-four, was sent to London in 1881 to serve as chief engineer of Edison's English Electric Company. There he built history's first central station for incandescent lighting, and designed elaborate electrical displays using Edison products for expositions in London and Paris. His EDISON sign was a marketing device to promote the company at those fairs.

The little hand-operated display was only ten feet long and not more than three feet high. It was installed above a pipe organ in the concert room of the Crystal Palace and unveiled on January 14, 1882. Hammer turned it on with a large, hand-operated knife switch, then used a hand-operated commutator to turn the lamp-filled letters off and relight them again one at a time, spelling the boss's name. A photographer was on hand to record the historic event—Edison, knowing he was writing history, never missed a photo op—and the famous time exposure that resulted shows light appearing to drift across the sign in eerie waves. There's no record of what was played on the organ at the electric moment, but surely it was something momentous.

As exciting as history's first sign turn-on was, Hammer's finest hour would come a year later, when he would demonstrate his automatic flasher, operating history's first automated electric sign. He was in Berlin by then, chief engineer of the German Edison Company, in charge of building all the Edison plants in Germany. The sign, a larger version of the first, was installed above the door of the Edison Pavilion of the Berlin Health Exposition. This time an electric motor drove the commutator, but the message was the same: EDISON.

A year later, Hammer built a flashing "Column of Light" and a model all-electric house for the Franklin Institute's International Electrical Exhibition in Philadelphia. In 1889, he built a display for the Paris Exhibition that entwined American and French flags made of colored lights and, using flashers and rheostats, made them wave—the true forerunner of the spectacular.

The stage was set for the birth of the sky sign.

## AMERICA'S GREAT WHITE WAYS

One of the least-known facts of the early twentieth century is that every city and town—not only New York—had its own White Way, a thoroughfare of light, entertainment, and electric advertisement that proclaimed local pride and suffused passersby with the glowing sense of possibility that the new lighting represented.

The original Great White Way was indeed in New York City—that portion of Broadway between Madison Square on 23rd Street and Longacre Square up in the 40s that was defined by its electric signs shortly after the turn of the century. The street's fame spread so quickly that everyone in the country soon knew what the White Way was—and knew they had to have one too. It was a sign of modernity—a premier value at the time—and it would be a shame to be left behind.

The opportunity wasn't lost on the new electric power industry. General Electric and Westinghouse teamed up with local public utility companies to sell electricity, equipment, and services. Soon, any town that could afford it had a generating plant.

The typical hometown White Way consisted of a street-lighting system—arc lights in the early days, incandescent lamps later—that illuminated the central business district, usually the main street and town square. Everyone knew that the dazzling new light attracted business. Merchants tapped into the system, and advertisers built electric signs along the thoroughfare. The town's moving picture theater got a sparkling new marquee. The citizens of Portsmouth, Ohio, and Wichita, Kansas, walked proudly through their light-as-day White Ways and imagined they had brought a piece of New York-style glamour to their own front yards.

The inauguration of a White Way was always a gala civic event. The celebration that welcomed the White Way to New Haven, Connecticut, on the night of December 15, 1911, included a Grand Parade with nine brass bands, every motorized vehicle in town, and uniformed marching units, including the Businessmen of New Haven bedecked in silk top hats and wearing American flags draped over their right shoulders. "Let everyone decorate," urged the *New Haven Times Leader.* "Let everyone be on time and autos and floats display their numbers." The newspaper laid out the order of the parade and the route in detail, and every man, woman, and child in New Haven turned out.

It is evident that this advance had not been without opposition. The *New Haven Register* ran an editorial cartoon depicting a high brick wall in ruins, opening a path to a prosperous main street ablaze in brand-new streetlights. "Three Cheers," said the caption. "The Wall of Rock, ribbed with conservatism, is busted."

White Ways were everywhere. An announcement in the Fall 1909 *Signs of the Times,* headlined "Will Have Gay White Way," informs readers, "A new lighting system has been ordered for the amusement center in Redondo, California. Two thousand incandescent lamps will be used."

Those who had been to the big cities had seen the future and brought home amazing stories about what the home folks had to look forward to.

In San Francisco, where more than a million people lived in 1916, Market Street was the Edison Company's first "Path of Gold," an "intensive White Way" illuminating the interiors and exteriors of hotels, opera houses, and restaurants, as well as the street leading down to the Ferry Union Depot, which was surrounded by a semicircle of electric signs as big as buildings.

Campus Martius in Detroit, where all the main streets came together like the spokes of a wheel, was surrounded by buildings with signs that were four and five stories high. One had a chariot race in electric lights with moving horses and yellow dust.

Chicago had given much of the country its first look at the magic of electricity on a grand scale at its glorious Exhibition of 1894. Within fifteen years it boasted a modern electrified wonderland called the Loop, blazing with light, where sophisticated ladies and gentlemen stepped smartly from touring cars under sparkling theater marquees, and huge signs that blocked out the stars told stories in colored lights.

Every city of any size had, in addition to streetlights, animated advertising spectaculars that seemed alive. These wonderful signs are long gone now. Even their ghosts have given up. They are remembered only by postcard collectors, librarians of a certain age, and veteran journalists who know what's in their papers' photo morgues. Unlike Times Square, the White Ways of these cities didn't survive past the 1950s, falling victim to urban decline, changing fashion, and unfriendly zoning. But they thrived for many years, and here they are, at the beginning, a reminder that the spectacular was an all-American creation, flourishing from coast to coast. Some examples:

- In the heart of Omaha, the Old Dutch Cleanser woman, a Vermeer peasant in floppy hat, apron, and wooden shoes outlined in incandescent lamps, chased dirt every night, attacking the offending unspecified contaminant and flailing at it with a big stick. The 38-by-54-foot display was built in 1909 for the Cudahy Packing Company. The slogan was: "Chases Dirt!"
- A merry family in a Stevens Duryea motorcar with spinning B. F. Goodrich tires chugged in place above Cleveland's Euclid Avenue in 1912. Nearby, a music roll revolved on an Everett Player Piano, inviting the viewer to imagine a favorite tune, and a sailboat glided toward Mathews & Gilbert Summer and Winter Homes on the bucolic Lake Erie shore—all drawn enthusiastically in bumps of electric light. This composition is a particular fa-

vorite of mine, as it embodies an entire constellation of elements of the Good Life, pre-World War I.

- What's for breakfast on Christmas morning? How about a nourishing bowl of oatmeal? Chicagoans doing last-minute shopping in the Loop on Christmas Eve 1913 went home with that message after watching the lighting of a four-story Quaker Oats spectacular. The display promised "The World's Best Breakfast," a giant bowl of twinkling brown oatmeal emitting silvery incandescent "steam."

- The Diving Girl, a bosomy bathing beauty in a daring swimsuit showing her shapely legs bare all the way up to her knees, stopped traffic at Fifth and Broadway in downtown Los Angeles in 1913. Smiling sweetly, she plunged from her diving board into the water with an electric splash, emerging an instant later holding aloft a refreshing bottle of East Side Beer, retrieved inexplicably from the cold, briny depths. Then, ever the frolicsome party girl, she announced in large block letters, "IT'S GREAT!"

- In 1909, the largest sign in the South welcomed friends and neighbors to Montgomery, Alabama. The display was mounted on a seven-and-a-half-story steel grid that towered over the town's railroad station. Paid for by the Montgomery Light and Water Power Company, the spectacular consisted of the city's name in 10-foot letters, a red 50-foot Key to the City, and Montgomery's message to the world: "Montgomery: Your Opportunity." The design was the result of a contest, honors going to Miss Anita Strassburger for the key idea, and to local newspaperman Gordon McKinley for the pithy slogan. Thousands turned out for the lighting ceremony, some traveling miles over dirt roads on mules and in horse-drawn wagons. The Montgomery Cavalry Band played "Montgomery: Your Opportunity," a march commissioned for the occasion. Fireworks exploded overhead as the sign's rainbow of colored lights began its dazzling show, spelling the brightest name in the heart of Dixie, and the crowd gave the Montgomery Light and Water Power Company three cheers.

- Montgomery may have claimed the largest electric sign in the South, but Atlanta claimed the most beautiful. The advertiser was Trio Laundry, urging its fellow Atlantans in 1916 to regard sartorial hygiene as a pressing matter. The 45-foot-tall downtown display, spanning two buildings, had a huge illuminated clock in the center, held in the talons of twin dragons equipped with fiery tails and shimmering wings. The animated dragons breathed electric lightning bolts into the message above the clock, lending it urgency: "Correct Dry Cleaning Laundering Time." That time, says the clock, of course, is . . . any time!

- San Francisco's Market Street Theater became the House of Movies in 1910, anticipating by seventy years the modern multiplex cinema. The latest Vitagraph and Biograph releases were shown continuously, but the electric show on the street topped them all. The arched two-story entrance was encrusted with Edison Mazda lamps—named for the Zoroastrian Force of Light—while above the arch twinkled the period's popular classical touch: the ubiquitous fountain of lights between flaming torches.

- In 1908, the F. W. Cook Brewing Co. of Evansville, Indiana, also opted for fashion over originality with its choice of skinny 50-foot torches flanking its logo and signature. The whole rather precarious-looking display was an amazing eight stories high and almost as wide, identifying for thirsty Hoosiers the home of Cook's Goldblume Beer.

Many of the first generation of electric signs were the work of local or regional sign companies. But national leaders emerged early. Foremost among them was Thomas J. Cusack of Chicago. Cusack's salesmen, like the billposters of yore, penetrated every corner of America—including Gude's New York turf—seeking customers with the wherewithal to realize an electric vision of themselves. If that vision proved to be nonspecific, Cusack's men were ready with a suggestion: How about a nice fountain? Thus the signature "Cusack Fountain," with its Romanesque base and willowy water spouts, adorned signs from Alabama to Seattle, and may help explain the rampant popularity of that image in turn-of-the-century electric signs.

The choice of imagery reflected the contemporary obsession with the Beaux-Arts style, a neoclassical hodgepodge of everything people thought was cultured and swell—dragons and lightning bolts, garlands and laurel wreaths, shields and weapons, lions and peacocks, ribbons and vines, and the overwhelming favorites: fountains and torches.

## SWEPT BY OCEAN BREEZES

*The modern advertising spectacular* was born in New York City on a hot July evening in 1892. Like every spectacular since, it was more than an advertisement for a product. It was a celebration of a compelling vision. Crude as it seems now, it aimed to push the viewer's buttons—and it succeeded.

The location was the V-shaped south end of Madison Square, the intersection where Fifth Avenue crosses Broadway at 23rd Street, on an assemblage of mid-nineteenth-century architecture known collectively at the time as the Cowcatcher Building. A wedge of one-story shops jutted into the vast expanses of broad boulevard spreading on either side, and the eight-story Cumberland Hotel towered over the shops, its bare front wall facing the teeming intersection. The broad brick facade, measuring 60 by 68 feet, was a wall dog's dream, and the space had long been filled with painted advertisements.

What was different on that night in 1892 was that the painted signs had been replaced by rows of raised letters—some taller than a man, some as big as the horses that pulled the carriages and omnibuses along busy, fashionable Fifth Avenue below. The 107 letters were formed of 1,457 16-candlepower red, blue, green, and frosted white Edison electric lamps. As night fell and a crowd watched in amazement, the rows lit up one at a time, spelling out this message:

BUY HOMES ON
LONG ISLAND
SWEPT BY OCEAN BREEZES
MANHATTAN BEACH
ORIENTAL HOTEL
MANHATTAN HOTEL
GILMORE'S BAND
BROCK'S RESTAURANT

The display was built by the Edison General Electric Company for a canny entrepreneur named E. J. Corbin, president of the Long Island Rail Road. Manhattan Beach was to the well-to-do what Coney Island was to the working class, and Corbin's aim was to trigger in the minds of his sweltering constituency a picture of the paradise that awaited just a short, comfortable train ride away—a resort offering fine dining, the latest in popular music, and other tasteful pleasures, all swept most reliably by ocean breezes. In an early and apparently successful venture into cross-marketing, Corbin plugged Manhattan Beach's various businesses too. Sousa's band soon edged out Gilmore's, Brock's eatery was replaced by Hagenbeck, and Pain's Fire-works offered one of the nineteenth century's favorite spectacles. It seems safe to assume Corbin didn't give this space away and the rail-road itself enjoyed a free ride.

Whether or not the LIRR enjoyed a surge in ridership, the sign was deemed a great success. It made international news, was both praised and condemned in newspaper editorials, and never failed to draw crowds every night. Reported the magazine *Western Electrician:* "This illuminated sign is not only a commercial success, but when all the lamps are lighted is really a magnificent sight. Its splendor is vis-ible from far away uptown, and its glow on the sky can be easily seen from the East and North Rivers. It is an immense step forward in the evolution of electric light."

Years later, Theodore Dreiser remembered the sign in his 1923 essay "The Color of a Great City": "Walking up or down Broadway on a hot summer night, this sign was an inspiration and an invitation. It made one long to go to Manhattan Beach."

At a time when most of New York City still had gas street light-ing and electricity in the home was still a novelty available only to the very rich, these eight rows of galvanized boxes with colored glass globes in them filling the night cityscape with dazzling illumi-nation were truly a wonder. And even more wondrous was the way the rows flashed on and off in sequence. The wall would fill, line by line, then go dark, and the sequence would start all over again, every three minutes from dusk to midnight. This miracle was executed nightly in a sweatily unmiraculous manner. In a little house on the roof of the building—today still called an electrical hut—workers pulled a series of levers, one for each row of letters. But the public's knowledge that a mere mortal with strong arms was the Great Oz behind the curtain, stage-managing this heavenly show, didn't di-minish its magic.

For the next ten years, until the Cowcatcher was razed to make room for the Flatiron Building, the north wall of the Cumberland Hotel was New York's premier outdoor advertising location. O. J. Gude took over the space by the mid-1890s. (Many later accounts credited Gude with inventing the Manhattan Beach sign. Not so, although it's possible that his company had a hand in its fabrication and installation.) A series of advertisers followed the LIRR, including the *New York Times,* promising "All the News That's Fit to Print," and politely nudging the reading public to try its Sunday magazine supplement ("Have You Seen It?").

The most controversial display on the site was built by Gude just before the turn of the century for the Pittsburgh tycoon H. J. Heinz, a manufacturer of 57 varieties of food products whose name has long been synonymous with the pickle. The Heinz display celebrated but five of the famous 57 "Good Things for the Table": Sweet Pickles, Tomato Ketchup, India Relish, Tomato Soup, and Peach Butter. At the top of this mouthwatering stack flashed the Heinz logo, a bright green pickle.

This was the mother of all pickles, fully 50 feet long, in dazzling pickle-green incandescent lamps. By all accounts, it flashed against its pulsating orange-and-blue background like nothing in the New York skyline had ever flashed before—or since, for that matter—so rapid had been the advances in lamp technology since 1892, and so daring was the conceit of this design, which easily puts later pop and psychedelic art in the shade. The "57," in white numerals eight feet high, flashed with pickle-matching intensity.

Vulgar! screamed newspaper editorial writers. Tawdry! pronounced the elderly veterans of Edith Wharton's genteel New York as they skirted Madison Square to avoid the affront. And people who lived blocks away complained about the eerie visual throb of green and white that nightly invaded their still-gaslit inner sancta.

Civic beautifiers loved to hate the great green monstrosity, which stood in such garish contrast to the lofty, floodlit, Beaux-Arts Dewey Arch across the way, erected to commemorate Admiral Dewey's victory over the Spanish fleet in the recent Spanish-American War. Never mind that the "battle" and the war that followed were more press-agentry than serious combat. Even the faded black-and-white photos of the time depict the Victorian garlanded patriotic Arch and the Pickle from Another Planet in full-tilt aesthetic collision.

Heinz, meanwhile, rejoiced in this bountiful harvest of publicity and stood his ground. He loved his great green pickle, and he wasn't going to turn it off for anyone.

Finally, however, the city did it for him. The Cumberland had to make way for the Gibraltar-like Flatiron Building, a monument to dignity and permanence that would never, ever be besmirched by electric advertising signs.

Heinz had the last word, however. His farewell to the neighborhood, written in lights beneath his beloved pickle, was a self-congratulatory verse of his own composition:

> *Here at the death of the wall of fame*
> *We must inscribe a well-known name*
> *The man whose Varieties your palate did tickle*
> *Whose name is emblazoned in the big green pickle.*

The face-off between the pickle man and the hero of the Spanish-American War was over, but the victory of the Dewey camp was a sour one. Admiralty cigarettes had already put up a spectacular on the north side of the square. Nearby restaurants in the elegant neighborhood had discovered the allure of electric marquees. And slowly the lights were spreading north on Broadway toward Herald Square, itself aglow even in 1902. The Great White Way was aborning, and there was no turning back.

One heroic-minded midwestern entrepreneur decided to bring his electrified vision to New York—with decidedly mixed results.

## "Leaders of the World"

*In 1909, an ambitious Dayton,* Ohio, sign salesman named Elwood Rice came to New York City bursting with an idea as big as the new century itself. Rice was determined to build the biggest electric sign in the world, towering over the bustling center of the country's largest city. The sign would portray a scene everyone at the time knew—the chariot race from *Ben-Hur*—and commemorate the "Leaders of the World"—a salute to a mighty nation and the American businessmen who made it great. A "talking" sign above the thrilling chariot race would recognize those Leaders who wished to pay—by the minute—to have their names and products thus exalted.

It seemed like a nifty scheme. In reality, it was a transcendent example of the over-the-top pre-World War I imagination. Rice's ego-driven extravaganza ultimately cost him a fortune. But he created a legendary landmark.

Motion pictures were the coming craze in 1910, but audiences were still accustomed to getting their doses of major spectacle live onstage. The popular theater obliged with shipwrecks, hurricanes, heaving rivers, volcanoes, and ice floes. One of the most popular stage spectacles of all time was *Ben-Hur*, based on General Lew Wallace's 1880 best-selling potboiler, *Ben-Hur: A Tale of the Christ*. After the stage version made its 1899 debut in New York, numerous productions were mounted all over North America, making it the most popular play since *Uncle Tom's Cabin*. And any stage *Ben-Hur* worth its salt had a chariot race with real horses, in which the scenery-chewing contestants and their steeds would clatter across the boards into the arms of waiting stagehands and be hurried out a door, through an alley to an entrance on the other side of the stage for yet another, and another, and another frantic crossing. This image, with its dramatic triumph of good over evil, would be the perfect leitmotif for Rice's lucrative and patriotic monument.

Securing a lease for the roof of the Normandie Hotel at 38th Street and Broadway, overlooking vibrant Herald Square, Rice built his sign in his Ohio factory and shipped it to New York in 1910 in eight railroad cars. Fielding an army of riggers and electricians, Rice had the sign up and running in a mere three months. The city had never seen such a massive display. Supported by a 60-ton superstructure, the sign measured 72 feet high and 90 feet wide, nearly dwarfing the eight-story hotel beneath it.

The chariot race struck the turn-of-the-century public as awesomely realistic. It was "more perfect and natural in its movement," reported the magazine *The Strand*, "than the finest colored cinematograph picture."

What Rice's audience saw in Herald Square topped even the most opulent *Ben-Hur* anyone had ever seen. The three-dimensional diorama depicted the stadium audience on a cylinder, rotating in a direction opposite to the racing chariots—creating an illusion of immense motion and speed. Sequences of flashing colored electric lights created the movements of the chariots, horses, and drivers in remarkable detail. The wheels spun so fast the spokes were a blur, the drivers leaned forward and cracked their whips, and the horses' legs galloped furiously. Rice attended to every detail—clouds of dust raised by the wheels and horses' hooves, the flapping of the drivers' robes, the waving of the horses' manes and tails.

The press and the public loved it. Throngs clogged the streets for weeks after the sign was turned on in June of 1910. Horse-drawn omnibuses inched through crowds gazing upward in amazement at the endless sequence of thirty-second races. A special police unit was assigned to Herald Square through the summer to keep traffic moving.

It captured for its amazed audience, not only the excitement of the contest but what it represented in the story: the triumph of Christianity over paganism. Rice made sure that the noble Ben-Hur, a Jewish convert to Christianity, was so clearly the winner, even his horses appeared more confident. The godless Roman prince Messala, on the other hand, strained mightily behind a panicked team, eating the yellowish dust billowing around him.

The business end of the sign, however, was its "talking" portion. Framed by a stage "curtain" drawn back and tied with jumbo lighted "tassels," it contained space for fifty-four four-foot letters operating on a ten-minute cycle, flashing ten different one-minute corporate messages. Rice landed a number of accounts, including *Scientific American* magazine, which devoted a multipage photo spread to this technological marvel. But, unfortunately, the paying advertisers failed to flock to the display with the same zeal as the press and the public.

Rice tried adding a magnificent bronze plaque to the display, permanently honoring his customers, the Leaders of the World. He printed up stacks of plaques and had himself photographed in front of them to demonstrate both their desirability and their availability. He gave away tens of thousands of minutes of what we now call public-service messages, honoring, for example, Colonel Theodore Roosevelt on his triumphant return from Africa.

But even then, businessmen didn't bite. Even the inducement of being named an Officially Recognized Leader of the World failed to persuade them to share advertising space with competitors.

Following the time-honored military tradition of "Declare a victory, and then retreat," Rice called his campaign a success, then returned to Dayton to rescue what was left of his sign business.

The episode contains a lesson, perhaps, that the *real* leaders of the world sometimes go unrewarded. For Rice's "Leaders of the World" was a remarkable achievement. Less than twenty years after the hand-operated "Swept by Ocean Breezes" flashed on and off—feebly, by 1910 standards—the city and the world were treated to a mechanized, electrified, fully automated extravaganza that foreshadowed even greater things to come.

## CROSSROADS OF THE WORLD

*By the time Elwood Rice's* chariot race was in full gallop in fashionable Herald Square, the neighborhood eight blocks up Broadway had developed an electrifying personality of its own. Times Square, so named for the New York Times Tower erected at the south end in 1904, offered a nightly outdoor light show that was one of the wonders of the new electric world.

Visiting British author Arnold Bennett was moved to describe Times Square in 1912 as:

> *an enfevered phantasmagoria....Above the layer of darkness enormous moving images of things in electricity—a mastodon kitten playing with a ball of thread, an umbrella in a shower of rain, siphons of soda-water being emptied and filled, gigantic horses galloping at full speed, and an incredible heraldry of chewing-gum.... Sky-signs!*

Times Square has always invited such poetic reach, but never more so than in the heady days of the early electric spectacular. "What a magnificent spectacle," remarked G. K. Chesterton, "for a man who couldn't read." The dream of being able to write, draw, and sculpt in the night sky finally had come true. And the oversize, surreal creations that resulted startled even the most sophisticated world travelers.

The sensitive English poet Rupert Brooke was determined to be offended by the unapologetic commercialism of the new American supersigns. But his awe is clear in his 1914 description of the drama of a sturdy dental health product defeating the devil of tooth decay:

> *... two vast fiery toothbrushes, erect, leaning towards each other, and hanging on to the bristles of them a little devil, little but gigantic, who kicks and wriggles and glares. After a few moments the devil, baffled by the firmness of the bristles, stops, hangs still, rolls his eyes, moon-large, and, in a fury of disappointment, goes out, leaving only the night, blacker and a little bewildered, and the unconscious throngs of ant-like human beings.*

Ant-like, perhaps, in the presence of such giants. But not unconscious. The parade of horse-drawn omnibuses loaded with wide-eyed sightseers never stopped, witnesses reported. And the Square was one of the first destinations of newly arrived immigrants, many of whom could not yet speak English. The language of the spectaculars was universal.

As the Great White Way rolled up Broadway to engulf Times Square and move on toward Columbus Circle, the turf battles that still pervade New York City political life raged on. Members of civic beautification organizations like the anti-sign Fifth Avenue Association and the Municipal Art Society lined up against businessmen-promoters and their ally, the Broadway Association. Ultimately, the city zoning ordinances of 1909, 1916, and 1922, putting a stamp on the inevitable, assured the future of the Great White Way as a milieu of unbridled commercial expression.

The first spectacular in Longacre Square, soon to be Times Square, was built in 1903, before the Times Tower was built and while the subway was still under construction. Big and spindly, it recommended Trimble's Whiskey to the thirsty workmen and merchants who spent their days and many of their nights in the still-drab neighborhood of shops, hotels, and saloons. The location of this pioneer sign is notable. It was on the face of a low building at the north end of the Square, on West 47th Street between Broadway and Seventh

Avenue—the site that would soon become the centerpiece of the Square's gallery of spectaculars, and remain so throughout the century.

The following year the subway started running, bringing crowds of new visitors to Times Square. Soon there was plenty for them to do. They frequented the row of fine new theaters that lined West 42nd Street between the Square and Eighth Avenue, attended the flickers, dined at Rector's and at Hammerstein's Roof Garden, checked out the latest news bulletins posted beside the door of the new New York Times Tower, and marveled at the blossoming garden of electric signs. By then, the spectaculars were as integral to the life of Times Square as the theaters, hotels, and restaurants were. The Crossroads of the World as we know it was already recognizable.

My grandfather, Jake, was in the middle of all this, which is right where he wanted to be. Strauss & Co. did a booming business in its second-floor Times Square factory, right behind the Trimble's Whiskey location. With Jake as chief engineer and general manager, Ben branched out from the theatrical displays and marquees that were his first love, and snagged a share of the other plentiful new sign business created by the advent of electric power.

Ben and Jake built their first advertising spectacular in 1914, on a rooftop on nearby Broadway and West 45th Street. The customer was Willys-Overland, then the number two automaker in the country. Willys-Overland was struggling to overtake the clever Henry Ford, whose affordable assembly-line-produced Model T was, hands down, the average American's car of choice. The sign showed a jaunty Willys-Overland and its happy occupants on the go. Ben and Jake rebuilt it several times—the last time, in 1924, in neon, making it the very first neon spectacular in Times Square.

Selling a spectacular in Times Square is never easy, and it can't have been any easier then. Ben and Jake had to go up against the formidable O. J. Gude, who dominated the territory.

Gude considered the Square his personal art gallery, a showplace for electric displays that demonstrated his belief in the convergence of fine and commercial art. Of the four spectaculars that stand out as the best of the best of the era, Gude built three.

The first was Miss Heatherbloom, the Petticoat Girl. The enduring success of this display can be measured by both the sign's revered place in historical memory and the sophistication of its artwork to the modern eye.

Built around 1905 by Gude at a staggering cost of $45,000, the incandescent Miss Heatherbloom walked delicately through a driving rain—depicted in slashing diagonal lines of lamps—concealed by a shell-like umbrella. The gale behind her whipped at her dress, revealing her shapely outline and, above her high-topped shoes, a daring glimpse of stockinged calf. Her skirt, with her ("Insist Upon the Label") petticoat peeking out, fluttered before her—the flutters rendered by twinkling lamps.

Unlike today's Times Square underwear models, she was fully clothed. All the viewer saw of her person was her shapely form, the glimpse of leg, and her delicate arm and hand holding the umbrella. But this mysterious young lady had sex appeal. As she tripped through the storm into the next decade, men and boys came to Times Square especially to admire her, and perhaps to imagine what they might say to win her if she ever turned to smile at them. But, alas, she never did.

In 1912, Corticelli Spool Silk, a brand of sewing thread, gave Times Square another object of affection that would be remembered long after the product was forgotten. Its classic display, built by the A&W Electric Sign Co. of Cleveland, dramatized what would happen if an adorable kitten 24 feet long endeavored to play with a spool of Corticelli—namely, nothing. Corticelli Silk, after all, "Does Not Knot."

The first Corticelli kitten capered on the roof of the Albany Hotel on Broadway at 40th Street, at the north end of what was becoming the Garment District. Replaced a year later by what *Signs of the Times* described as yet another cigarette-smoking "koochy koochy girl" (yawn!), the display was rebuilt in a more elaborate wraparound version a block north, at the corner of 41st Street.

On the Broadway side, the playful feline tugged the thread off the spool, becoming hopelessly entangled in the thin but clearly knotless product. On the north side, the kitten leaped up—in a series of four steps—from the roof to the top of the display, where a 30-foot New Home sewing machine whirred away. The sewing machine had moving wheels and a revolving belt that fed the smooth-running Corticelli through the needle bar, which pumped up and down. Avoiding the moving needle, the kitten snatched the thread and jumped back down to the roof, stopping the machine—a force of playfulness and innocence powerful enough to halt the mighty Industrial Revolution.

This repeating drama unfolded in the delicate lines of incandescent light that were the pen strokes of spectaculars then. The business of building animated electric signs was only twenty years old, yet the sequence was ambitious, even by today's standards. The kittens' tails waggled, their ears twitched, and their paws pummeled, pulling the silk off the turning spool in a blur and tangling the kitties in the loops. This sign was a popular hit not just because it was a technical marvel, but because it told a story with heart and humor.

The White Rock Table Water display, built in the premier spot at the north end around 1915 by Gude, was remembered for many years as the most beautiful spectacular ever built in Times Square. Indeed, that may still be true.

The centerpiece of this seven-story light sculpture was a wreath-bordered clock with Roman numerals, flanked by lion-headed fountains of light that gushed sparkling "water" into conchlike basins. "White Rock" was emblazoned across the top; at the bottom the slogan "The Water for All Time," in an elegant font devised by Gude, was framed in graceful swirls. The entire display had the size, symmetry, and presence of the celebratory arches that were so popular at the turn of the century. It captured the virtues of the Beaux-Arts style without its excesses, and showcased Gude's principle of marrying commercial and fine art.

In black-and-white photographs, the sign looks all-white. In fact, its colorful themes were carefully thought out, in contrast to the practice of less artistic sign makers who filled their signs indiscriminately with colored lamps of every hue simply because they were available. The fountains and sparkling streams of water were gold, and the face of the clock segued smoothly and very . . . very . . . slowly from blue to pink to yellow and back to blue. The sequence took an entire minute, and the effect was meditative. Witnesses reported that people came to Times Square just to stand quietly and watch the hands of the clock move.

Gude's crowning achievement, however, was the monumental Wrigley's Spearmint Chewing Gum spectacular he built in 1917, filling the roof of the block-long Putnam Building between 43rd and 44th streets with a tracery of 17,500 white and multicolored lamps.

Eight stories high and 200 feet long, it was the largest sign ever built in Times Square. Since then, only the Bond waterfall of 1947 has equaled it in size.

It was Gude's second display for William Wrigley, Jr., the Chicago chewing gum magnate who was a pioneer in the aggressive use of national brand advertising. The first, built in 1911 in Herald Square, was a relatively modest affair—an illuminated pack of gum and the less than urgent entreaty: "BUY IT BY THE BOX."

Wrigley needed something stronger. Since 1899, he had been in an all-out war with an alliance of six competitors known as the Chewing Gum Trust. Advertising was his artillery, and it was time to call up the big guns. The staggering price O. J. Gude wanted for his Times Square rooftop location—$100,000 per year—was not too much to pay. What was at stake was nothing less than the hearts, minds, and jaws of a masticating public.

The 1917 display, mounted on an open steel gridwork, was a festival of late Victoriana. Twin peacocks faced off on a tree branch, their tails forming a feathery canopy over the central portion of the display. Beneath the branch were the familiar Wrigley's signature, and the flavor of the gum—Spearmint—its very name promising the tangy breath of a cool forest morning. Flanking the text were six animated "Spearmen," three on each side, sprites in pointy hats who might have been soldiers in some fairy-tale army. Brandishing spears, they comprised a drill team that went through a series of twelve calisthenics the populace quickly dubbed the Daily Dozen. Flanking them were fountains spraying geysers of bubbling water, and the whole spectacle was framed in vinelike filigree.

Like the White Rock display, the Wrigley spectacular was beautifully composed. The message of the chewing gum—a promise of energy, sharp taste, and luxurious well-being—is clear. But the sign told an additional story: the ultimate realization of pre–World War I spectacular art.

It was the pinnacle of Gude's career. When he retired in 1919, the sign was still delighting the public, its full-time maintenance crew diligently installing new lamps on a daily basis. The Wrigley extravaganza became Times Square's longest-running display at the time, remaining in place until 1923. It was replaced by another celebrated but short-lived Gude Company roof-size spectacular, for Clicquot

Club Ginger Ale, with an Eskimo motif. In 1924 the Putnam Building was torn down to make way for the Paramount Building. But a generation of New Yorkers couldn't pass by the spot without thinking of the green-clad Wrigley drill team doing its Daily Dozen.

These were the great Times Square spectaculars of the first two decades of the electric century. But there were hundreds of other good signs too in this amazingly fertile and sadly forgotten period. A few whose images have survived:

The Egyptienne Straights Cigarette Girl gracefully strutted the length of a tightrope, using her parasol for balance, stretching, cavorting, kneeling, and dancing—and she never fell off. Presumably these gymnastics were meant to dramatize the joie de vivre to be had from the sponsor's product—Egyptian and Turkish being code words, in those days, for tobacco laced with marijuana, which was legal at the time.

Fists flew furiously in the "Man-Boy Boxing Match," in which a chap with a mustache and a hearty lad half his size engaged in energetic pugilistics. The product was Porosknit Summer Underwear, complete with tail flap—the long johns of choice, we're doubtless meant to surmise, of the upright male.

How did the regular New Yorker spell laxative? Just as the Times Square spectacular spelled it: P-A-R-T-O-L-A. It was candy-mint-flavored, and, we imagine, worked as smoothly as the sign itself.

Lipton Tea, in "Air Tight Tins Only," poured merrily in big drops of light from a chubby teapot. Perrier showered the night sky with a zillion-lamp white fountain of its French Natural Sparkling Table Water. Coronet Dry Gin, equally serviceable in both rickeys and fizzes, showed how sensible it would be to keep two bottles on hand.

Trimble's Whiskey was replaced in due course by C&G Corsets, offering reliable rustproof comfort, and then, quite efficiently, by CC Ginger Ale, the letters being in the same spot on the sign as the C&G. The ginger ale enticed the parched with a multicolored animated display in which a cork popped from a bottle, spraying forth a shower of bubbly golden beverage.

Budweiser moved uptown, abandoning the spot in Herald Square it had occupied since 1905, with another early version of its famed flying eagle. Haig & Haig Scotch saluted its own authenticity with an animated pictorial of a kilted Highlander doing an intricate fling. And

Regal Shoes, not content to keep the wearer's feet firmly on the ground, identified itself with an eagle of its own, complete with great feathery wings in majestic flight.

Photographs from that time tell the story of a fresh and often naive sense of the possible, of an untutored hunger for grand artistic expression, of an unabashed capitalistic spirit, and of a veneration of the engineer's burgeoning science. There was no precedent for designing and building advertising displays like the early electric spectaculars. A large part of their ebullience, originality, and charm stem from ignorance of what could or could not be done.

Buffeted by the same wind and weather that bedevil us today, most of these signs didn't last long. Lamps were short-lived, flashers were fragile, and construction techniques primitive. Like fireflies, these signs lived their short, bright lives and then disappeared.

World War I gave the nation its first lesson in what happens when the lights go out. Shortly after America entered the war, the Square, like other business hubs all over the country, was blacked out to conserve energy. The great Wrigley display, a reliable friend giving light and warmth every night, was cold and silent, like its neighbors. Newspapers reported that theater attendance and restaurant business plummeted immediately. Merchants stared out their windows at the dim streets, searching in vain for customers who waited out the war at home.

When the lights came back on in 1918, the Square was filled with an air of jubilation. The *New York Times*—like other institutions throughout the country—recognized the symbolic and patriotic importance of the return of the lights by outlining its entire tower in large white lamps and erecting a lighted American eagle, with flags, on top.

When the Square came back to life it was with a quicker pulse, a sharper edge, a keener sense of urgency. Prohibition was only a year away, and a host of other social changes were peeking over the horizon. The world was about to change profoundly.

*3.* *The Neon Age*

A t dusk on a cool night in 1928, a truck with a motion pic-

ture camera mounted in the back cruised Broadway, a

river of light that connected Herald Square to Times

Square and then flowed on up to Columbus Circle. The anonymous cameraman was shooting routine background—for a Hollywood movie, perhaps, or footage for the endless newsreel documentaries of American life and times that were so popular in the days before TV, when audiences were still awed by the miracle of motion picture photography.

Yesterday's B roll, however, is today's archival treasure. And as I "stand" in the truck bed with the cameraman moving through a stream of square black cars and boxy trucks, looking at his forgotten world, I'm amazed anew at the richness and vitality of the electric landscape. On this evening, we're three decades into the electric century, deep into an era bursting with a spectacular sense of its new-found freedom and prosperity. And the signs, as always, tell the story.

Both sides of Broadway are aglitter with lights in action—layers of electric signs on shops selling cigars and hats and shoes and hairdos, hundreds of rows of lamps chasing around dozens of theater marquees, Public Chop Suey and other restaurants spelling in neon their messages of populist affordability, emporia trading in fashions for the lady and gentleman with neat signs that might have been hand-lettered in electric light.

There's no plot in this film, no characters, no expected shift of scene to the curb where the taxi pulls up and Gloria Swanson steps out in cloche hat and white gloves. No sound track either, but we can almost hear the growl of the unmuffled engines, the clang of the trolley, and the shouts of vendors. The camera remains trained on the street and the traffic and the dense crowds of real people on the sidewalks, there to earn money or spend it, and moving toward those common goals at a shared tempo that makes us understand where the term "pulse" of the city came from.

Up ahead, the river widens into a great lake of electric effervescence called Times Square. We see a slice of it, bracketed on our left by the back side of the Times Tower, on our right by the east cliff of the neon/incandescent canyon that contains the Square. We slide through the mouth of the river into the lake of light, in its full, fabled glory.

Straight ahead is the stack of signs at the north end, the Square's familiar Ground Zero. But what a change since Miss Heatherbloom braved the elements and the elegant White Rock light sculpture cast a spell over tarrying pedestrians with its hypnotic colored clock. In those days, a spectacular took about three minutes to run through its entire show. Now the tempo is quick-time by comparison, paced to a new America on wheels. And the stack is higher, wider, and has a lot more company on all sides.

At the bottom, a ruddy-faced all-American businessman, his hat rakishly tilted over his forehead, grins at us with a lighted Camel tucked into the corner of his mouth. Above him, in the premier center spot, a giant framed color extravaganza rejoices over the dental dazzle made possible by Squibb Dental Cream. Higher still is the first of several Chevrolet spectaculars, the familiar flying rectangular logo already taking shape. And at the top, twin Maxwell House Coffee cups drip their famous last drops down the sides of the stack.

A left turn at the center of the Square, then a right. We're surrounded by towering displays—the Palace, Columbia, and Loew's State theaters, electric movie ads four stories high; a huge, round, happy face lathered up and waiting for a "real shave" by an Eveready Safety Razor; a twinkling invitation by "toasted" Lucky Strike to "See Them Made Below."

Then the river narrows again, and flows north, its shores packed with more shops, more marquees, more pinwheeling, starbursting, razzle-dazzling, fast-breathing neon signs. The next electric lake is Columbus Circle, ablaze with spectaculars years before the Coliseum, Lincoln Center, and Huntington Hartford's hole-pocked folly (now home to the New York Convention and Visitors Bureau) gave the neighborhood a new identity.

The sidewalks are jammed along this leg of the trip too. Once in a while, a face turns to notice the cruising camera, and then turns away. Most of these citizens of the 1920s pay no attention. The lullaby of Broadway is their daily marching music, and the hip-hooray and ballyhoo call to them constantly.

I wonder how many of these snappily dressed, savvy-sauntering folk on the go knew that they were the real stars of their Age of Liberation—not the passionate icons who clutched each other on the silver screen, or the glamorous moguls and molls who appeared in daily newspaper accounts of love-nest carryings-on, or the flamboyantly pious, robed evangelists who led so many sinners into the Cleansing Flood to be Washed in the Blood of the Lamb.

This wondrous light show was there solely for the benefit of the man and woman in the street. And the courting of the American consumer, my ride with my ghost photographer showed me, had reached electrifying proportions.

## SIGNS OF PROSPERITY

*It's easy to reduce the* 1920s to a series of jazzy images driven by a Charleston beat: a montage of flappers, flagpole sitters, bottomless martini glasses, bathtub gin, tommy-gun-toting gangsters riding the running boards of long black sedans, and the stock market ticker tape climbing relentlessly upward. To most Americans, however, the roar of the Roaring Twenties was no louder than an automobile engine, the sound of the Jazz Age was filtered tinnily through the speaker of a radio or gramophone, and Hollywood sex scandals and gangland shoot-outs were racy events in faraway places.

What consumed consumers, then as now, was the business of daily living. And life wasn't anything like one of Jay Gatsby's endless parties. The American working man of the mid-1920s toiled fifty or more hours per week for a wage that, in uninflated dollars, was less than half of today's average. His wife worked equally hard—cooking, baking, canning, cleaning, laundering, ironing, sewing, mending, raising the youngsters. It's doubtful that they complained much, however. They knew they were far better off than their parents, and lucky to be living in an age of amazing technological advances, most of them made possible by electricity.

People remembered growing up in pre-electric days, freezing on winter mornings until the wood stove in the kitchen was stoked up, feeding quarters into the gas meter or cleaning the kerosene or coal-oil lamps, bathing weekly in the same big washtub in which Mother scrubbed the clothes. They could remember her sewing on her treadle sewing machine, sprucing the family up for a slow ride downtown in a horse-drawn conveyance. Automobiles, store-bought duds, and household conveniences were only for the well-to-do. In the modern age, however, one could dare to dream of bigger things.

And the 1920s was an era of the biggest of big dreams. The War to End All Wars had been won. Men built skyscrapers into the clouds and bridges across vast bodies of water; piloted flying machines across the Atlantic; sent voices and music through the air without wires; brought exhilarating, tearful, titillating stories to life in pictures that moved on a screen, and made plans to tame the great rivers that routinely ravaged huge regions. And the happy journey into a wonderful future could be made in a fast new automobile, driven at breathtaking speeds of up to thirty-five miles per hour on the network of paved roads and macadam highways that was spreading rapidly across the country.

Advertisers too reached for the sky—sometimes quite literally. In 1924, New York City dwellers who heard the drone of an aeroplane engine at night might look up to see "Smoke Chesterfield" or "Fox Photoplay—Lyric Theater" flashing in electric light overhead. The advertisement was attached to the underside of a Curtiss C6 biplane nicknamed "Iron Horse" by its operator, Night Aero Advertising Corp., which charged a whopping $2,750 per flyover. And in 1927, another ambitious company introduced the Projectograph, announcing that this marvel of the age would revolutionize outdoor advertising by projecting "reading matter" onto clouds, steam, smoke, banks of fog, trees, office buildings, riverbanks, boulders, sides of ships, and hillsides "either green or barren."

This atmosphere of imagining dreams come true translated into a more practical vision for the working family of the 1920s. Prosperity seemed within reach, and literally could be seen on the horizon. The signs there promised beauty, contentment, sex appeal, and—best of all—time, blessed time, thanks to new labor-saving electrical appliances. Time for the family, time for work outside the home, time for art, culture, politics, and play. Mother may have been middle-aged at twenty-five, exhausted by the effort of bearing, feeding, and clothing six or seven tots, but her thoroughly modern daughter could expect to remain in bloom at thirty, thirty-five, and even longer.

## THE LIBERATED CONSUMER

*Technology, more than any other* social force, liberated women from domestic drudgery after World War I. Margaret Sanger founded the American Birth Control League (later the Planned Parenthood Federation of America) in 1917, and suddenly, women were planning careers. The Nineteenth Amendment to the U.S. Constitution, giving women the right to vote, was ratified only three years later. A destiny defined entirely by domesticity was clearly going the way of the bustle, the corset, and the high-button shoe. Suddenly, time was a commodity that could be bought.

As the big 1922 O. J. Gude billboard for United Electric Shops promised, "Electrical Appliances Save Labor and Preserve Youth." The proof was right there on the sign: a pretty woman, lithe and lovely, as free as the breeze fluttering her knee-length skirt, her youth clearly intact and unthreatened by old-fashioned housework.

Better yet was the 1926 Times Square spectacular that dramatized liberation from two of women's most onerous tools of toil, the washtub and washboard. A company named Maytag of Newton, Iowa, invented a motorized aluminum washing machine that took the elbow grease out of laundry forever. The spectacular, at 48th Street and Broadway, told the story in 6,000 lamps: clothes tumbled in the mechanized tub until clean, the lid opened, and, one by one, items of family apparel—underwear, stockings, towels, baby clothes—passed through the machine's automatic wringer and appeared on the 70-foot electric clothesline that spanned the sign. The spotless clothes then flapped in a sweet-smelling breeze while the sign explained that Maytag "Washes Faster and Cleaner."

The Dover Manufacturing Company of Dover, Ohio, went Maytag one better a year later by advertising two new labor-saving appliances on the same sign. Their display, above the northeast corner of Times Square, promised "Better, Quicker" coffee from a Dover Table Percolator with Vea Heat Unit—at 24 feet high, the company boasted to the press, "the largest percolator in the world." Then, like magic, the percolator dissolved into its nifty kitchen sister, the Lady Dover Electric Iron, also—you guessed it—"the largest iron in the world."

What to do with all the time thus saved but invest it in culture? The family piano was an essential in the American parlor of the 1920s. And what better way to enjoy the 88s, suggested a 1920 Times Square spectacular, than by gathering around the upright and singing Stasny Songs like "Girl of Mine," "Lullaby Land," and "My Gal" from

Stasny Sheet Music. The sign celebrated the sweetness of Stasny with a rustling butterfly sipping nectar from a huge electric rose.

And a rose by any other name might spell Sonora Phonographs: the mahogany talking machine box was depicted in its 1920 display alongside a giant rose. Pealing bells below signified Sonora's clear tone and lifelike sound reproduction.

Hooven Typewriters strove to be the secretary's best friend with a nimble 1920 spectacular at 48th Street and Broadway. The characteristically intricate work of the O. J. Gude Company, it sported a giant typewriter with working keys, a space bar, a revolving platen, and American Typewriter type that tapped out messages extolling the machine's virtues on a sail-like sheet of paper emerging from the cylinder.

Royal topped Hooven in 1925 with a larger, more detailed display at 47th Street. Amazed by its lifelike action, *Signs of the Times* enthused: "Up and down, up and down the flashing keys go busily—for all the world as if one of the most efficient of the many pretty, bobbed-haired stenographers gazing at it from below was making them go with her dainty, manicured fingers."

Remarkable new products were not just for the ladies. One of the greatest wonders of the modern world—clean drinking water—is so pervasive that it is routinely taken for granted. But it wasn't always so. In its 1927 Times Square spectacular, Standard Plumbing Fixtures chose a thundering waterfall in white, green, and orange light pouring into a foamy blue river to dramatize to the world, as a spokesman told the gathering at the lighting ceremony, that "the plumbing industry has arrived." The waterfall, the spokesman explained, "is the symbol of the plumber's gift—flowing water and purity in every home."

The Geo. P. Ide Co., Inc., a collar and shirt manufacturer in Troy, New York, was proud of its six-story 1923 display built by Thomas Cusack in the premier spot at the north end of the Square, "the biggest advertisement in collar and shirt history." A frenzy of yellow, red, and green lamps ran riot around the Ide logo in "Daylo Blue," while the display reminded the well-dressed man of the trio of Ide options: "Idaflex," "Streetline," and "Starched."

Where to buy an Ide was not a mystery. Shoppers on the Great White Way found Macy's in their line of sight wherever they turned.

Macy's maintained four huge spectaculars, one on each side of the Square, all simultaneously inviting viewers to "The World's Largest Store," symbolized by a great, glowing, gold-and-white star.

Meanwhile, the electric courtship of the 1920s consumer was proceeding with ardor in other American cities too.

Residents of Dallas witnessed the lighting of their city's largest electric sign to date in 1923. The two-story display, for Fishburn Dyeing & Dry Cleaning, philosophically counseled taking the long view when choosing to color clothing: "Not How Cheap But How Good."

In Boston, a mysterious medicine called Zonite that claimed to be the "greatest household agency known to materia medica for protection against infection and disease" employed a huge traveling display to beam its salubrious messages down on Boston Commons in 1923. The Anheuser-Busch eagle began to fly on the other side of the Commons in 1926, the same year Gillette lighted a spectacular more than six stories high on South Station that could be read far out into the harbor.

In 1928, Procter & Gamble, a pioneer of electric advertising in its hometown of Cincinnati, placed a five-story-tall minidrama for Ivory Soap on the highest roof in town, overlooking the city's Fountain Square. The sign, which attracted crowds to Fountain Square every night, showed a tot in his birthday suit jumping from a diving board into a clear pool, wherein floated a large cake of Ivory. The tot landed with a great splash and sank, while, naturally, the 99 and $^{44}/_{100}$% pure soap did not. The story had a happy ending, however—the smiling child bobbed to the surface with Ivory in hand, clearly eager for his ablutions.

P&G's animated spectacular, which took at least half a minute to tell its story, was designed to dominate the city's principal gathering place, Cincinnati's White Way, where people strolled or cruised slowly by in cars. To that audience, being there was much more important than getting there.

In Indianapolis, Standard Oil had a different constituency in mind for its 1922 Red Crown Gasoline spectacular—a new consumer to whom getting there, and getting there fast, was the whole point, and toward that end applied shoe leather only to the accelerator, clutch, and brake of his brand-new American automobile.

Standard Oil placed its four-story, five-color display on the roof of a downtown building overlooking the main approach to the Indianapolis Speedway, home of the already renowned International 500 Mile Sweepstakes automobile race. Geared to the speed-minded viewer, the display simply alternated the name of the product with a glittering image of a jeweled crown.

Resourceful salesmen from the O. J. Gude Company sold Standard Oil on the merits of the pricey $25,000 spectacular by means of the new science of marketing statistics. They painstakingly clocked 800 automobiles per hour passing the site during the day, another 1,200 at the time motoring America would soon come to know as the evening "rush hour," and an amazing 1,300 per hour for the entire two days preceding the opening of the Indy 500.

## "Gentlemen, Start Your Engines!"

*Nowhere was that famous instruction* heard more clearly than in Times Square, ironically—then as now—the pedestrian's turf. True enough, a pair of crisscrossing streams of vehicular traffic honked and growled their way through the Square inch by inch virtually around the clock. But the masses were on foot, and most were New Yorkers who weren't likely to own cars anyway.

Nonetheless, advertisers celebrated America's emerging car culture with a gusto unmatched anywhere else, in a competition for size and brightness that was surpassed only by the Las Vegas casino industry a generation later. By the 1920s, the giant automakers and related businesses that would drive America's greatest industry—and, to a great extent, steer the nation's economy—already had emerged. And their Times Square signs were their racing flags.

Fisk Tires staked its claim to a piece of the sky over the Square early on with an electric version of its logo—a boy in a nightshirt carrying a tire over one shoulder and a candle in his other hand—so high over the West 50s that it seems literally to float in the photographic nightscapes of the day.

Richland Oil chose altitude also, at the very top of the north end's "tower." So did its competition, the Pure Oil Co., with a huge spectacular for its "Twins of Power," Purol Gasoline and Tiolene Oil, on a roof on West 54th Street. In 1923, it was the Great White Way's second-largest spectacular, the largest being the Wrigley extravaganza on the Putnam Building, then nearing the end of its run.

Taking a more intellectual approach, U.S. Tire placed a painted billboard on the Claridge Hotel (the site of the "smoking" Camel sign two decades later), duplicating in jumbo size the "Historical Books" highway signs the company built all over the country. Each open book carried two messages: a synopsis of a historical event that took place on the site of the sign, and the fact that "United States Tires Are GOOD Tires." The Times Square copy read: "You are now in Times Square, the Crossroads of the World. New York, biggest city on earth, is now the commercial, financial, and amusement center of the planet. New York typifies the enterprising spirit of the American People." And the display also typified the enterprising spirit of the Claridge Hotel management, who decided that the sign rental revenue outweighed rendering some rooms unrentable by blocking their windows.

General Motors weighed in in 1925 with an 82-foot-tall sign atop its headquarters building at Broadway and 58th Street, overlooking Columbus Circle. The eager-to-inform 5,000-lamp display told the world that Chevrolet, Oldsmobile, Oakland, Buick, and Cadillac cars and GMC trucks are all General Motors products and all have bodies by Fisher. Flashing across the bottom was the GM slogan: "A car for every purse and purpose."

Commanding as this sign was, however, it was overshadowed in both brilliance and chattiness by the 13,000-lamp La Salle–Cadillac spectacular that went up two years later at Broadway and 42nd Street. Most of the animated illumination was devoted to a colorful depiction of the explorers Robert Cavelier, Sieur de La Salle, and Antoine de la Mothe, Sieur de Cadillac, and their faithful crews, bravely oaring through uncharted waters in longboats. Explaining the connection, a motograph ran a lengthy message that advised: "Out of the bog of claims and counterclaims, Cadillac prestige stands as a beacon light, pointing the way to luxury and distinction, and to motor car value that brings abiding satisfaction." And the elegant discourse went on from there.

The following year, the Dodge Brothers outdid them all with a spectacular that had a foot in the next decade and beyond. On Broadway between 46th and 47th streets, the six-story display was notable not merely for its size but also for its stunning luminosity, its forward-looking technology, and its very modern sense of graphic animation. Simply spelling "Dodge Brothers" in blue and white, its letters breathed, filled, and spelled on, generating a pulsing excitement that foreshadowed the great Canadian Club and Admiral spectaculars of the 1950s.

The Dodge Brothers display was said to be the first spectacular to use a message center driven by a continuous ribbon of tape to flip the switches that made the letters appear to "travel" across the face of the display. Indeed, with its lamps installed in a corrugated concave mirrorlike trough, it was designed to look like a ribbon fluttering. The sign was one of the first to enjoy the services of an ace p.r. pro—none other than Edward Bernays, whom history credits as the Father of Public Relations. Little wonder, then, that it was the most hyped spectacular of the 1920s.

Impressive as this display was, however, it was hard pressed to outclass, in sheer drama, a Times Square spectacular of the same period, embodying a different form of transportation, that lasted less than a year. Today this sign would be considered grossly politically incorrect, but in its short life it set a standard of storytelling spectacularity that few have matched.

Known in 1924 as the "Four Little Eskimos" sign, it replaced the 1917 Wrigley display on the roof of the Putnam Building, and was completed—to the dismay of its backers—just months before the building was torn down to make way for the Paramount Building. The advertiser was Clicquot Club Ginger Ale, a Prohibition-era favorite that doubtless found itself mixed with illicit beverages in the speaks that thrived behind the scenes all around the Square. A block long and five stories high, it used 19,000 dazzling white and colored lamps and 29 flashers, and consumed four times as much electricity as any other spectacular built to date.

The sign played like a scene from a CinemaScope epic of three decades later. First, a crimson glow spread across the night sky, slowly growing brighter, filling with streaks of yellow, rose, lavender, and blue, eventually revealing a pudgy, grinning Eskimo boy clad in white fur, speeding across sparkling snow on a sled carrying a 30-foot bottle of ginger ale. He cracked his whip over a team of three other Eskimo boys, identical to himself but smaller, their little legs running furiously. Each time the driver cracked his whip, another word in the sign's slogan appeared: "Clicquot... Club... Ginger... Ale... World's ... Largest... Seller." And as the thirsty team arrived in camp, the aurora borealis reached a blazing climax.

This spectacular may have been the first to appear on the radio. In a multimedia blitz that dramatized the vigor and growing sophistication of the advertising industry, the Gude Company's advertising manager, S. N. Holliday, delivered a ten-minute talk, "Four Little Eskimos on Broadway," on a national radio hookup. The show was advertised in advance by direct mail, and photographs of Holliday talking about the sign on the radio were published in newspapers the next day.

The business of building and leasing electrifying outdoor advertising displays had matured, and was about to be transformed into an industry. In 1925, the Gude Company, Thomas Cusack, and a host of smaller outdoor companies were absorbed by a new nationwide corporation, the General Outdoor Advertising Company, its management comprised of Holliday and key executives of both the Gude and Cusack companies. Both Gude and Cusack themselves, their reign over, died within the year. The Second Generation was officially in charge.

Business was booming, and was only going to get better. And something new was on the horizon—the glamorous new light from France.

# Neon Wars

While the gangsters that Prohibition spawned were busily hijacking each other's booze-laden trucks and gunning each other down in the streets, another turf war was being fought—a bloodless war that was nonetheless just as ferocious in its own way, with big money at stake. This was the war, fought on legal terrain, for control of America's blossoming neon light industry.

The combatants were the forces of Georges Claude, the French businessman-chemist who invented commercially viable neon tube light, and a series of American challengers who sought to circumvent the canny foreigner's claims with similar inventions of their own.

**The bane of civic beautifiers:**
Printed bulletins covered entire street corners in
pre-electric days. 42nd Street and Seventh Avenue, New York, circa 1890.
© *Collection of the New-York Historical Society*

**The first electric sign:**
William J. Hammer spelled his boss's name in
lights at the 1882 London International Exhibition.
*Hall of Electrical History, Schenectady Museum*

**The first electric spectacular:**
Viewers in 1892 said they could almost feel the promised
"ocean breezes." Fifth Avenue and Broadway, New York.
© *Collection of the New-York Historical Society*

**Same site, green light:**
The great electric Heinz pickle that replaced ocean breezes in 1898 annoyed
neighbors who still dined by gaslight. Fifth Avenue and Broadway, New York.
© *Collection of the New-York Historical Society*

**Fanfaring the flickers:**
A fountain and a pair of torches, popular images in early electric spectaculars,
welcome crowds to San Francisco's House of Movies in 1910.
*Hall of Electrical History, Schenectady Museum*

**When Motown glowed:**
Woodward Avenue, from City Hall Square
north, was Detroit's White Way in 1910.
*Hall of Electrical History, Schenectady Museum*

**Signs of the good life:**
A new car, a summer home,
a player piano, and a night on the
town advertised on Euclid Avenue,
Cleveland's White Way, in 1912.
*Hall of Electrical History,*
*Schenectady Museum*

**An eight-story spiderweb of steel,**
ready for "Leaders of the World" at
38th Street and Broadway in 1910.
*Museum of the City of New York,*
*The Byron Collection (93.1.1.10811)*

## The Wonder of Herald Square:

"Leaders of the World" was New York's favorite free show in 1910. *Museum of the City of New York, The Byron Collection (93.1.1.17914)*

**The "Leaders" chariot race** from *Ben-Hur*, complete with clouds of incandescent brown dust. *Museum of the City of New York, The Byron Collection (93.1.1.10807)*

Times Square, 1909

**Times Square,** looking north in 1909,
is already a gallery of electric art.
*Postcard, Collection of Artkraft Strauss*

**Having a ball:** The last and largest version of the Corticelli kitten
frolicked above 42nd Street between Broadway and Seventh Avenue in 1913.
The Great White Way stretches south from Times Square.
*Hall of Electrical History, Schenectady Museum*

**Nightly cat capers:** The Corticelli kitten debuted in 1912, endlessly doing battle with a spool of thread that never broke. 39th Street and Broadway.
*Hall of Electrical History, Schenectady Museum*

**Sculpture in lights:**

The artistically ambitious White Rock spectacular of 1915 was resplendent in gracefully changing pastels. 47th Street between Broadway and Seventh Avenue.

*Brown Brothers, Sterling, Pa.*

**Electric Victoriana:**
Lush with peacocks and fountains, bristling with Spearmen in action, Wrigley's
block-long Times Square extravaganza pulsed from 1917 to 1923.
*Brown Brothers, Sterling, Pa.*

**Northern lights:**
The aurora borealis lit the way for Eskimo boys hauling ginger ale
over the tundra in Wrigley's short-lived replacement.
*© Collection of the New-York Historical Society*

**Stream of syncopation:**
By the early 1920s, the Great White Way was a river of jazzy, many-colored, animated signs and marquees. Broadway looking north from 46th Street. *Museum of the City of New York*

**"It's Over Over There":**
The Times Tower outlined in lights to celebrate the Armistice that ended the Great War, 1918. *Brown Brothers, Sterling, Pa.*

**"Happy New Year":**
The first New Year's Eve Ball, photographed a few days before December 31,
1907, when it made its first descent from atop the Times Tower.
*Brown Brothers, Sterling, Pa.*

**Dancing in the rain:**
Times Square on a wet night in 1920, looking north from 45th Street.
© *Collection of the New-York Historical Society*

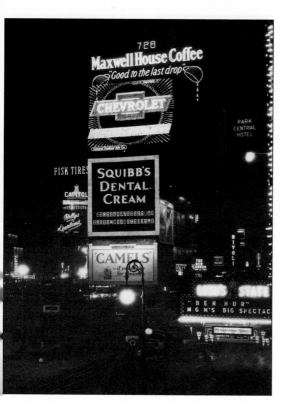

**The "Tower" of signs at the north end of Times Square in 1927:**
Coffee, cars, and a winning smile for sale.
© *Hall of Electrical History,*
*Schenectady Museum*

**The "Tower" by day in the early 1920s:**
Monster letters on grids of steel.
© *Collection of the*
*New-York Historical Society*

**Secretary's friend:**
Royal's 1927 typewriter in lights sported working keys, carriage
return, and letters that wrote messages extolling the machine's virtues.
© *Collection of the New-York Historical Society*


**What Depression?**
In the late 1930s, Times Square looked like this.
*Collection of Artkraft Strauss*

Claude was a tough foe, however. A consummate image maker, well financed and well connected, he was a masterful self-promoter and a tireless litigator. Armed with six patents on process and equipment granted by the U.S. Patent Office in 1925, he established a national network of vassals: licensees and franchisees, all committed to defending Claude's process. Each of these was a successful and powerful sign company in its own right—and many of them survive to this day.

The neon wars raged on into the next decade, ending only when Claude's last patent expired in 1932. By then, many fortunes had been made, and lost—and America was aglow in the light that Claude, with his characteristic poetic panache, called "the Living Flame."

Neon was the night light of a bold new age in which young people stayed up late doing shocking things that dismayed their parents and appalled their grandparents—drinking giggle water from hip flasks, dancing in raucous speakeasies to the wanton new music called jazz, smoking cigarettes and even maryjane, roaring around the countryside in fast cars, necking and petting with gosh knows who.

Neon light in its rainbow of colors was bold and supple and sensuous and exciting, like the Jazz Age's perception of itself. The tubes could embrace the graceful curves of theater marquees, or project a name in giant letters into the sky like fireworks, or create huge, flowing animated characters that gave outdoor advertising displays the jaunty personality of movie cartoons. A great neon sign on the roof of a factory announced to the world that a mighty manufacturing center, a corporate city-state that nurtured an army of workers and their families, pulsed within.

Neon—named for the Greek word *neos,* meaning new—symbolized quality and sophistication. This may be hard for us to imagine, since for so many decades that followed, neon was disparaged in our popular culture as the saloon light of the tawdry and the fallen. But in the 1920s, businesses craved its stamp of modernity and prosperity just as dignified professional men of the nineteenth century yearned to see their names embossed in gold leaf. Neon was worn like an architectural badge of achievement. Its texture was so smooth and even, its glow so deep and mesmerizing, it seemed to elevate whatever it was attached to into a higher realm.

Neon holds a mystique that is not shared by its sister technology, fluorescent lamps, which seem to light up objects rather than being cynosures—eye attractors—in themselves. Perhaps this is because they work in different ways. In fluorescents, the phosphor coating the insides of the tubes gives out light when excited by high voltages, while in neon tubes, the light is produced by the excitation of the gas itself. Or perhaps something more profound is at play.

Urban dwellers have long noticed that no self-respecting storefront Gypsy would be without a neon sign, usually in one of the argon shades of pink, orchid, or turquoise, often containing mystical symbols, but sometimes simply the proprietor's name and the words "Fortunes Read" or the like. I had often wondered about this, and finally Mrs. Rosa on West 54th Street, after I'd crossed her palm with the appropriate amount of silver, explained it to me.

"Neon vibrates at a very high frequency," she said, as accurately as a science teacher, "just like people's astral bodies. The presence of neon sets up harmonics that not only make the astral bodies easier for me to read, they also act as filters, clarifying the clients' concentration." I have no doubt that twenty-first-century scientists will confirm Mrs. Rosa's observations.

Besides its psychic benefits, early neon devotees promoted its physiological benefits as well. Blue argon, for example, was thought to be particularly effective in dissipating arthritis, and thousands of handheld devices, with more attachments than a modern vibrator, were sold for this purpose.

But during its first heyday in the 1920s, neon was primarily thought of as an architectural embellishment. It was widely used to accent the proud and alluring contours of Art Deco buildings and theaters, including walls, ceilings, and floors; to ornament fountains and statuary in public gardens; and even, in keeping with the evangelistic fervor that paralleled the hedonism of the day, to delineate religious symbols in the night sky. In 1928, someone counted more than sixty neon crucifixes in the mid-Manhattan skyline guiding the way to churches and cathedrals. Why shouldn't God be accorded equal attention in the cityscape along with shoes, soap, and tires? A neon sign was a beacon, visible from far greater distances than the incandescent bulbs that, by then, seemed dull, yellowish, and old-fashioned.

As new as luminous tube light seemed, however, it wasn't really new at all. Claude's competitors (and counterlitigants) were fond of pointing out that the concept of generating light by electrifying gas trapped in a vacuum tube dated back to experiments with static electricity in the 1600s by Francis Hauksbee the Elder, French scientist Jean Picard, and others.

In 1745, Johann Heinrich Winkler, a professor of physics at the University of Leipzig, bent a glass tube into the shape of the name of a wealthy patron, sealed the ends, and lit it up briefly with a newly invented Leyden jar, creating what could be considered the first luminous tube sign. (Sadly, the name of Winkler's patron—the first-ever neon advertiser—has been lost to history.)

Nineteenth-century experimenter Heinrich Geissler added platinum electrodes and tried to sustain the light in a sealed tube that thereafter bore his name. The search for a sustainable tube light that burned cooler, brighter, and longer than the incandescent bulbs of the day was under way in earnest.

In 1891, Nikola Tesla, Thomas Edison's nemesis, took the process a step further. Ever the showman, he dazzled lecture audiences in London, Paris, and New York by bombarding gas-filled, phosphor-coated Geissler tubes, shaped to spell the word LIGHT, with the alternating current he championed, in doses of up to a million volts, with spectacular results that nearly—literally—brought the house down.

By 1892, patents had been granted in the United States and Britain for improvements in the Geissler tube intended for use in signs. A General Electric researcher, Daniel McFarlan Moore, invented a way to pump more gas into the tubes at higher pressure, increasing their longevity. The Moore tube was the first to be used commercially. Moore himself used his tubes in a sign he built for a Newark, New Jersey, hardware store in 1894. And E. Machlett & Son, a New York sign company, installed a sign made of Moore tubes in a post office, where reportedly they burned for 10,000 hours. Machlett later became one of Claude's principal challengers.

With improved tubes available, luminous tube lighting now seemed destined to succeed. But General Electric, committed to the supremacy of Edison's incandescent lamp, bought up Moore's patents and buried them, effectively squelching the spread of the new technology in the United States for the next twenty years.

In Europe, however, research continued. In 1897, Sir William Ramsay and Morris W. Travers developed a process for extracting four of the six "noble" gases—neon, argon, krypton, and xenon—from distilled air.

The noble gases, which also include helium and radon, are called noble because, like their "noble" human counterparts, they possess extraordinarily limited reactivity. (Ever try to tell a joke to a roomful of dukes?) Colorless, odorless, tasteless, and nonflammable, they have highly stable outer electron rings that they rarely share with other, "baser" elements. These noble—also called inert—gases vibrate more brilliantly and durably than the common atmospheric gases that had been used before. Ramsay and Travers demonstrated their discovery in 1897 during a commemoration of Queen Victoria's Diamond Jubilee by erecting a sign in London that spelled out VICTORIA REGINA in three glowing colors—neon's orange-red, argon's celestial blue, and krypton's pulsating orchid.

Claude's discovery was the by-product of a different search. The innovative industrialist was looking for a way to produce oxygen cheaply and in commercial quantities. What he got instead was a large supply of the noble gases. He filled Moore tubes with the gases, bombarded them with electricity, and contemplated the fascinating commercial possibilities that resulted.

Experimenting with color-impregnated glass tubes, he also discovered, following Tesla's example, that coating the insides of the tubes with various phosphorescent powders produced a complete array of gleaming colors: pinks, yellows, oranges, greens, and whites, as well as the already known reds, blues, and purples. (Today, using Claude's method of varying combinations of colored glass, phosphor coatings, and inert gases, we can produce any color except brown—although a brownish-purple cola-like color is possible.)

Claude unveiled his new light in 1910 at the automobile show in Paris's Grand Palais. A jazz band imported all the way from Storyville in New Orleans wowed the fashionable crowd, thus cementing the bond among the new music, the new transportation, and the new light. In 1915, Claude developed and patented a greatly improved, corrosion-resistant electrode. And a new industry was born. Within a few short years it would become a global enterprise.

In 1912, Jacques Fonesque, Claude's master salesman, sold what was probably Europe's first neon business sign to a Paris barbershop called Palais Coiffeur. The first neon sky-sign, spelling CINZANO in white letters a meter tall on the roof of a building, went up a year later. By 1919, when a Claude sign was lit up over the entrance to the Paris Opera, the City of Light was beginning to take on a new character, basking in the electrifying glow of "New Light."

Claude's neon finally came to America in 1922, when Fonesque met a vacationing Los Angeles car dealer, Earle C. Anthony, in Paris and pitched him the idea of erecting a neon sign on his Packard showroom at Seventh and Flower streets in LA. The sign contained the familiar Packard logo in metal channel letters filled with orange-red neon, framed in a blue argon border. Anthony could boast to his fellow Angelenos that the colors were identical to those used in the Paris Opera sign—colors then known in the trade as Couleur Opéra.

The now-legendary Packard sign, America's first neon business sign, quickly became one of the city's most popular attractions. America was on wheels by then, and a goodly portion of the population of Los Angeles found its way to the corner of Seventh and Flower. Traffic backed up for blocks as family buggies crept past the dealership, the windows of the cars lined with wide-eyed faces. Everyone loved the sign—except the Los Angeles Police Department.

His American debut a certifiable hit, Claude took the next logical step. He offered to sell General Electric the exclusive right to use his technology for five million dollars. GE, still stubbornly wedded to the Edison incandescent lightbulb, turned him down. The Edison establishment continued to believe it could turn America's lights on and off at will. So mighty were they in their own self-perception, they imagined the bruised Frenchman would simply take his toy and go home.

Instead, Claude sought and was granted six U.S. patents. The most important was a patent on his durable corrosion-resistant electrode, the invention that proved to be his key advantage in the neon wars that ensued.

# THE GASMAN COMETH

*Claude himself came to America* and opened a New York office in 1924. He immediately entered into a franchise agreement with Strauss, and together they sold the first American neon spectacular, advertising Willys-Knight Overland Motors at 45th Street and Broadway. The display was fabricated and installed under the foremanship of my grandfather, who had built the original in candescent display for the same customer on that site ten years before.

Then, with stunning rapidity, Claude went global, franchising the manufacture of Claude Neon all over Europe, Latin America, China, Japan, Australia, New Zealand, the United States, and Canada. He enlisted a network of shrewd partners from sign companies that were already well entrenched—in some cases, forming new companies with them; in others, granting licenses. Companies bearing some version of the Claude name still survive, under different ownership, throughout the world.

The largest of the new U.S. companies was the Claude Neon Federal Co. of Chicago, a sister of the huge Federal Sign Co. that dominated the Windy City and much of the Heartland—and in 1998 reached its own century mark as a subsidiary of a multibillion-dollar public company, Federal Signal. By 1928, Claude Federal had branches in Dallas, Duluth, Houston, Indianapolis, Lexington, Kansas City, Louisville, Memphis, Milwaukee, Minneapolis, New Orleans, and Shreveport.

Electrical Products Corp. of Los Angeles, Denver, Seattle, and Salt Lake City was Claude West. The Bellows-Claude Neon Co. of Detroit, with branches in Cincinnati and Cleveland, served as a major supplier of parts and materials. Claude Neon Lights of New York City and its local franchisees, including Strauss, had the electric sign capital of the country covered, and Claude Neon Lights of Maryland took care of Baltimore and Washington, D.C. Other licensees flew the Claude flag in Pittsburgh, Boston, Atlanta, Toronto, Vancouver, Philadelphia, Jacksonville, Miami, Richmond, in GE's own back yard in Schenectady, and in dozens of other smaller cities. By 1930, the Claude empire encompassed more than a hundred companies throughout North America.

One of those smaller cities—Lima, Ohio (pronounced like the bean, not the South American city)—was a burgeoning neon center, with dozens of glass shops employing hundreds of tube benders (as well as thermometer makers and radio-tube fabricators). "Lima was the hotbed of neon," says Dan Kasper, the president of Harmon Signs in Toledo. "Many major companies of today got their start there." One of those companies was Artkraft Signs, a Claude-franchised company that was to play a major role in my family's history and ultimately in the history of Times Square.

Artkraft, originally a porcelain enamel company making bathtubs, stoves, and other appliances, started making signs in 1921, and by all accounts was hugely successful, sending signs and marquees all over the country. Today, collectors prize the exquisitely crafted signs of porcelain enamel and neon the company built for bars and bakeries and department stores, haberdasheries, restaurants, and theaters, as well as for spectacular advertisers. By the end of the decade, Artkraft's vast, warehouse-like facility was bursting at the seams with new work. And the company had acquired a new partner in faraway Gotham— my grandfather.

By the late 1920s, Jake, ever the entrepreneur, had left his comfortable berth at Strauss and started his own company, Starr Engineering, in the Bronx. Neon was filling the city skies, and Jake wanted to be in on the action. So he hopped on the train to Lima.

I can just see Jake, the quintessential immigrant from the Big Apple in his homburg and rumpled suit, explaining to the Midwesterners in his gruff voice and thick accent how he would make thousands of dollars for them by selling their glorious neon signs in the fabled, glittering Emerald City. And whatever he said to them did the trick, because he went home with a contract in his pocket. Jake was now the president of the New York division of Artkraft Signs.

Soon Artkraft's first New York spectacular, for a local cement company, went up in Long Island City facing the East Side of Manhattan, its reflected glowing tubes sparkling in the East River. Shortly afterward, the immense landmark Pepsi-Cola sky-sign—replicated in 1994 from the original blueprints—went up nearby. Henceforth Artkraft Signs was a player in the New York outdoor business.

By the early 1930s, Jake had taken over Artkraft and merged it with Strauss, forming Artkraft Strauss. It was the bottom of the Depression, and both companies were broke—proving that, as my father, Mel, used to say, "Zero plus zero sometimes makes three." Shortly thereafter, Jake bought out Strauss. A dozen years later, Artkraft Strauss would be the principal builder of signs in Times Square. But we're getting ahead of our story. In 1928, when Jake's first neon spectacular took up its nightly vigil along the dark river that reflected the lighted concrete towers of Manhattan, it was enough just to own a neon franchise. Jake knew this. He could see the future, and its story was written in neon.

Within a few years after Mr. Anthony lit up his Packard dealership, neon light swept the country like a prairie fire, transforming towns and cities everywhere.

The first of more than 200 Claude creations in Boston lit the way to the John Ward Shoe Store in 1925. Boston's first spectacular, for Willys-Knight Overland Fine Motor Cars—the same satisfied customer as in New York—went up a year later on Commonwealth Avenue. An immense structure 85 feet long and 48 feet high, it was said to be visible for more than a mile to the traffic on "Boston's great automobile highway."

Oregon proved to be especially fertile ground for Claude. By 1930, more than 1,200 Claude displays bathed the night streets of the state's cities and hamlets in neon glow. Enlightened customers included hotels, banks, and, especially, churches.

One such display in Portland, reported *Signs of the Times* in 1925, was "gaining a world-wide reputation for its novelty and practical results in religious work." Surmounting the Apostolic Faith Mission on the corner of Sixth and Burnside, the sign proclaimed "JESUS The Light of the World." The magazine noted, "Remarkable results are reported from the effects of this sign. People have been converted just from looking at it, and one man, on the point of committing suicide, saw this sign just in time to bring him back from the pit of despair and into the ark of safety"—certainly an impressive achievement, even by modern marketing standards.

The first neon sign in Oregon was built for the W&R Donut Corp. of Portland, makers of Sugar Crest Doughnuts. Thanks to a frosty, sugary-looking Claude confection above the storefront, a display whose thick letters and swirling ornamentation might have been drawn in electrified icing, Sugar Crest became Portland's dunker of choice.

Twenty years earlier or later, a sign for a doughnut shop probably would have included an animated pictorial—a piping hot doughnut, for instance, emitting steam, or a strutting baker toting a trayful fresh from the oven. But in the 1920s the emphasis was on elegant typography. A neon sign above a store or business was an echo of the enterprise's business card, only writ huge in electric light. The art of exquisite hand-lettering was still alive and well in the 1920s, and neon users and sign makers—perhaps as a reflection of neon's architectural, Art Deco roots, perhaps in reaction to the medium's linear quality—often strove for simple, brilliant lettering effects.

Thus Mrs. Pickett identified her Atlanta Tea Room in a simple, jolly script contained in a hexagonal box; Murray W. Sales & Co. Plumbing Fixtures of Detroit chose a clean, sans serif Moderne; Mayflower Cab Co. of Baltimore opted for a flowery Parisian Bold in bright yellow; the New England Bakery of Salt Lake City promised "Oven to You" freshness in a well-fed Bodoni; Graham Paige, Denver's swanky haberdasher, opted for a marine green version of its stylized pyramid-shaped Deco lettering; and classy clothiers Crowley Milner's of Detroit, Alexander & Oviatt of Los Angeles, and Best & Co. of New York's Fifth Avenue simply duplicated their craftsmanlike metalwork Deco logos in neon.

But while the glamorous new light may have been a relatively easy sell, nothing sells itself. Claude's marketing acumen and aggressiveness were major factors in his success. By the 1920s, American advertising had matured into a sophisticated communications industry. Its practitioners understood the nuances of image and attitude, the necessity of celebrating values, the power of association with an icon. In this arena, Claude was right at home.

He knew he was selling more than gas-filled tubes that gave off attractive colored light. Though his discoveries were the accidental by-product of another quest, he recognized their creative potential immediately. When early neon signs inspired rhapsodic responses from onlookers, Claude paid attention and adopted their language in his ongoing sales pitch. Nurture the romance! Cultivate the myth!

Make people *want* to write poetry about neon! In its advertising, Claude Neon portrayed itself as the one, the true, the *legitimate* neon. To build a sign with inferior, makeshift products by patent-infringing imitators was tantamount to giving your beloved a piece of glass and calling it a diamond.

So brilliant and aggressive was the marketing campaign, Claude Neon became a household word. Most people believed that all neon was Claude Neon. Some even thought Neon was Claude's last name. In 1928, Claude's best year in the United States, sales topped $19 million—hundreds of millions of dollars by today's standards. By 1930, industry analysts estimated that at least half the incandescent lamps in all outdoor advertising signs in America had been replaced by neon tubes.

The aggressiveness of the Claude enterprise can be discerned in an advertising flyer distributed throughout the Great Lakes region by one of Claude's adversaries, the makers of Everbrite Electric Signs in Milwaukee. Entitled "The Truth About Neon Tube Signs," the flyer noted, "For some time, many people interested in buying signs made of Neon tubing have been disturbed and harassed by having the question of patents and lawsuits injected into the talk of Neon salesmen." Somewhat inconsistently, Everbrite both dismissed the threats as groundless and promised to indemnify its customers against the inevitable costs of litigation. (Everbrite had the last laugh, however. Founded in a Milwaukee garage in 1927, by century's end it had grown into a global sign and display company employing more than 1,200 people.)

For three years, beginning in 1928, Claude published a newsletter, *Claude Neon News,* in which he kept the faithful abreast of Claude projects, chronicled Claude's wins (but not his losses) in his ongoing legal battles, saluted those with the taste and class to buy a Claude Neon sign ("The men who have chosen Claude Neon signs are invariably the progressive and successful merchants in each city..."), and entertained with knee-slapping neon humor and inspirational poetry.

A sample of the former: "What does 'estic' mean, Papa?"

"It means 'Hotel Majestic' when all the bulbs ain't working on the electric sign."

A sample of the latter, by poetess Elizabeth W. McDevitt of Los Angeles:

> *They thought the "Stars" made Hollywood;*
> *Of all the jokes sublime!*
> *The thing that made our Hollywood,*
> *Was the NEON ELECTRIC SIGN!*
>
> *We'd ride all night 'till broad daylight*
> *And think—how the sun does shine,*
> *But the light that lit up Hollywood*
> *Was the NEON ELECTRIC SIGN!*
>
> *A studio searchlight here and there,*
> *But the richest joy that's mine,*
> *Is to ride up Hollywood Boulevard*
> *And read the NEON ELECTRIC SIGN!*

Loath to allow a perky verse by a mere woman to speak for itself, the *Claude Neon News* editors, covering all bases, prefaced it with this patronizing commentary: "Man may never understand the process of feminine logic, but he knows that the results are usually sound. [The ladies] are severe critics, but appreciative of merit. A greater part of the success of Claude Neon lighting is due to its attraction for and approval by the ladies."

Thus womankind, ever the demanding nurturer, could bask in the glow of neon. But it was understood that Man, not Woman, was the Giver of Light. And no light giver ever generated more glow—by his own account—than Georges Claude.

"When a man achieves the degree of success which has crowned the work of Georges Claude," intones the lead article in the first issue of *Claude Neon News*, "he ceases to be an ordinary mortal and becomes, in the public mind, almost a mythical superbeing." But don't worry, the *Neon News* assures its readers, Georges the superbeing hasn't totally transcended his humanity. "He retains the human qualities that make him loved and trusted by all those who know him." This becoming humility notwithstanding, however, "his discoveries and inventions in the scientific field make the world eternally his debtor. He is one of the foremost living scientists, and [is] sometimes termed the 'Edison of France.' "

There follows a recitation of Claude-begat inventions, some of which were fanciful, and all of which reflected the notion that gas-filled tubes would represent the ultimate communications devices of the future: fog-piercing neon lights for airports; neon screens for early versions of television, telephoto, and transatlantic televideophone transmission; a method of synthesizing ammonia; a device to localize short circuits in electrical railway systems; an early form of sonar.

However, the most successful early invention of this consummate gas man was an interesting array of caustic explosives and suffocating gases for use in World War I. For this, the French government awarded Captain Claude the Legion of Honor. And French universities and science academies fell over each other in their rush to award prizes to Citizen Claude, Doctor of Science.

## FLASHY DIGNITY

*Neon, the strictly honky-tonk* light of a later time, stood for richness and stability in the 1920s. Eminent institutions like the Republic Bank of Dallas outlined their edifices in neon. Republic chose to "stand out in the night sky like a flaming jewel," *Claude Neon News* reported, its dome and eighteen Doric columns accented in ribs of red, its wraparound stone loggia limned in blue.

Power providers like Seattle's Puget Sound Power & Light Company, the Kansas City Power & Light Company, and the Rockland Light & Power Company of Middletown, New York, not satisfied merely to provide power and light, demonstrated both with displays that ran the length of their plants and towered over them. The Utilities Light & Power Company of Asbury Park, New Jersey, added a parapet covered with 1,500 feet of red and green tubing.

Churches all over the country sought to demonstrate an even greater power with neon signs like the red, blue, and white Opalite plaque-shaped emblem surmounted by a white crucifix on the roof of Hinson Memorial Baptist in Portland, Oregon. The color combination, the *Neon News* judged, "appeals to men's finer instincts and creates a feeling of reverence which lingers in the minds of those who pass by."

If a lighted crucifix can create a feeling of reverence, a mighty newspaper's name floating in the night sky above all the other signs may inspire trust and even awe—identifying as it does the exact geographic location of the Moral High Ground.

Newspapers had long regarded themselves as institutions, like banks. Wisely, they knew very well they were selling more than information and entertainment. They were selling image, a public perception of unswerving trustworthiness and the strength to oppose the forces of avarice and tyranny. Solid, proud newspaper buildings, like those that headquartered the *Chicago Tribune,* the *Detroit News,* and the *Baltimore Sun,* assured the reading public that the Truth was protected therein just as surely as their hard-earned cash was safe behind a bank's great granite walls and thick Greek columns. Attesting to this, all boasted proud new neon signs that could be seen for miles.

No newspaper edifice was a more imposing symbol than the New York Times Tower. It didn't matter that the *Times* had long since moved its operations to a larger home nearby on West 43rd Street. After characteristically careful deliberations, the *Times* decided in 1928 to install two architectural embellishments that guaranteed the building's future as the paper's icon for the next fifty years: the wraparound traveling message device that quickly became known as the "zipper," and the name TIMES in 30-foot-high white neon block letters near the top of the 26-story tower.

And not just any neon, of course, but Claude White, a new white neon described by Claude marketers as the next best thing to the "mechanical efficiency in light as given off by the firefly." What could be more reassuring to a restless city than the name of its greatest newspaper spelled in the calm, cool, steady light of a trillion fireflies, unflappable above the red, blue, green, and yellow neon hurly-burly of Times Square?

Around the corner on West 42nd Street the New Amsterdam Theater had names in neon lights too: Eddie Cantor in Florenz Ziegfeld's new show, *Whoopee.* The New Amsterdam's new Art Deco marquee and six-story vertical sign were built by Strauss & Co.—as was the original marquee that graced the theater when it was opened in 1903 by Oscar Hammerstein I. In 1928 it looked much like it does now, thanks to the splendid restoration completed in 1997 as part of the 42nd Street Development Project. An immense electric poster lettered as neatly in neon as if Ben Strauss himself had penned it by hand offered *Midnight Frolic* in the rooftop theater with George Olsen and His Music. ("Orchestra," apparently, was a bad fit.) The wedge-shaped bottom display announced the name of the main show, the name of the star, and the name that guaranteed spectacle and elegant sex appeal: the "glorifier of American girls," Florenz Ziegfeld.

The fabled impresario was pleased as always with his friend Ben Strauss' work. "I confess to you," he wrote to the *Claude Neon News,* "the name of Ziegfeld looks mighty good to me in those alluring tubes of color."

There's no way to tell from the black-and-white photographs what colors were used in Ziegfeld's displays, though the *Neon News* boasts of borders of alternating blue and green made of "special welded glass." But neon signs of the 1920s were nothing if not colorful. Sign makers and customers alike reveled in bright reds, greens, blues, pinks, yellows, oranges, and whites, commonly using most or all available colors in a sign. Chroniclers of life in the Square in the 1920s and 1930s reported that red, not white, was the dominant color of the Great White Way. So chances are Ziegfeld's display contained rows of every hue, spelling on and flashing in jazzy sequence. His show literally started on the sidewalk, and inspired Eddie Cantor to dub it "the swellest thing in lights in all show business."

Ben Strauss' daughter, Florence, was in grade school at the time, and she recalls the 1920s as a golden time for her family. "My father loved what he did," she says. "He loved the theater, and he understood better than anyone else that the show begins on the street. Times Square was magic then, so full of light and life. And I felt that it was our place, that we helped make it all happen.

"Every Saturday afternoon I went to the Square. I wore my best dress and I always had a ribbon in my hair. I got to pick the show I wanted to see. Any one. I just walked up to the door. The ticket takers all knew me and found me a seat. I was Ben Strauss' little girl. Then afterward my father would take us to Toffenetti's for ice cream. It was the best of times."

The Strausses attended the opening night of *Whoopee* on December 4, 1928. They stood briefly on the chilly sidewalk, watching the big boxy black limos growl to a stop in front of the theater and disgorge men in top hats and tails and women wrapped in furs—all bathed in the scintillating, multicolored light of the new marquee. On such nights 42nd Street blazed with a fury of luminescent glamour that hasn't been seen since. The great entertainment palaces poured light into the streets and into the sky, battling with each other for the hearts, minds, and pocketbooks of an amusement-hungry public.

Ziegfeld saw it that way. His Claude/Strauss display, he wrote to *Neon News,* "stands out on Forty-second Street like a light-rocket over a battlefield."

Though Ziegfeld had his own war for the box office in mind, the nightly light show on West 42nd Street and contiguous Times Square was a principal battlefield of the neon wars too. And by 1928 the decisive engagements were about to take place.

## The Final Battle

*As mighty as Claude's forces were*—six U.S. patents, a formidable marketing and public relations machine, and a national network of American partner companies, all of them with substantial investments at stake—eliminating the competition proved to be impossible. For all of its mystique, the technology was no secret. Moore and Machlett, among others, had created luminous tube light before World War I. Thus challengers argued that the fundamental process itself, like the lever, the pulley, and the wheel, is unpatentable.

Claude was, in addition, a victim of his own success. The glamorous image he nurtured for his product helped the copycats too. By 1927, only five years after the historic Packard sign created traffic jams, *Signs of the Times* magazine counted six major neon manufacturers in addition to the Claude group—contenders with lit-up names like Rainbow, Tubalite, Starlite, Sun-Ray, and Aurora. Innumerable small sign companies bootlegged Claude knockoffs, and other folks flocked to the patent office to circumvent Claude by registering processes with exotic names like Muon, Xeon, Harmon, and Zuon. Patent enforcement became a pricey—and ultimately fruitless—proposition.

Claude, however, took on all comers. He and his licensees invested more than $400,000 in legal fees—a fortune at the time—filing more than six dozen federal suits against alleged infringers. The tangle of cases took years to work its way through the courts, and ended only when his last patent expired, in 1932. He fought on all fronts: *Claude Neon Electrical Products* v. *Aurora Products, Inc., Southern California; Claude Neon Lights* v. *Air Reduction Co., Inc., New York; Claude Neon Lights, Inc., and Claude Neon Federal Company* v. *David Hilgenberg d.b.a. The Chicago Neon Sign Company; Claude Neon Electrical Products* v. *Brilliant Tube Company of Washington State*—to name just a few.

The landmark case was *Claude Neon Lights* v. *E. Machlett & Son,* the early developer of luminous tube lighting. Claude contended that Machlett's Rainbow Light, Inc., infringed all of his patents. After two years of suits, countersuits, and appeals ending in 1929, however, only one Claude patent was left standing—the patent on the noncorroding electrode. It proved to be enough to assure Claude's dominance of the industry, at least temporarily.

But Claude's legal troubles weren't over. Some of his licensees rebelliously teamed up with some of his enemies and continually formed new companies, keeping Claude lawyers busy through the end of the decade.

Claude's empire, like his patents, proved difficult to defend. Like the Roman Empire, it grew too large and expensive to administer properly—especially for someone who was spending so much of his time and resources on lawsuits. Eventually, Claude withdrew from his personal involvement in the United States, selling his remaining plants to his former franchisees and devoting his remaining days to new experiments, including an intriguing but costly undertaking to generate electric power from temperature differentials in the ocean.

And remember General Electric, the company that declined to buy the exclusive right to manufacture and market Claude's inventions in the United States for a mere five million dollars? Realizing it had blundered, GE moved to keep the Claude network away from GE's bread and butter, the interior lighting market. Operating under an unwritten agreement, the two stayed away from each other's turf for many years. In 1938, they made a formal agreement in which Claude Neon was granted the exclusive right to make and sell certain GE outdoor lamps. Thus Claude and his neon were kept outdoors in the United States while in Europe low-voltage interior neon lights were being developed.

The expiration of Claude's last patent in 1932 sparked a neon rush that almost equaled the splashy American debut of the glamorous French light ten years earlier. The carefully protected Claude electrode was readily available then, and everybody got into the act. Neon sign production had declined after the stock market crash in 1929, but it soared again in 1932. The country was once more awash in neon, much of it the product of countless small manufacturers who appeared almost overnight.

Neon became ubiquitous, and lost its mystique. The Living Flame became as common as the corner streetlight. Every bar, restaurant, gas station, bakery, and haberdasher had one. Every city's tenderloin came to be known as the "neon district." Neon had become democratized.

At the same time, thousands of magnificent neon signs—including a new generation of Times Square spectaculars that would take the medium to new heights—were built in the 1930s, as advertisers continued to crave bigger and more elaborate displays.

The blush of first romance with the glamorous light—like the youthful blush of the decade that spawned it—was ripening into a marriage.

A taxicab zips down Broadway on a cold evening in the 1930s, en route to a posh Park Avenue address. Nick and Nora Charles are its passengers—he rakishly tipsy in black tie and stiff stand-up collar, she unflappable and rotogravure sleek inside a fluffy mountain of fur. Through the oval window behind them, between the steady swipes of a single wiper blade, we catch a glimpse of a rainy Times Square, its spectacular nightly light show in full swing.

Depression-weary America of the 1930s loved scenes like this and understood them perfectly, even though most people had never traveled more than twenty-five miles from their hometown and would never take such a ride on the Great White Way. The Charleses—Dashiell Hammett's stylish husband-and-wife detective team indelibly incarnated by William Powell and Myrna Loy in the popular *Thin Man* films—epitomized thirties sophistication and fueled the fantasies of millions.

While ordinary folks struggled to keep biscuits and gravy on the table, Nick and Nora awoke every morning to breakfast in bed at the Waldorf, their neatly creased newspaper served to them alongside the linen napkin and egg cup. Independently wealthy, effortlessly witty, and capable of endless alcohol consumption without apparent ill effect, the Charleses were the smartest of the post-Prohibition smart set. Hard times never touched them—or their turf, the Great White Way, the national symbol of unsinkable swank—and an America that knew better wouldn't have had it any other way.

Not that the Great White Way and its images were impervious to the devastating impact of Black Thursday, October 24, 1929, the day the stock market crashed. The costly Dodge Brothers spectacular was among the first to disappear, followed by several other auto-related advertisers (although Chevrolet and Fisk Tires stuck it out), as hard-hit industries began to fall back and regroup. But the vacant spaces weren't vacant for long. Pulling the plug on advertising was clearly *not* the way to bolster a beleaguered business. Furthermore, as the Depression deepened, entertainment evolved from an affordable luxury into a morale-boosting necessity. So spectacular Times Square barely missed a beat.

Just a few blocks in any direction, however, signs of the Depression were everywhere. By the spring of 1930, New York City had six thousand apple sellers at makeshift street-corner stands, with hundreds of them lining Sixth Avenue alone. The city had its share—of the 3.2 million workers who had lost their jobs by then (a figure that would rise to an unbelievable 12 million by 1932); of the 1,352 banks that failed that year; of the 26,355 businesses that went under; and of the $5.64 billion deficit suffered collectively by the 450,000 American companies that managed to stay open.

But like Errol Flynn as the dashing Captain Blood, grinning indomitably in the face of his adversaries ("Ha-ha! Take that, you varlet!"), Times Square played out its swashbuckling destiny. The spring of 1930 brought the lighting of the biggest and most ornate spectacular since the Wrigley extravaganza of 1917. The six-story Pepsodent toothpaste display, in the premier north-end spot vacated by its competitor, Squibb Dental Cream, was a rococo tour de force that had one foot in the world of ornate pre-World War I light sculptures and another in the slick new Deco age of swank.

By far the brightest display in the Square, it was framed in sinuous boughs and Victorian feathers. A clock large enough to be read a dozen blocks away sat at the top. And below the clock—here's the swank—a shapely, scantily clad lass swung back and forth on a swing, leaning eagerly forward with knees bent at one end of the arc, leaning languidly back with legs thrust forward at the other end.

If she looked like a chorus girl, it's because she was modeled on one: a certified Ziegfeld Girl, doubtless selected for her resistance to vertigo. Florenz Ziegfeld, ever the Glorifier of the American Girl, supplied her services to General Outdoor's designers, who rigged a swing on a nearby rooftop and filmed the young woman in her short but exhilarating flight.

The image was familiar to patrons of New York's rich nightclub scene, in its heyday through the 1930s both during and after Prohibition. Posh clubs like "21," El Morocco, and Hollywood on Broadway, clustered in and around Times Square, competed against one another with elaborate floor shows featuring legions of chorus girls in Busby Berkeley–style production numbers, sometimes swinging in formation high over the heads of diners and dancers.

The other Hollywood, the one in California, took the rest of America into such spiffy places too, following Nick and Nora and their elegant ilk down broad marble staircases to gleaming dance floors flanked by tiers of tables with little shaded lamps on them. Everyone got the picture: swank starts with white teeth and sweet breath.

Depression? What Depression?

# Signs of Success in the Great Depression

*Although no one knew it at* the time, the Depression wouldn't end for good until the country channeled its industrial might into wartime production. But if an economic recovery remained a hopeful illusion throughout the 1930s, a renewal of the American spirit of enterprise certainly didn't.

America celebrated its ability to build. Our faith in our technology was stronger than ever. Technocracy—a system of government in which all economic resources, hence the entire social system, would be controlled by scientists and engineers—was seriously advanced by its proponents as the world order of the future.

The reach for the sky that began in the teens and flourished in the twenties caught a second wind in the thirties, as skyscrapers like the Empire State Building—built entirely, from excavation to dirigible mast, in only eleven months in 1930–31—continued to redefine the skyline. Putting America to work, the Public Works Authority built dams like the Boulder to tame the Colorado River, and the Tennessee Valley Authority brought electricity to a vast region of the Southeast. The great sculptured portraits on Mount Rushmore were completed. Anyone could fly around the world for the (admittedly hefty) price of an airline ticket. Radio networks united the country as nothing ever had.

The great signs of the times were more than advertisements for products. They were, as Frankfort Distillers promised with its Four Roses Whiskey spectacular in Times Square, expressions of "confidence in a recovering economy." More to the point, they were expressions of confidence in American technology.

The spectaculars built across the country during that decade were dramatizations of industrial power and magic. Like the signs of the twenties, they grew larger and larger, employing ever-greater technical virtuosity. Their innards filled entire rooms with clattering metal fingers, cams, and switches. With their great letters and sweeping fields of neon and incandescent lamps, they were man-made wonders of the world.

The times were ripe for energetic entrepreneurs with a flair for technology who could see opportunity where others were tempted to despair. And that description exactly fit my grandfather, Jake, who moved through the Times Square of the thirties like a whirlwind.

By the late 1920s, Jake and his former employer, Ben Strauss, were keen and prosperous competitors. *Signs of the Times* magazine chronicled each new and colorful theatrical display by Strauss & Co. At the same time, it noted, "Those Artkraft boys seem to be busy everywhere, building many of the new signs that are filling the streets along the Great White Way."

Then came the Crash.

"In 1929 I lost everything, I'm not ashamed to say it," Jake told me nearly fifty years later. "I had real estate, stocks, bonds, other holdings, it all went down the drain. I was broke, I did not even have carfare. They shut off the water, the gas, the electric; I ran around on foot to borrow the money to turn it back on."

Commodities he wasn't short of were energy and drive. By the end of 1929 he had started his own consulting company, Starr Engineering, and was investing every cent he made into the leasing of rooftops from cash-strapped property owners. Equipped with the Artkraft neon franchise and the ability to design and build economically, he began leasing and selling signs to national advertisers, augmenting the on-premise business identification signs that had been his ordinary stock-in-trade.

By 1932 he had accumulated enough cash to buy a half interest in New York Artkraft, and in 1933 he bought out his partners. In 1934 he renewed his association with Strauss, whose reputation was still golden but whose recovery from the Crash was proceeding less fortuitously than his own. In 1935 the two companies merged, forming Artkraft Strauss.

The new company pursued a classic full-service approach—from sales, leasing, art, and design to engineering, fabrication, and maintenance. Soon it would start to overtake General Outdoor as a major Times Square presence. Along the way, Jake acquired a number of other companies, including their customer lists, employees, and know-how. In 1937 he bought out Ben Strauss, who stayed on as general manager until his retirement in 1959.

*Signs of the Times*'s observation that "those Artkraft boys seem to be busy everywhere" certainly applied to Jake during those years. He shipped big displays all over the country, including a series of huge blue-and-white logos for the roofs of Ford assembly plants and elaborate, ornate marquees for the entire Loew's theater chain. He built and maintained advertising displays for both his own advertising locations and those of his competitors, and was the uncredited subcontractor on many others. He experimented with every new technology and incorporated it into his signs. He learned about politics, union politics, and strategic alliances. But most important, chastened by his 1929 experience, he learned about finance: the management of cash flow and debt, the leasing of signs and equipment, the trading of signs for equity in cash-poor companies, the development and marketing of advertising space. Whatever it took, he kept the factory humming—he was determined never to have his lights shut off again.

The year of the Artkraft-Strauss merger, 1935, was also the year the company moved into the plant on Twelfth Avenue between 57th and 58th streets, hard by the Hudson River, that is still our home. The building was then only ten years old and located in the heart of the busy industrial West Side adjoining the piers, where the Pennsylvania Railroad once ran by.

Today the bustling Port of New York is mainly a memory, and so is the railroad—a developer named Donald Trump is turning the old rail yards next door into high-rise luxury housing—but we're still here. The factory hasn't changed much, though the plumbing and wiring may be somewhat improved, and the roof, ramps, and doors have been through several incarnations.

One of the last surviving New York City manufacturing plants, the brick factory is a favorite with movie location scouts, magazine photographers, and music video producers. When I had our parapet sign repainted in 1997 in honor of our 100th birthday—we do this every sixty years whether it needs it or not—I retained the original design, including the words "Sign Corporation" in chunky blue Arts and Crafts script and the proud "Plant No. 1" in its red medallion, doubtless Jake's idea. (Plants No. 2 and up have tended to come and go over the years.) The plant provides a small glimpse of old New York, a landmark to regular motorists on the West Side Highway.

No one has ever counted the signs that have come out of our big doors. There have been tens of thousands over the years, including virtually every major spectacular built in Times Square since World War II and many of the classics of the 1930s.

Among some of the most memorable were the landmark displays we built for Jake's favorite sparring partner, the great Times Square sign impresario Douglas Leigh.

## BOW TIES AND BIG IDEAS

*Douglas Leigh was another classic* success story of the Great Depression. A master salesman and deft self-promoter who came to New York from Alabama in 1931 with a meager few dollars in his pocket, he was David taking aim at the mighty General Outdoor Advertising Company's Goliath in the battlefield of Times Square.

General Outdoor, a giant so big it reached clear across the country, marked its turf with torrents of incandescent lamps and waves of pulsing neon tubes. Leigh, a dapper warrior who confessed to owning more than sixty bow ties, fought for a foothold with puffs of steam, dancing silhouettes of cartoon characters, pocketfuls of big ideas, and a carload of southern charm. And if Leigh didn't actually slay the giant, he certainly bloodied it.

He had a unique sense of what Times Square's supersigns ought to be about—a blend of nineteenth-century three-dimensionality and modern cinematic spectacularity that owed as much to show business as it did to graphic art. Though his body of work was relatively small—in 1941, his best year, he had just sixteen signs out of some four dozen in Times Square—his impact was large.

Leigh and his engineers pioneered the application to spectaculars of what we now call "special effects"—a movie term identifying the use of technology to create an illusion. Principal among these was the use of steam from a building's heating system to serve as the steam wafting from a hot cup of coffee or the smoke rings drifting from the mouth of a giant cigarette smoker. His three-story box of Super Suds detergent released real soap bubbles into the air. The clock in his Gillette Razor sign announced the hour with Westminster-style chimes. Passersby also caught a whiff of the lemony aroma emitted by his lemon-colored Sunkist Smell-O-Rama display further down the same block.

By 1940, Leigh virtually owned a large chunk of Times Square. Douglas Leigh, Inc., he proudly told reporters, was a $1 million business. Pretty good for a kid from Anniston, Alabama, who, just seven years earlier, was making only $30 a week.

Leigh was a handsome, mannerly, ambitious, all-American underdog. He came to New York to work for General Outdoor at $50 per week, hoping to sell signs in Times Square. But when the company cut his pay to $30 in 1933 and tried to confine his sales territory to Brooklyn, he quit and started his own company, capitalized with $150 from the sale of his old Ford.

He swapped the St. Moritz Hotel a wall sign in the Bronx for a suite the hotel probably couldn't rent anyway—and away he went. Doing business on the fancy hotel's stationery while dining at the Automat on his food budget of a dollar a day, he sweet-talked, bluffed, and otherwise huckstered landlords and advertisers with his spectacular schemes until, barely a year after he started, he gained his first foothold in General Outdoor's Holy Ground, Times Square.

His story of getting the better of what the movies called "Old Man Depression" was tailor-made for *The Saturday Evening Post,* and the magazine profiled him in 1939 under the headline "Young Man of Manhattan." *Time, Life,* and *The New Yorker* followed suit. Thus a legend was born. And Broadway had a new Lamplighter.

"Leigh was kind of mythic. His legend seemed to grow in the dark decade of the 1970s," recalls neon historian Rudi Stern, who started his studio, Let There Be Neon, in 1972—and wrote an influential book of the same name—to help keep the craft alive at a time when neon had gone hopelessly out of fashion. "Old postcards of Times Square from the thirties were treasured by neon aficionados," remembers Stern. And Leigh happily took his place in the neon pantheon.

Leigh in the thirties was a public relations man's dream come true. Not only had he built a successful business from scratch in difficult times, he also possessed mastery of the razzle-dazzle promospeak of his day. No New York newspaper account of anything related to signs in Times Square was complete without a quote from him.

And Leigh believed he had a lot to say, on matters far weightier than the number of lightbulbs on the Great White Way. *The Saturday Evening Post* reported that he had political aspirations and planned to start a new party for businessmen. Toward that end, said the *Post*, "he is now dickering with a radio network, offering to promote it on a Broadway spectacular in exchange for fifteen minutes of radio time a week in which to expound his political philosophy. 'The old days must have been great,' says this child of the Depression with a sigh. 'How can a capitalist make any money the way things are now?' "

Leigh's idol was Henry Ford, with whom he shared a dislike of bankers and Wall Streeters—and all they symbolized. So fierce was his admiration for the isolationist auto pioneer that he stormed out of a Columbia University night course in philosophy, never to return, after the professor made a disparaging remark about his hero.

Punditry proved to be a dead end for Leigh, but capitalism did not. The world may have ignored his political opinions, but his pronouncements on the state of signs in Times Square were always taken as gospel.

Like a skilled Broadway producer, he had a knack for surrounding himself with talent. He was a brilliant salesman and a professional dreamer of dreams. But, he told reporters, he deliberately avoided knowing too much about the "how" of his signs on the grounds that excessive focus on nuts and bolts might hamper his creativity.

At Artkraft Strauss, Leigh was famous for marching in unannounced and dropping some outrageous concept—a waterfall, an erupting volcano, a smoke-puffing giant—on my grandfather's desk. "Jake," he'd say, "here's what I just sold. You can build it now, can't you?" This would invariably unleash one of Jake's storms of spluttering rage. Then Jake would calm down, figure it out, and build it—for a price.

Leigh also readily admitted to a fear of heights, an inconvenient phobia for a builder of massive roof displays. So he supervised his projects from the sidewalk, leaving the intricacies of engineering and construction to his colleagues—Jake, and his right-hand man, Fred Kerwer. Kerwer, a fixture in the New York sign industry since the teens, was a sign man's sign man, a perfectionist widely respected for his inexhaustible skills as a painter, draftsman, metalworker, porcelain craftsman, electrician, mechanic, tube bender, carpenter, and rigger.

Jake was a kindred spirit to both men. As an inventor, he shared

Kerwer's technical ingenuity. And like Leigh, he was a brilliant businessman. But hampered by his immigrant origins—and always conscious of them—he lacked salesman Leigh's gift of gab. Together, the trio made a formidable team.

The three joined forces in 1934 on the first of many spectaculars Jake built for Leigh—a three-dimensional steaming A&P coffee cup on the corner of Broadway and 45th Street. It was one of Jake's last projects as president of the New York branch of Artkraft of Ohio—a year later, he would found Artkraft Strauss, and Kerwer was his employee. In the course of the collaboration, Leigh hired Kerwer away from Jake—then as now a professional no-no. But there were signs to be built and money to be made. So the three worked together for many years, creating dozens of fabulous displays, including their masterpiece, the "smoking" Camel sign of 1941, and their engineering marvel, the Bond waterfall, in 1947.

Leigh and Jake were like Gilbert and Sullivan—and their relationship was similarly rocky. Personality differences aside, Leigh doubtless resented having to employ his strongest competitor to engineer and build his extravaganzas. But there was no one else who could interpret his dreams. In 1994, Leigh, then eighty-six, described the long collaboration as "a nice fifty-odd-year sparring match."

And their rivalry continues. Today, when I run into Leigh at meetings of the Broadway Association, he fixes me with a gimlet eye. "How old was your grandpa when he died?" he demands.

"Eighty-four, Mr. Leigh," I reply.

And he grins with an old man's triumphant glee.

But if the two could never be considered friends, exactly, they clearly respected each other. And the ingenuity and professionalism of their work speaks for itself, long after the displays themselves have vanished.

## THE RETURN OF "THE CUP THAT CHEERS"

*"Mother's in the kitchen /* Washin' out jugs," went a popular Prohibition-era ditty, "Sister's in the pantry / Bottling the suds / Father's in the cellar / Mixing up the hops / Johnny's on the front porch / Watching for the cops."

America's first great experiment in social engineering—the Eighteenth Amendment to the U.S. Constitution, prohibiting the manufacture and sale of alcoholic beverages—was a resounding flop. It replaced a legal industry with a criminal (and nontaxpaying) one, made a mockery of law enforcement, and invested drinking with the allure of forbidden fruit.

In 1927, someone counted the speakeasies in New York City and reported to the newspapers that they outnumbered the old-time saloons. And, unlike the oaken, spitoon-equipped, all-male inner sancta of yore, they all admitted women. Sugary mixed drinks with cute, pseudo-sophisticated names were added to the bibacious menu, both to appeal to the ladies and to conceal the taste of rotgut.

Bad home brew was said to account for more than 1,500 deaths per year. The nation's long coastlines and 3,986-mile unfenced border with wet Canada proved impossible to police. By 1928, the Treasury Department reported, it had fired 706 Prohibition agents and prosecuted 257 of them for taking bribes. And in 1929, New York authorities dropped liquor charges against thirty nightclubs because it was certain no jury would convict.

During the thirteen years of Prohibition, Times Square, like all business districts, was cleansed of liquor advertising, all the better to protect a populace which, in the optimistic view of one Episcopal Church official, had "learned to drink milk as never before." Nothing harder than Clicquot Club Ginger Ale—its Eskimo boy display now in its second incarnation at Broadway and 47th Street—beguiled smart Square-goers in search of the high life. Never mind that real happy water was as near as the nearest speak—third brownstone on the left, knock three times, tell the eye that peers through the little door, "Joe sent me."

The campaign to end Prohibition was almost as vociferous as the campaign that began it. Breweries and distilleries that limped through the twenties making everything from root beer and "near beer" to cattle feed and soap led the fight, promising their parched Depression-plagued constituency not only a return of their favorite beverage but thousands of new jobs as well. And no one rejoiced at the prospect of Repeal more than the outdoor advertising industry.

The first signs that the end was near appeared simultaneously in six cities—New York, Chicago, Philadelphia, New Orleans, St. Louis, and Kansas City—on November 4, 1932. The advertiser was Anheuser-Busch, whose eagle had flown only on behalf of soft drinks for thirteen years. Each spectacular contained the familiar eagle logo, Budweiser spelled in script, a huge clock, chimes, and the word "Malt" in the lower right-hand corner. Everyone knew, however, that Anheuser-Busch didn't spend this kind of money just to advertise this important component of malted milk shakes or its nonalcoholic malt beverage, "near beer."

The spectaculars, the largest and most colorful of which was in Times Square on Broadway at 46th Street, were turned on four days before the 1932 presidential election, a neon message to both candidates intended to be read as handwriting on the wall. The Democratic candidate, Franklin D. Roosevelt, who strongly favored Repeal to generate a tax infusion for the cash-starved government, was elected. A year later, in December 1933, the chimes on the clocks tolled the end of Prohibition.

And by early the next morning—when a great wagon pulled by a team of Clydesdale horses delivered a load of thank-you brew to the front door of the White House—the word "Malt" had disappeared from the signs and been replaced by what *Signs of the Times* coyly described as "a four-letter word meaning an amber-hued liquid brewed from malted grain." Namely, "Beer."

Breweries were back in business overnight, and America quaffed their product as quickly as they bottled it. By 1936, Americans were drinking 53 million barrels of beer annually. New Yorkers, claiming the nation's largest thirst, accounted for 8.5 million of those barrels. Budweiser didn't have any city's night skyline to itself very long.

Schaefer weighed in with a block-long display next door to Budweiser's in Times Square, between 45th and 46th streets, that promised, "Our Hand Has Never Lost Its Skill." To demonstrate this, a 16-foot neon man on a flying neon trapeze flew across the sign and did a somersault in midair before he snagged another trapeze for the return trip.

A block farther south, Trommer's White Label, a local brew, opted for height with a six-story neon spectacular in which two surefooted gnomes balanced on a giant horizontal long-necked bottle as if it were a floating log, draining bottle after gnome-sized bottle of "Genuine Ale" without falling off.

The best of the Depression-era beer spectaculars, however, was Douglas Leigh's 1936 Ballantine Ale display on the roof of the Brill Building on Broadway at 48th Street. At four stories high, it wasn't the largest. But it was the most sophisticated, the embodiment of the spectacular swank that characterized the great neon signs of the day.

Leigh began with the company's logo—a set of three interlocking rings—and with the rather unlikely circus theme of Ballantine's advertising campaign: "It's a three-ring show." The company claimed the logo had its origin in 1840 when founder Peter Ballantine drained his ale in three "lifts" of his glass, forming a moist ring on the table each time he set it down. How the brewery's ad agency got from that charming anecdote to a three-ring circus remains a mystery. But Leigh and his production team, working with these givens, stayed with the program and delivered a stunning neon pictorial of a clown tossing rings at a post. Striving to achieve motion-picture-quality animation, the Leigh team produced a twelve-second Broadway show that turned heads blocks away.

The story was simple enough. The clown bent to pick up a ring, stood up, and tossed it with an outstretched arm, winking engagingly, his red nose flashing, as the ring skittered across the sign and settled perfectly on the post. At the same time, a 40-foot beer bottle turned into a giant beer tap that filled a mammoth frosty mug with tempting brew.

What distinguished this rather odd combination of images was the execution. The neon overlays were so densely packed—the clown ring toss sequence alone required 54 individual movements—the animation appeared seamless, and created an illusion of depth. The rings—3,780 of them every night, and every time a bull's-eye—grew larger as they approached the post, seeming to fly off the face of the sign, a precursor of movie 3-D, a fad of a generation later. Like the great spectaculars of the 1950s, it celebrated its own modernity and technical wizardry—and invested its advertiser with a touch of its own classy brand of spectacularity.

The Ballantine advertising campaign of 1936 didn't earn a place in beer marketing history alongside "Tastes Great! Less Filling!" But the Ballantine spectacular was one of Broadway's greatest hits of 1936—and every year thereafter, until World War II darkened Times Square.

Beer was a proletarian beverage, meant to be consumed at Oktoberfests accompanied by polka music, around campfires after thirsty days of fly-fishing, and in wooden bleachers overlooking the sacred ground of emerald green upon which America's national sport was played. Whiskey, on the other hand, had a different image to rebuild. Whiskey was rich, sophisticated, regal. Demonized by the Drys as the soul-destroyer of "1000 Nights in a Barroom," and with the Good Stuff in precious short supply for so long, whiskey had a willing, worldly-wise constituency waiting for its legal return. And like the breweries, the distillers believed their customers were all men.

Despite the determinedly coed culture of the speakeasy, the perception remained strong after Prohibition that imbibing was primarily a male activity. Mama might dip into the cooking sherry now and then, or sip a pink lady, a grenadine-flavored manhattan, or even a martini in a nightclub. But the image of serious boozing was an exclusively male one. Even Alcoholics Anonymous, founded in 1935 by two men who kept each other sober through lengthy mutually supportive conversations while their wives supplied them with coffee and sandwiches, didn't admit women until after World War II.

Downing a straight shot, or two or three, was a rite of male passage. A man of business was known by his brand of whiskey as surely as he was known by his smokes, his automobile, and the label on his suit. The regiment of swanky bottles, dramatically backlit behind the bars of the dark, leather-upholstered lounges where men conducted business, had a hierarchy of its own. Perception of prestige determined position in that hierarchy. Drinkers had a choice again, and advertising dollars replaced machine-gun bullets in the Whiskey Wars of the 1930s.

Millions of those dollars were spent on spectacularly macho outdoor displays. Distillers competed in size and swagger—big and bigger were the order of the day—as well as in technical virtuosity. Cartoon graphics were generally eschewed in favor of emblems, heraldry, and classy typography. Even when cartoons were used, they were intended, like Ballantine's ring-tossing clown, to impress with their technology, not to amuse with their antics. A man's whiskey took its stand with a BIG sign, a virtuoso loaded with hardware, bursting with power, its message a grand slam that made its competition look feeble by comparison.

The first post-Prohibition whiskey spectacular in Times Square was built in 1934 by Hiram Walker, a 42-by-109-foot blockbuster launching a series that would culminate with the long-running 1952 Canadian Club spectacular on the fabled north tower. Other imposing Hiram Walker displays followed throughout the decade all over the United States and Canada. One of them, on HW's headquarters in Windsor, Ontario, is still operating.

These signs were big, but they weren't big enough. In 1937, Hiram Walker topped itself with a gargantuan spectacular built by Federal Sign on Chicago's White Way, at Randolph Street and Outer Drive. At $111\frac{1}{2}$ feet high by 250 feet wide, it may still hold the record as the largest spectacular ever built.

It wasn't, however, the tallest. Seagram's apparently holds that record. Its 1935 display on Michigan Avenue in Chicago, also built by Federal, was 117 feet high by 114 wide, and offered a nifty piece of neon animation—a 60-foot red neon seal balancing a rotating Seagram's ball on its nose. The 1938 rebuild lost the seal and added a massive crown, a two-story clock, the name of the product illuminated with ferocious new intensity, and six more feet of girth.

Seagram's wasn't finished with animation, however. A year later, identical seven-story Seagram's spectaculars depicting a neon racetrack complete with a thundering pack of Thoroughbreds took their places in Times Square and on the Boardwalk in Atlantic City. The ponies ran 500 races nightly, post time every minute, tempting friendly wagers by onlookers fortified with a sufficient quantity of the sponsor's product. "Can do, can do, the guy says the horse can do..."

The guy who would bet on a neon horse race apparently wasn't the target customer that one of Seagram's competitors, the aggressively intellectual Calvert Distillers, had in mind. In 1937 Calvert blitzed the nation with spectaculars, from Miami to New York to Chicago to Los Angeles and major points in between, all portraying variations on the theme: "Clear Heads Call for Calvert."

Representing clearheadedness was a robust-looking chap with a savvy smile on his face. If this in-the-know look didn't persuade, the viewer needed only to come back at night for a more literal demonstration of a clear head. When the sun went down and the lights came on, the man's cranium became transparent, revealing the electrified brain within. The neon folds of the Calvert man's brain, doubtless in the throes of Calvert-fueled clear thinking, glowed and throbbed all night long. The company was deadly serious about this macabre display, explaining it was intended "to create a national consciousness for the Calvert name."

The brainy approach appealed to Schenley's too. Opting for art instead of anatomy, Schenley's put up theater-themed displays in places like Cleveland's Playhouse Square, portraying a bright bottle of 100 Proof Cream of Kentucky Straight Whiskey at center stage, presumably basking in its audience's accolades.

Schenley's on the road was a nice show, but Schenley's on Broadway was simply smashing. The company elected to make its mark at the corner of 42nd Street and Seventh Avenue, the entrance to the fabled Deuce, on the roof of the Rialto Theater. In 1936 they erected an 80-foot crystal glass and neon tower topped with a giant star beaming shafts of floodlight skyward. *Signs of the Times* said the tower, which might have been the identifying spire of a space city in a Buck Rogers serial, "gleamed like a giant pearl." Glass was seen as gleamingly modern by forward-looking 1930s designers and architects, and the Schenley Tower was touted as the building of the future.

A great shaft bursting with light and power, it was the ultimate expression of masculinity. The tower was perfectly located, Schenley's said, citing studies purporting to show that more men than women passed through the intersection. Perhaps they were drawn by the proximity of Minsky's burlesque, perhaps by the numerous neighborhood bars.

If Schenley staked out the south end of Times Square as a

male preserve, Frankfort Distillers, the makers of Four Roses Whiskey, did the same at the north end. Its exquisite Four Roses display, a Douglas Leigh creation, crowned the "tower" at the north end of the Square, its ruby-red neon roses climbing the sides like a trellis.

Leigh dramatized the great size of the display by reporting its dimensions in "girl units." Each spray of roses, he declared, was "thirteen girls in height," while each of the letters was "six girls in height." Two girls perched in the trough of the O for a pre-turn-on photo op, and more bevies of girls fanned out through Times Square on the night the sign was illuminated, bestowing roses on passersby from baskets carried on their arms. And none of them, of course, touched a drop.

## EPOK AND WONDER

*Two spectacular displays that were* virtually fraternal twins marked the Times Square debut of the large-scale animated lamp bank, the forerunner of the modern outdoor video screen. These were Leigh's Epok sign of 1938 and Artkraft Strauss' Wondersign of 1939. The Wondersign was artistically and technologically superior, but the Epok is better remembered. This is partially due to Leigh's incomparable promotional skills—but also the Epok seems simply to have had more charisma. Like Leigh himself, it was undeniably cuter.

Lamp banks—solid matrixes of lightbulbs—had been used before, of course, going all the way back to 1909's "Leaders of the World" and its contemporaries. But the earlier displays were alphanumeric, flashing letters and numbers only. True cartoon animation, as on a movie screen, had to wait for the advances in electrical controls that came along in the 1930s.

The Wondersign was a French invention, the brainchild of famous poster artist Jean Carlu of Paris. Under the name "Luminograph" it had won the grand prize at the Paris Exposition of 1937. Artkraft Strauss, its exclusive American licensee, installed it on the front of the Palace Theater building on Broadway at 47th Street in time for the opening of the 1939 New York World's Fair. Nine more installations in various cities were planned, and advertising was to be sold on a space-and-time basis: $4,500 for a twenty-second showing every twelve minutes for a year. Piel's beer, Enna Jettick shoes, La Palina cigars, Hamilton watches, and, inevitably, Wonder Bread were among the first advertisers to sign up. "Thirty-six Spectaculars in One!" cried the headline in *Signs of the Times*.

The display panel was 28½ by 23½ feet in size and contained 27,000 lamps on two-inch centers. But the most wondrous thing about the Wondersign is that it was full-color—its red, green, amber, and clear lamps could combine to display the entire spectrum.

The flashing equipment consisted of nine relay racks, each containing 3,000 individual relays. They were activated pneumatically, like a player piano. A giant roll of paper was hand-perforated in the designs of the artwork, and as it rolled past a series of pneumatic flutes, puffs of air coming through the perforations flipped the switches.

The Wondersign went dark for two and a half years during the war, but was relit in 1945, now exclusively to promote RKO films, with the addition of a neon identification, a changeable attraction panel, and a Trans-Lux traveling message. The first movie it advertised was *Along Came Jones,* a Western starring Gary Cooper and Loretta Young.

Movie advertising for sophisticated audiences would require a finer hand in the design department than the simple cartooning of dancing products that had sufficed before. And along came Kreisberg—Irving Kreisberg, then a young artist from Chicago seeking to make his mark in the Big Apple. Kreisberg has since enjoyed many exhibitions and awards, but his stint at the Wondersign holds a particular place in his heart.

"On July 4, 1945," he wrote to me fifty years later, "I arrived from Chicago at the bus station in Times Square . . . , noted the ubiquitous logo, and telephoned Artkraft Strauss. The meeting place an hour later was a tiny office above the Palace Theater.

" 'Are you an artist?'

" 'Yes, I am.'

"Mel Starr put a large sheet of paper on the table in front of me. 'Can you draw a hand holding a lasso?'

" 'Yes, I can.' The image of the rope hugged the edges of the paper, for I knew that titles would fill the central space.

" 'Can you start work tonight?'

" 'Yes, I can.'

"The next day I met George the electrician seated on his outdoor scaffold waging his hopeless daily battle against burnt-out bulbs; and I met Victor the technician who would be my partner.

"I was never formally introduced to the boss, whose office abutted our workspace, but his presence was abundantly manifest. [Jake], between volcanic outbursts of anger in his office, would fling his door open and pace the floor near my drawing table, his restless hands behind his back jangling his stacks of coins.

" 'Bombard them!' he barked hoarsely, 'Bombard them!' His words straining with phlegm, he cast his smoldering eye at me and at every other intractable object that hemmed him in. 'Bombard them!'

"George the electrician, if he heard the directive, would mutter in remonstrance but never audibly, 'But Boss, we're burning the relays! We're burning the whole thing up!'

"The papers on which I plotted my drawings were stamped with grids comprising the 27,000 tiny circles. These drawings, encumbered with instructions, were placed on a machine frame where Victor with his magic needle pierced each indicated circle and translated the drawing into a huge player-piano roll of paper. That was magical, but the whole situation, for me, heaved with fiery magic.

"I must tell you that in the weeks before and after my arrival in New York, I had been reading Thomas Mann's huge novel *Joseph in Egypt*. In my mind, the parallel with my own removal to another land was inescapable.

"I had traveled from my home grounds not by camel but by Greyhound yet clearly I had arrived at the fleshpots of Egypt: Times Square in New York. And at once I had found myself in the employ of the priests of Moloch. The huge false gods of stone, breathing fire, their great arms made to move by creaking pulleys, their false grimaces lit up to stupefy the rabble below....

"From my drawing table I looked the length of the corridor that housed the long serpentine coil of paper—the monstrous player-piano roll—whose perforations sparked the great flashing banks of circuits. And to keep the roadway of paper supple and rolling, huge pots of steam lined the route. While from its back we could see this crackling monster breathing fire and billowing smoke, the front of the Wondersign amazed the crowds in the Square and we could hear their multitudinous cries and squeals as the 27,000 colored electric bulbs bombarded their senses.

"And true to my Joseph character, I was dedicated to the idea of loyalty. I remember especially a long speech I made to your father. In exchange for flexible hours I was offering twenty-four-hour availability. My task was to assure him of my absolute fidelity; I was serving Potiphar but my loyalty and reliability were absolute. . . .

"Mel finally stopped me and said with ease, 'Okay, Irv, okay. I never asked you to marry me.' No further words.

"I had total freedom of hours and design for the Wondersign; and at all times I gave the spectacular whatever was needed whenever it was needed.

"And thus I served my master for three years as animator for the Artkraft Strauss Wondersign."

Kreisberg's later work, now in museums and private collections around the world, is an original and vibrant reweaving of many threads of modernism. But his work for the Wondersign—including sequences of Frank Sinatra crooning and Judy Garland belting out hits—was fine portraiture: nuanced, shaded, rhythmic, pointillist.

Leigh's Epok sign down the street, installed a few months earlier, was almost identical to the Wondersign in size—30 by 24 feet—but it was in black and white only, and contained fewer than one-sixth the number of lamps: 4,104, to be exact. But its cartoony charm earned it a place in history.

Otto Soglow, the creator of Felix the Cat, was the Epok's animator, and his sequences, which ran for five minutes—a remarkably long time—had the angular edginess that is Felix's hallmark. The first advertiser was Old Gold cigarettes, and the initial sequence—a new one was to be created every two months—featured the romantic adventures of a Soglow-created, pointy-headed character called Goldie and Goldie's nameless girlfriend.

According to the description in *Signs of the Times,* Goldie "walks into a tobacco shop, where he buys a package of cigarettes. He then strides along smoking and makes his way to his sweetheart's home. While he stands in front of the door blowing smoke rings, his girl comes to the balcony window. There she catches whiffs of the smoke, is delighted by it, and steps onto one of the smoke clouds to ride gently to the ground. She takes the cigarette from Goldie, smokes it, and the two go off together to be married." An outcome like that is enough to turn almost anyone into an Old Gold smoker.

The Epok technology was invented by Kurt Rosenberg of Austria, from whom Leigh licensed the American marketing rights. Leigh installed several of them over the years, and never wavered in his view that it was the ultimate in technology. It was indeed a clever device.

The Epok was controlled by a vertical bank of 1,026 photoelectric cells, each connected to a switch that turned four lamps on and off. Ordinarily, the mechanism was operated by projecting black-and-white film strips onto the photoelectric wall, and the silhouettes would appear on the board. But the Epok was also capable of operating "live." For one memorable turn-on, Leigh hired a stripper, who did her number in front of the photoelectric sensors. The sight of the twenty-foot-tall ecdysiast dancing her duds away was literally a traffic-stopper, causing a rash of fender benders.

In 1979, after a career spanning nearly half a century, Leigh sold his remaining fourteen locations and left the Square. He didn't retire, though. His new business, the design of municipal lighting projects, was well under way by then. Leigh is responsible for the multicolor lights that illuminate the Empire State Building at night and for the golden glow of the Helmsley Building. He has also done projects in Florida and designed master lighting plans for the cities of Cincinnati and Atlanta.

But Times Square and its spectacular advertising signs remained in his blood. As recently as 1990, he still had a few Epoks stashed away in a warehouse in New Jersey. He convinced Coca-Cola officials, then in the early design phase of their forthcoming new Times Square spectacular, to come have a look. They did, and waited patiently as warehouse guards cleared away decades of dust and pried open the ancient crates. The brass listened politely as the octogenarian legend of the sign industry extolled the virtues of his 1938 technological marvel. It must have been a poignant scene, like Gloria Swanson attempting her last comeback in *Sunset Boulevard*. I wish I had been there.

## Neon's Desert Song

*Times Square's first serious rival* as the center of the neon world took root in the Nevada desert in the 1930s. The place was Las Vegas, a dusty little town whose claim to future fame was its cluster of gambling casinos. Within two decades, Las Vegas could boast more miles of neon and square footage of spectacularity than anywhere else on earth, a claim that remains unchallenged.

Ironically, the sign man who in 1931 planted the seeds of the neon garden that came to be known as Glitter Gulch didn't gamble, drink, smoke, swear, or consort with fast women. He was drawn to little Las Vegas, not by the seductive whir of the roulette wheel or the fantasy of instant wealth pouring from a slot machine, but by the obvious market for his product—electric signs.

Thomas Young—kindred spirit of Jake, Doug Leigh, and a legion of other Depression-era entrepreneurs—was a hardworking Mormon traveling salesman, patriarch-to-be of a burgeoning family, and proud proprietor of the prosperous Young Electric Sign Company (YESCO). Born in England, Young heeded the call of prophet Joseph Smith and migrated with his family to the Promised Land in the American West. There, he and his brothers opened a sign shop in Ogden, Utah, in 1920.

Tom was the Outside Man, and the entire Depression-parched Southwest was the territory he staked out for his company. He drove thousands of miles in the big Packards he favored, over pavement that sometimes ended before he got where he was going, looking for towns with businesses that needed—and could pay for—his services. He found them, in tiny desert towns miles apart, throughout Utah,

Nevada, California, and Arizona. By the time he died, in 1971, YESCO was one of the largest sign companies in the world, with plants in all those states. And YESCO had provided the glitter in Las Vegas's fabled Glitter Gulch.

"Regardless of the temperature, Dad never left the house without having on a suit, white shirt, and tie," recalls his son Tom Jr., now the patriarch of the family business. "He'd take off on those long trips, and come back with a big satchel full of order forms all filled out, and a bunch of drawings of what his customers' signs would look like—some on linen napkins. He'd just take 'em down to the shop and say, 'Here, have this finished in two weeks.'"

So it's easy to get the picture of Tom Sr. on his first foray to Vegas: bow tie smartly in place, sleeves of his white shirt rolled up, suit jacket neatly folded next to him on the front seat. He cruised down sun-bleached Fremont Street, peering through his dust-covered windows at the handful of gambling halls and small hotels and shops, and saw money to be made.

And before he left town, he sold his first Las Vegas sign—an electric display that made the Boulder Club the brightest spot on the sleepy street. That sale, he knew, was just the beginning. The biggest and the best was yet to come.

Only twenty-five miles away, Boulder Dam (renamed Hoover Dam in 1947) was being built to harness the power of the Colorado River. Young could feel the power in the making. "Dad would come home and say, 'Mama, all that power's going to be generated down in Las Vegas,'" Tom Jr. remembers. His dad had been watching the progress of the project for a long time. The dam's planners, representing the seven states that would reap this amazing harvest of power, sat down in 1920 to do their work. The surveying and geophysical analysis of the mighty river and its twists and turns took several years and had teams of scientists on mules boldly going where only frontiersmen had gone before. The political wrangling over proper apportionment of the project's bounty took several more years. By 1930, the first crew was ready to go to work.

In 1931, the same year the state of Nevada legalized gambling, the work to divert the Colorado River around the dam site began. By the time the dam was completed in 1935, ninety-six workmen had died building it. And Las Vegas had enough power to become . . . Las Vegas.

Men worked in temperatures up to 138 degrees, many living with their families in open-sided lean-tos in a colony they called Ragtown. The work was murderously hard, yet men came from all over the country and lined up to apply for the jobs. This was the depth of the Depression, after all, and the pay—fifty cents per hour—was worth risking life and limb for. Anyone who complained might be labeled a Communist and surely fired.

The dam made it possible for Las Vegas, Nevada, a town so insignificant its mail sometimes got misrouted to Las Vegas, New Mexico, to become the gambling center of the nation.

When the dam was completed, President Roosevelt officiated at the dedication ceremony on September 20, 1935. Then his motorcade returned to Las Vegas and cruised down Fremont Street on its way to the presidential train. The people lined the street and cheered the man bringing them the New Deal. He grinned, chomped on his signature cigarette holder, and waved to his constituents. There's no record that FDR took note of Las Vegas's first major attraction—the massive new marquee of the Boulder Club that was lighted the same year—but if he had his eyes open, he couldn't have missed it. This was Tom Sr.'s first hit, the display that sparked the Las Vegas sign war—a race for supremacy that continues to this day.

The wedge-shaped marquee had a vertical "blade" sign on top that thrust 50 feet into the air, the highest sign the town had ever seen. The real attraction, however, was the sparkling representation of Boulder Dam that wrapped the marquee.

It was called a Scene in Action, says Tom Jr., trademarked by a Los Angeles company of the same name. It was the first animated sign in the Southwest.

Tom Sr. had designed the sign on a big sheet of butcher paper taped to the wall of his hotel room, and sold the idea to the owner of the Boulder Club the following morning.

The scene, bordered in neon, was 16 feet high, a vertical view of Boulder Dam with realistic-looking water pouring through its spillways. The sign had openings corresponding to the spillways, and behind each set of openings was a cylindrical screen. Inside that was another cylinder covered with lightbulbs. The heat from the lamps turned the outer screen, creating a rippling, refreshing effect suggesting water endlessly flowing.

The "water" flowed through the spillways of the sign until well into the 1950s. By then it was surrounded by YESCO's other classic Vegas spectaculars—massive walls of light for the Horseshoe, the Golden Nugget, and the Las Vegas Club, among others. The towering neon cowboy Vegas Vic, endlessly winking with a knowing leer and repeating his scratchy greeting, "Howdy, partner," welcomed high and low rollers alike. A desert hamlet of squat buildings dedicated to the legal pursuit of sin became a neon oasis in the desert, singing a siren song that is now heard around the world.

But the hand of the man who gave the Gulch its glitter never shook the hand of a one-armed bandit.

## GOING HOLLYWOOD

By the mid-1920s, virtually everyone who was old enough in the 60 million-plus U.S. population went to the movies two or three times a week. Hollywood, the motion picture capital of the world, was more than a place: it was a national state of mind.

The Hollywood Dream Factory fueled fantasies as no form of entertainment ever had. Moving pictures of torrid romance, heart-stopping adventure, sidesplitting comedy, and sweeping historical epic reached every corner of the country.

The humblest hamlet boasted a movie theater—sometimes nothing fancier than a converted store equipped with wooden benches, or even a sheet tacked to the side of a barn. At the opposite end of the spectrum, in every major city, were sumptuous entertainment palaces with exotic motifs—Oriental, Aztec, Mayan, Egyptian—the grandness of the place underscoring the richness and power of the fantasies that were played out inside. Main Street, U.S.A., sported spiffy new movie houses too—jewel boxes, many of them, with the same exotic themes as their central-city counterparts—with glittering marquees that towered two or even three stories into the air. To the local citizenry they were every bit the equal of anything Minneapolis or Chicago or New York had to offer.

The movies shown on these thousands of silver screens were the same everywhere. When Theda Bara or Rudolph Valentino turned a smoldering gaze directly at the camera, the millions of pairs of eyes that made contact with theirs in the darkness shared the thrill of seduction. The cult of movie celebrity was born. The consensus on what was sexy and smart and what the human heart yearned for was set, for better or worse, by the movies.

The onset of the Depression rocked Hollywood just as it did the rest of the country. But Hollywood rebounded and, as the 1930s deepened, thrived. Its role expanded to that of national morale booster. Reality may have been watered soup, newspaper lining the soles of worn-out shoes, and signs that said "Closed" and "Not Hiring." But escape to a world of romance, opulence, and hope was available for just a few coins.

The soda jerk and the counter girl could hold hands in the cool balcony of the posh, dark movie palace and pretend they were Fred and Ginger dancing on a moonlit veranda. Shirley Temple's unshakable optimism despite the meanness of her orphanage home was invariably rewarded with the news that she was, after all, the tycoon's lost daughter. And when Kind Old Grandfather's pension of a whopping $1,000 finally came through, his grandson and the other members of the ragtag Our Gang celebrated with mountains of ice cream and cake served by a comical English butler.

Hollywood, the state of mind, was pervasive, and its signs—growing both in physical dimension and in the thundering boldness of their promises—were ubiquitous from the start. Builders of spectacular signs and producers of spectacular movies enjoyed a symbiotic relationship that was forged the instant the first electric lightbulb twinkled on a theater marquee, and symbolically cemented when Warner Bros. titled the "first 100-percent talkie," in 1928, *The Lights of New York*.

Moving pictures, like illuminated signs, swept the country as soon as electricity was available to give them life. By 1910, Loew's New York Theater ballyhooed the endless stream of new releases from Biograph and Vitagraph with three-story electric displays. By the end of World War I, Times Square had three theaters built just for movies—

the Strand, the Capitol, and the Rivoli, which routinely devoted the entire wraparound facade of its corner building to animated electric displays. Older theaters like the Criterion offered movies along with vaudeville and live variety shows. The names of theaters and their new stars competed with shirt collars, pipe tobacco, and coffee in the night-lit gallery.

Hollywood, the place, labeled its larger-than-life self in 1924 with a 45-foot-high, 750-foot-wide sign spelling HOLLYWOODLAND across the arid foothills north of Los Angeles. It was visible for seven miles in those pre-smog days. Electrical Products Corporation built it for S. H. Woodruff, a real estate developer who vowed the barren landscape would one day become a garden of sensual and financial delights. His detractors scoffed, of course. Nothing could survive there but jackrabbits and snakes. The sign's heavy galvanized iron letters and related electrical equipment had to be dragged up the scruffy mountainside on a tractor-drawn sled, an operation compared to the assembly of Egypt's pyramids in Cecil B. DeMille's silent spectacle of the previous year, *The Ten Commandments*.

The sign has had a hard life. The H disappeared in a mudslide in 1925, the first of several such losses of letters over the years. The LAND was removed for good in the 1940s when the city took over the site. The great kitschy icon, as Los Angelean as carhops on roller skates and Bar-B-Que stands shaped like pigs, fell into disrepair after World War II, surviving the predations of vandals only to be reviled by the Formica lovers of the 1950s and 1960s who couldn't demolish the past quickly enough.

But the sign survived and, like a fallen movie star, staged a spectacular comeback. Today HOLLYWOOD is a historic site, protected by the Hollywood Sign Trust behind a chain-link fence that prevents a new generation of romantic adventurers from risking encounters with jackrabbits and snakes to dally in its shadow.

Though the sign was originally built to inspire a land boom, it served to give a sense of place to the new home of the motion picture industry. Moviemakers abandoned their roots back East for the little suburb with the bucolic name. Though the stars went West, however, their movies came back East to premiere in Times Square.

For almost half a century, every major movie opened officially in Times Square, where it enjoyed a First Run. The longer a film played on Broadway, the better it was received elsewhere; hence the importance of a spectacular Times Square promotion. In a 1945 article in a motion picture business journal, my father wrote, "If you were to ask Jake Starr, Broadway's Lamplighter, why the Broadway houses put up such tremendous spectacular signs, he probably would answer, 'Good pictures deserve them; the others need them.'"

Having one's "Name in Lights on Broadway" was a component of the American Dream, an undeniable certification of star status. That's why William Randolph Hearst, the newspaper baron who was the model for Orson Welles's *Citizen Kane,* spared no expense in erecting electrified monuments to the unmonumental works of his lady love, Marion Davies. The most grandiose of these, built in 1923, was the largest and brightest movie spectacular of its day. Filling the front of the Criterion, it was 35 feet high by 60 feet wide, and blazed forth the name of Mr. Hearst's inamorata 10 feet high, in 2,200 50-watt lamps—twice as big as the title, *When Knighthood Was in Flower. Signs of the Times* marveled, "Marion Davies has the distinction of having her name inscribed in the largest letters ever written in incandescents for a movie actress."

Hearst's electric valentine to Ms. Davies was the work of a company that carved out a small but memorable niche in the history of the spectacular. For a few years in the 1920s, the Norden Company, founded by Mortimer Norden, formerly a General Outdoor engineer, was to Times Square's movies what Strauss & Co. Signs was to the legitimate theater. Norden's specialty was the three-dimensional action diorama that strived to reproduce, in metal and light, a moment of the movie's irresistible emotional impact.

Elegiac loneliness was the theme of a five-story-tall display for Paramount's now-forgotten *The Covered Wagon,* which premiered in 1923 at the Criterion. The scene was a river, in the middle of which sat a covered wagon, abandoned by the early settlers who rode it that far and no farther in their struggle to settle the West. The water "ran" through the wheels of this forlorn symbol of pioneer bravery. Stereopticons with color wheels supplied the effect, which was considered quite realistic at the time.

In 1926 Norden created another huge and sentimental vision of the frontier, also at the Criterion. The film was Famous Players-Lasky's *The Vanishing American*, Zane Grey's elegy for the Native American. The display depicted an Indian brave slumped sadly on his horse in the center of a vast prairie, contemplating a sunset symbolic of the end of his way of life. Fading sunlight glimmering through slowly moving clouds cast a red glow on horse and rider—"an atmosphere of statuesque beauty," said *Signs of the Times*.

Meanwhile, on the Warner Theater farther up Broadway at 52nd Street, a Norden seascape portrayed the essence of the whaling epic *The Sea Beast* with John Barrymore. A sheet-iron whaling ship with canvas sails rocked in a restless sea in a dramatic face-off with a breaching whale spouting real water. Up above, indifferent stars twinkled through yet more drifting clouds.

Wind, water, and rolling seas became Norden trademarks, and brought him his trickiest job ever in 1929—the last-minute installation of a working Noah's Ark on the marquee of the Winter Garden. The eleventh-hour scramble wasn't Norden's fault, however. Warner Bros. had shrouded its new all-talking spectacle in secrecy, and wanted to astonish public and press with a dramatic unveiling of its ambitious project.

Norden and his crew were given just five hours before the film's opening to install the Great Flood, complete with a tossing tempest, torrential rain, and bobbing Ark. Norden kept the secret and, at the appointed hour, unleashed the rain. A gaping crowd gathered in time to see the downpour stop and rainbow-colored light beam through hissing steam, suggesting great flames licking the hull of the Ark.

Students of the Bible didn't remember any mention of a fire, or of Warner's interpretation of how Mr. and Mrs. Noah passed the time until the waters receded—"Two Glorious Lovers Who Loved for All Eternity"—but what the heck. It was a good show. So good, in fact, that police had to be stationed near fireboxes and hydrants to prevent unnecessary alarms.

Soon after that, Norden vanished from the Times Square stage: nobody seems to know what became of him. But he left a legacy. In

1937, the first Hollywood production number of the new Artkraft Strauss Sign Corporation was a Norden-like seagoing spectacular for the MGM maritime epic *Captains Courageous* with Spencer Tracy and Lionel Barrymore.

Jake and Ben turned the front of the Astor Theater above the marquee into a realistic piece of the chilly North Atlantic, on which sailed a 45-foot Gloucester schooner built by a Brooklyn shipyard. The three-dimensional wooden ship, rocking on storm-tossed seas, had working canvas sails and authentic rigging. A fan kept the sails billowed when the real Times Square breeze was insufficient. The ship plunged through the "waves" on four rollers, sending up alternating sprays of real water from bow and stern.

That same year, Jake and Ben also built lavish displays for two other MGM blockbusters at the Astor—a 50-foot smoke-breathing dragon for *The Good Earth* and mammoth silhouettes of Leslie Howard and Norma Shearer for *Romeo and Juliet*. Soon the factory was turning out movie spectaculars at the rate of nearly one a week. And they were not simple displays. The sign for *How Green Was My Valley*, 75 feet by 100 feet in size, was made entirely of plate glass on which was painted a detailed mural depicting a Welsh mining town, glowingly illuminated from within.

All this quick-change artistry required some innovation—or at least recycling. To get everyone's custom-made spectacular Name in Lights up on Broadway overnight, Jake standardized the fonts and letter sizes, eventually developing a "library" of 8-, 10-, 12-, and 16-foot-tall electric letters that he kept stacked on the roof of the plant.

As the cult of celebrity blossomed, props, scenes, and names in lights simply weren't enough. The faces of movie stars—faces sometimes more evocative and familiar than those of one's own family—filled entire building facades. To promote *One Hour With You* in 1932, a 20-foot, three-dimensional Maurice Chevalier protruded from the front of the Rivoli, his giant eyeballs rolling from side to side, directing equal measures of suave toward the kissers of his curvaceously three-dimensional co-stars, Jeanette MacDonald and Genevieve Tobin.

The grandest physiognomic display was a 30-foot head of Greta

Garbo on the front of the Astor Theater in 1934, with the five letters of her last name forming a 20-foot-tall halo. No need to mention her first name. And the title of the movie? Another trivial detail. Those who cared could read it on the marquee. Garbo in something new was all they wanted to know.

By the time World War II began, Artkraft Strauss dominated the surreal world of oversize and often outlandish Times Square movie advertising. That era ended in the 1960s when the movie industry itself went through wrenching changes, abandoning the studio system, and with it its Dream Factory mystique. Today's movies premiere everywhere at once, and multiscreen cineplexes have marquees that are for the most part unadorned menus—efficient and informative, but sadly dull compared to the days when the movie, the entertainment palace in which it played, and the advertising extravaganza outside were all part of the show.

## FISH STORY

*The greatest spectacular of a* great decade of spectaculars was the 1936 Wrigley Times Square aquarium display in which the chewing gum company's trademark Spearman floated in a sea of neon waves and bubble-blowing fish. A beautiful design with an insightful and innovative advertising psychology behind it, the towering neon extravaganza was the zenith of the art of the spectacular, which was still less than fifty years old.

*Signs of the Times* called it the largest spectacular in the world, and in 1936, it was—eight stories high and a full block long. "A skyscraper of color!" enthused the magazine. Since then, nothing larger has been built in Times Square, although the Bond and Pepsi waterfalls of the post-World War II era came close.

The Wrigley display shared something else with the waterfalls—its choice location. The display dominated the east side of Times Square, on the roof of the Bond Building between 44th and 45th streets. And, perhaps anticipating its successors, it used the soothing effects of flowing water as the key to its appeal.

Regular Square-goers, many of whom doubtless were devoted gum chewers, were startled by the giant animated color scene that flashed into action on March 28, 1936. Wrigley was hardly a newcomer to the Square's repertoire of outdoor shows, and the lighting of another Wrigley spectacular starring its trademark Spearman was rather like the appearance of a beloved movie star in yet another vehicle. But something was different—the Spearman had stepped out of his typecasting this time. It was as if Errol Flynn had put down his sword and become a pacifist.

Until 1936, all the Spearmen in Wrigley's several Times Square spectaculars had been feisty fellows. The lush 1917 light sculpture atop the Putnam Building had two squads of three Spearmen each, all armed with spears, going through a series of calisthenics the press dubbed the Daily Dozen. The military tempo was just right for the patriotic fervor that accompanied America's entry into World War I. Wrigley donated the sign's message center to the War Department, and wannabe doughboys who would soon sail for France to fight the Hun marched to the Times Square recruiting station in step with the tireless Spearmen. The sextet kept up the pace until the sign came down in 1923.

But Wrigley, a pioneer in spectacular outdoor advertising, was never absent from the cityscape for long. Another Times Square spectacular in 1932, replicated all over the country, also starred the Spearman, sans weapon, enthusiastically performing what any veteran of the Big War would recognize as PT (physical training). They could almost hear him count cadence, something like: "Chew-your-gum-all-day-and-night. Wrigley's-Spearmint-tastes-all-right. Sound off... one, two ... sound off ... three, four ..."

In 1935, Spearman, fully a civilian by then but still an elf with a mission, made another appearance, this time on the tower at the north end of the Square, beating out the message "The Perfect Gum" on a big bass drum. That sign was turned on just before midnight on New Year's Eve, reportedly to the delight of the partying multitude.

So imagine everyone's surprise when Spearman turned up a year later just floating placidly in a big bubble ... sitting quietly ... smiling contentedly ... presumably just chewing. He was surrounded by gently lapping waves and a school of neon fish serenely blowing neon bubbles that rose slowly to the surface. The tempo of the sign was un-hurried, calm, relaxing. Overnight, Wrigley had gone from a message of gum that invigorates to gum that relaxes.

The sign was designed by Dorothy Shepard, an interior designer known for her sea-life motifs. Installed on a new spiderweb steel structure, the fish ranged from 12 feet to 43 feet long. The innovative neon colors, specially developed for the sign, included ultramarine blue, sea green, and a new, iridescent chartreuse—according to *Signs of the Times*, "all the colors that a vivid sunset reflects on green waters, or that can be discovered at the bottom of a tropical sea." The ani-mation, rivaling the intricacy of the ring-tossing clown, kept the fish swimming with their huge tails and fins aflutter, and blowing slow-moving bubbles up to three feet in diameter.

The models for the fish, Wrigley said, resided in Ms. Shepard's own California aquarium. The authenticity of her designs surely were appreciated by serious ichthyophiles. Included in the hyperrealistic school were the giant Angelfish, orange and blue in this interpreta-tion; the finny and breathtakingly iridescent Veiltail Fighting Fish; the Pompadour, a striped marvel from the Amazon; the long, thin, and alarmingly endangered Bloodfin, which Wrigley was pleased to report "has recently reappeared in tropical waters in gratifying numbers"; the hardy and colorful *Rasbora heteromorpha;* and four minnows of the sort that were improbably "said to make South America the angler's paradise."

Thus Wrigley switched overnight from a message of gum-induced pep to a message of meditative calm. "Steadies the Nerves," promised the sign. It was the first spectacular since O. J. Gude's pioneering White Rock to employ a slow, hypnotic tempo. And it worked equally well. Just as people came to Times Square in 1915 to watch the lighted hands circle the face of the pink, blue, and yellow White Rock clock, pedestrians stood still and gazed at the serene, oversized un-dersea scene.

Though no one explicitly said so, the Wrigley fish display was a morale booster. It was gospel to express confidence in the American economy, and building a huge, expensive technological marvel in Times Square was a grand way to do just that. Wrigley intended the fish to keep swimming there for at least a decade, and if the World

War II dimout hadn't intervened, it probably would have. "Steadies the Nerves" was a reassuring message to a Depression-fatigued audience—some of whom often settled for no more than a stick of chewing gum for lunch.

Go placidly and steadily, said the sign. Like the becalmed Spearman, ride out the waves.

At the end of 1941, Times Square still pulsed every night with the energy of hundreds of electric signs, dozens of theater marquees, and the light of some of the best spectaculars in its history. Neon peanuts cascaded endlessly from a giant bag of Planters, urging "A Bag a Day for More Pep." And what would go better with salty nuts than an icy Coca-Cola, its big sign twinkling red and white beneath the cascade of nuts, suggesting a quick stop at the nearest lunch counter for "The Pause That Refreshes"? The neon fish swam placidly in the Wrigley sea, as they had since 1936. And two sunbursts competed nightly—Sunkist's bright yellow solar logo and Chevrolet's neon aurora borealis.

December 7, 1941, transformed everything. In a matter of months after Pearl Harbor, Times Square looked like someone had pulled the plug. And that is exactly what happened. Under orders from the War Department in April 1942, all illumination above street level was forbidden. The Square appeared to be closed for business. In the shadowy ambient light, the neon fish and the cheery little Spearman in the boat looked cold and lifeless. The peanuts were just glass rings wired to sheet metal, and the sunbursts, similarly eclipsed, became spidery and sinister.

In a heartbeat, the business of America became waging war, not selling chewing gum, beer, cars, and cigarettes. With its lights out, Times Square instantly lost its value to its traditional advertisers. At the same time, without anyone planning it, the Square just as quickly acquired a new role—in the marketing of the war effort. Deprived of the very spectacularity that made it a symbol of national energy and prosperity, a dimmed-out Times Square became a symbol of national sacrifice. Even New Year's Eve, since 1907 a celebration of ebullience and optimism centered on a globe of light, became a solemn occasion, the traditional glowing Ball replaced by amplified chimes both prayerful and melancholy.

A dark Times Square also became an internationally recognized symbol—like cultured London in flames and romantic Paris flying swastikas—of a beleaguered free world struggling against oppression. Newsreels reporting on the grim fighting abroad and the steadfast citizen support of the war effort back home routinely ended with a shot of a dimmed-out Times Square and a voice-over resolutely promising that, after the inevitable triumph, the lights would, indeed, come on again one day.

That day proved to be more than three and a half years away. By then, Times Square had adjusted to wartime conditions as well as it could and even managed to enlarge its role as a symbol of the fighting home front. Theater marquees learned to sparkle, more or less, without lights. And a giant replica of the Statue of Liberty, built by Artkraft Strauss, became a widely publicized morale booster and rallying point for war bond drives.

## THE DIMOUT TAKES ITS TOLL

*The Square had been darkened* once before, during World War I, to conserve electricity. Now, twenty-five years later, there was an additional reason. The light from the Square was so bright it could be seen glaring in the sky off Rockaway Beach. The light could silhouette freighters in the coastal shipping lane, offering tempting targets for German submarines prowling the Atlantic.

In 1942, as in 1917, people knew why the dimout was necessary. They could easily imagine Hitler's U-boats skulking offshore, the skipper scanning the dark coast of New York for the shapes of defenseless cargo ships. They knew Times Square wasn't closed, that the Broadway theaters, restaurants, clubs, and shops were open. And yet ... repelled by the darkness, the people again stayed away in droves, stayed in their homes, blinds drawn, huddling beside the radio.

Times Square wasn't the country's only no-lights zone, of course. Every other city turned down its public lighting too, for energy conservation or national defense, or both. On the West Coast, where the possibility of Japanese air attack was very real, especially in the early months of the war, the blackouts had a special sense of urgency.

But Times Square was the world's window on the American personality, its barometer of the American spirit. Everybody knew what the "Broadway rhythm" felt like, the joyously raffish and uniquely American beat of life in the fast lane of bright lights and exuberant commerce. To dim those lights, of all the lights in the country, was symbolically to hush the soul of a nation.

The dimout also wreaked havoc with Times Square business. The early effect was devastating. Stores closed, and some never reopened. Plays and movies struggled for audiences. Belt-tightening was the order of the day.

The Broadway Association, the Times Square business community's vocal advocate, was stuck between the proverbial rock and hard place. To oppose the dimout was unpatriotic. But allowing Times Square to turn into a ghost town didn't seem like a worthy contribution to the war effort either. So the Broadway Association argued for increased street-level lighting, pointing out that newsreels of London showed theaters lit up except during air-raid warnings.

Unmoved, the city countered by asking for even more stringent measures—the closing of all stores at 8 P.M. "in order that the dimout might be more effective, to conserve electricity, or to permit employees to serve as air-raid wardens or in other civil defense activities." The Broadway Association replied angrily it would support the curfew only if ordered to do so by the Army. The debate continued, and so did the dimout.

As the months passed and the war dragged on, Times Square became a magnet for GIs. The Stage Door Canteen and USO Center attracted a lively young crowd that was a natural audience for theater and movies, and business picked up. But the dimout, like food and gasoline rationing, was a restriction that Americans, long accustomed to an endless supply of everything their mighty industrial nation could produce, never really got used to. Newspapers were endlessly fascinated by it, and painted word pictures of citizens in darkened neighborhoods threading their way home by hurrying from one meager public light source to another. For light-hungry Americans, the dimout couldn't end soon enough.

## SIGNS OF WAR

*Most of my family spent* the war at home, in Times Square. My father, Mel, to his chagrin, was classified 4-F—despite his repeated attempts to volunteer. Jake, of course, was too old to go. Cousin Gene, who came to work for Artkraft Strauss in 1940, joined immediately after Pearl Harbor, along with many other employees, and didn't return until well after V-J Day. We were soon shorthanded. With both military service and civilian jobs opening up to women, we couldn't keep a switchboard operator, so my mother filled in. (She, along with Jake's leather-tongued sidekick, Miss Rose, and Ben Strauss' statuesque and witty assistant, Miss Blanche, formed Artkraft's entire female cohort. It would be another forty years before the number of women at Artkraft Strauss ever exceeded three.)

World War II united this country like nothing has since. Everyone did his or her part to ensure victory. Everyone made sacrifices, and the sign industry was no exception. Outdoor companies donated billboard space. Stores donated their windows. Banks allowed their vitrines and identity signs to be covered with inspiring war posters.

Like other manufacturers of consumer goods, sign companies retooled and went into war work too. Federal Sign manufactured signaling equipment. YESCO and many others did specialty sheet-metal fabrication. Artkraft Strauss built metal containers for use on aircraft, as well as custom airplane wings—required in numbers too small to justify tooling up an aircraft manufacturing facility. Sometimes the government paid in money, sometimes in equipment. More than fifty years after the war, we were still using a German-made Pels punch press of 1925 vintage that Jake accepted as payment for one of his war jobs.

Meanwhile, sign makers faced new challenges as sources of materials dried up. And even if metal and glass and wire and paint had been available, and even if electricity weren't being rationed, there was still no point in building electric signs—they couldn't be used anyway, in the blackouts and dimouts that darkened cities and towns around the country.

As the war progressed, even the simplest sign had to be built from recycled, scrap, or previously unthought-of materials. Everbrite of Milwaukee, for example, made innovative use of Masonite, wood, and glass to create electric-looking commercial and point-of-purchase displays. Many sign people toted car batteries around, recharging them on their service vehicles to get maximum mileage from scarce gasoline—enabling whatever lights were permitted to light up. Resourcefulness and experimentation were the orders of the day.

Jake is credited with inventing a technique that was widely used until the dimout ended, both in Times Square and in other blacked-out cities: the use of mosaics of tiny mirrors to reflect ambient light. The motion picture industry was by then a mainstay of the sign industry, and the dimout immediately cut movie attendance in half. This was equally alarming to theater operators and sign makers—and to the War Department too, because movies were an essential propaganda tool.

Jake's idea was to replace lights with patterns of one-inch-square mirrors in varying hues of gold, blue, green, red, and yellow on marquees and on the massive vertical displays that often rose five or six stories above the marquees themselves. The mirrors, like diamond-cut gems, caught and reflected whatever light was on the street—auto headlights, streetlights, the minimal light that was still permitted in store windows.

The first movie display to use the technique was the one for *The Pride of the Yankees*, with Gary Cooper as Lou Gehrig. The sign contained no steel, no wire, no lamps, not even one metal screw. Tiny blue and gold mirrors mounted on canvas spelled its message in letters 10, 12, and 20 feet high. The display sparkled clearly if not brilliantly in the perpetual dusk.

The little mirror squares cost about one cent apiece. "It was like making a whole sign face out of pennies," my father remembered. At $1.44 a square foot, it wasn't really cheap. But it worked. Soon the whole Square was atwinkle.

Jake used the same idea on a larger scale in the beautiful red, white, and blue Pepsi-Cola display Artkraft Strauss built at the bottom of the north tower, above the entrance to the USO Center, in the summer of 1942. The face of the sign was rippled glass that reflected and magnified light too, like the surface of a lake. It shimmered in the ambient light until the end of the war, when the lamps inside could be turned on. Even then, it required less electricity for its size than other spectaculars, an example of energy-efficient technology forced by the war. It was so classically refined, many who saw it after the war thought it was made of stained glass.

## LADY LIBERTY

*Like other sign companies,* Artkraft Strauss was called on regularly to build displays aimed at boosting morale. These included a 30-foot birthday cake for FDR and a 25-foot glass Red Cross for a blood drive.

But the best of all—and certainly the most valuable to the war effort—was the giant replica of the Statue of Liberty that presided over the Square in the last years of the war, sponsored by the New York Area Motion Picture War Activities Committee.

The 60-foot statue stood atop a two-story pedestal built in the shape of a giant cash register, on the traffic island on 43rd Street between Seventh Avenue and Broadway, in the middle of the Square. A stage occupied the second story, with a traveling message center above it and a banner below that said, "Fifth [or Sixth, or Seventh] War Bond Drive."

A free show was given on the stage at noon every day, attracting a big lunchtime crowd. Some days there was jitterbugging in the streets to the music of Artie Shaw or the Dorseys. On other days Alfred Drake and company filled the Square with a rousing "O-O-O-O-Ok-lahoma, where the wind comes sweepin' down the plain..." Movie producers furnished celebrities, and gave free movie passes to those who bought war bonds. Impresario Mike Todd supplied visitations by the bevies of chorines who populated his stage spectacles. Even the cast of the long-running *Life With Father* showed up to do a scene now and then. Best of all, bond buyers saw their names displayed on the traveling message center—"Your Name in Lights on Broadway!"—and heard their individual patriotism praised from the podium by the likes of such visiting show biz royalty as Bob Hope, Bing Crosby, and Betty Grable.

Like so many wartime jobs, the statue had to be done in a hurry. We built it in eleven days. The armature for the 9,000-pound statue was fashioned from government-provided steel in 38 horizontal sections. Sculptors Rochette & Parzini mixed a weather-resistant plaster and concrete compound for the sculpture itself, using crushed lava rock instead of sand to keep the weight down. (Three years later, the same technique was used to built the 70-foot nude statues that flanked the Bond waterfall.) A few months before the end of the war, Artkraft Strauss and the two sculptors added to the traffic island a replica of the statue of the flag-raising on Iwo Jima, a symbol of the impending victory in the Pacific.

The blend of potent, spectacularly oversized patriotic symbols was right at home in Times Square. The display became the center of all wartime activities in the Square after that. Crowds came daily and dug down deep. The War Activities Committee claimed that $60,000 worth of war bonds were sold at each show.

More important, however, was the way the statue reenergized the war-weary Square. During World War II, more than ever before, Times Square was America's town square. All the war news that was fit to print spun forth daily on the New York Times news zipper, and newsreel cameras were always there, carrying the communal images across the country and around the world. Before TV, newsreels were the animated information medium that the whole nation shared, and a victory headline on the zipper followed by the jubilant reaction of the watching citizenry became a stock shot, an upbeat counterbalance to the standard dark-Square-at-night newsreel closing.

Photographers loved the spectacle of the incongruously huge Lady Liberty, as tall as a six-story building, towering over a reveling, feisty, all-American populace. At dawn the cameramen climbed to the tops of buildings and recorded her in silent vigil, her long shadow falling across empty streets. At dusk they caught her as the low lights at her base and in her torch came on, one brave candle in an ocean of darkness.

Newspaper feature writers loved her too, because she never failed to provide good copy. First there were all the stories about people who actually believed the real Lady Liberty had somehow conveyed herself to Times Square. Then there were the daily crowds around her, the great man-on-the-street stuff, the sights and sounds, the million New York war stories played out under her silent gaze.

Public displays of emotion have always been permissible, and even encouraged, in Times Square. A place to laugh and cheer—to share the exultation of New Year's Eve, the jubilation (or disappointment) of election night, the national sense of relief that comes with the end of a war—Times Square is also a place to weep. New Yorkers went there to grieve on April 12, 1945, when FDR died, just a few months into his fourth term. He was a father figure to a generation that lived through the Depression and the war together. The most beloved President in history, his photograph was on the wall of millions of American homes and businesses. Thousands, sharing what amounted to a family loss, gathered around Lady Liberty to receive the sad news from the *New York Times* zipper, the newsreel cameras recording their sorrow, a mirror of a nation in mourning.

When the end of the war finally did come in 1945—first V-E Day, May 7, then V-J Day, August 15—Lady Liberty stood vigil as the ecstatic masses swirled around her, in every shot, a symbol of enduring struggle now become the symbol of victory.

"For every generation, there's a place where it all happens," says one New Englander, a high school student at the time, who, like so many others, on hearing the news of V-J Day, hopped a train and headed for the Square. "For the generation of the 40s, that place was Times Square. That's the place where the war ended. Not on the USS *Missouri*, where the formal surrender took place, but where Alfred Eisenstaedt caught the picture of the sailor kissing the girl. That was the defining moment. It caught everybody's attention. It galvanized the nation." Even Lady Liberty seemed to be smiling.

When the lights came on again, however, the newsreel cameras were pointed the other way. It was beautifully staged: a sweeping vista of the north end of the Square, the lights all surging on almost simultaneously, as if someone threw a single giant switch. (In reality, weeks of maintenance on long-unused signs, several rehearsals, and the coordinated services of some four dozen electricians were required.) Lady Liberty had done her job and was about to be forgotten. The Iwo Jima statue went to the lawn of the Veterans Hospital in St. Albans, Queens. Lady Liberty just disappeared, a vestige of a war everyone wanted to put behind them as quickly as possible.

## THE MOST FAMOUS SIGN OF ALL TIME

*No one was more dismayed* by America's imminent entry into World War II than Douglas Leigh, who knew that war meant a blackout, and that meant watching his business disappear with the flick of a switch. Never shy with the press, Leigh spoke out against a dimout, though he must have known it wouldn't do any good. It didn't, and when the unavoidable arrived, he joined his fellow sign men all over the country and turned off his displays.

By that time, however, Leigh's fallback position already was in place. Never at a loss for ideas, he had imagined a Times Square spectacular that would have its greatest impact in daylight, and sold it to a national advertiser. It was already up and running, on the Claridge Hotel between 43rd and 44th streets, by the time the lights went out.

The world-famous "smoking" Camel cigarette sign was a sensation from day one. Conceived by Leigh, designed and engineered by Fred Kerwer in collaboration with Jake, and built and installed by Artkraft Strauss in June of 1941, the display was plain, simple, and absolutely brilliant.

The 30-by-100-foot red painted plywood billboard pictured a man's face just left of center, flanked by his raised left hand holding a cigarette. His mouth formed a perfectly round, satisfied O. The heroic smoker had just taken a big drag on his Camel, and, savoring the deep fulfillment and rich taste, he exhaled. Out of the mouth came a smoke ring that spread to ten feet in diameter and, on a calm day, drifted placidly across the Square. This happened every four seconds, eighteen hours a day, from 7 A.M. to 1 A.M.

The "smoke" was really steam, collected from the building's heating system into a reservoir behind the sign. A piston-driven diaphragm forced the steam through a small hole, producing a series of rings emitted from the smoker's "mouth."

To make his smoker as lifelike as possible, Leigh engaged a modeling agency to furnish him with a photograph of an all-American smoker in action. The agency hired a handsome, lanky Jimmy Stewart type named Lyman Clardy—ironically, a nonsmoker. For a fee of five dollars, Clardy spent a morning before a camera in a downtown studio posing with freshly lighted Camels in his hand and trying to blow smoke rings.

"I'd never heard of any such thing before, and it sounded nuts to me," he recalls. "And I didn't really like cigarettes. But five bucks was five bucks.

"I got the hang of it finally, after a couple of packs, and fortunately I didn't have to inhale. But the smoking wasn't the most important part. What they were after was the look on the face and the shape of the mouth. Especially the shape of the mouth."

Clardy came through with just the right expression of contentment, the perfect tilt of head, the right touch of theatricality in his debonair two-finger hold on the Camel, and a circular orifice that could launch a zillion smoke rings.

His run as the Times Square Camel smoker was short, however. When the war began, he was replaced by a soldier, who was later replaced by a sailor, who was replaced by an airman, who was replaced by a marine. By then, Clardy was in uniform himself, serving as a naval officer in the South Pacific.

After the war, he resumed his modeling career, appearing in national magazine advertisements for numerous products, notably Stetson Hats. He was still at it half a century later, summoned whenever a distinguished octogenarian in an ascot was needed.

Leigh put on a uniform too, joining the ranks of American advertising men in military intelligence. But not before he went national with his smoking Camel sign. First he chose a dozen cities that were heavy war production centers—more workers, he reasoned, meant more smokers. Then he went to his delighted customer, R. J. Reynolds, with a sales presentation built around a map of the United States. Holes were punched at the targeted cities and tiny puffs of smoke were blown through. I'm guessing RJR didn't need much convincing, however. A nation of cigarette smokers at war had already taken Leigh's sign to heart.

By Labor Day 1942, new smoking Camel signs were blowing rings in Baltimore, Boston, Buffalo, Chicago, Cleveland, Detroit, Los Angeles, Milwaukee, New Orleans, Philadelphia, Pittsburgh, and San Francisco. Each became a landmark overnight.

Pete Waldmeir, a veteran columnist for the *Detroit News,* remembers the Motor City's version. As a teenager during the war, he often rode the trolley down Woodward Avenue, Detroit's main drag, to Grand Circus Park, then the city's equivalent of Times Square. "The trolley would come to the corner, and even before it made the turn, you could see the smoke rings shooting out there over the park," Waldmeir remembers. "Every time I go there now, I think of it. I don't remember when it came down. In my memory, it's still there."

The smoking Camel sign has, indeed, lived on in memory—so much so that a huge number of people who can't possibly have seen it insist that they remember it—a perfect example of image superseding reality. RJR has received many times its money's worth, as the sign continues to "play" in people's minds long after the display is gone.

After the war, a neon border and channel letters were added, but the display's chief attraction, the contented smoker, remained the same. Sometimes he wore hats, sometimes glasses. For a while he was Phil Silvers as TV's lovable con man, Sergeant Bilko. But whoever he was, he didn't puff his last until January 3, 1966. The display lasted twenty-four years—one of only a handful of signs in Times Square history to approach the quarter-century mark.

Today, a "smoking" sign would rub people the wrong way. But during World War II, when American cigarettes were so popular that GIs used them as currency overseas, it was a sign of its time—perhaps the greatest of them all.

## HOME AGAIN

GIs came home with dreams they never thought possible, to a country where all dreams could come true. A wealthy, powerful nation had bestowed upon them the best package of veterans' benefits ever devised, and they made full use of every one. No strangers to standing in line, they queued up at university registrars' windows and union halls, confident that they would fill the ranks of a new army of professionals and skilled workers manning the mightiest business juggernaut the world had ever seen.

They married and had children in record numbers. They bought homes in new suburbs and filled them with the latest appliances. They were a willing and eager constituency for a Detroit that hadn't built a car in three years.

At a time when pent-up consumer demand had reached explosive proportions, American industry dominated the world. And the signs that filled up the war-darkened Times Square in the next fifteen years celebrated the vision of that dominance.

Douglas Leigh sometimes took that vision into fantastic realms. As early as November 1945, three months after V-J Day, he was drumming up support for his new fantasy of Times Square that would turn entire buildings into giant American-made products. By March 1946, he was able to go to the newspapers with a startling rendering, by architect Hugh Ferris, that depicted Times Square as, quite literally, a commercial theme park.

Left to his own devices, Leigh announced, he would rid Times Square of the bright reds, greens, and blues that hitherto defined its neon personality and replace them with the softer glow of pastels shining through plastic. He imagined entire buildings in the shapes of coffee cans, soap boxes, and soft-drink bottles, all representing the enterprises of the principal tenants. One such building would look like a perfume bottle, its stopper the penthouse, a spray mechanism on top spritzing the crowd below with scent. Another would resemble a jumbo glass that would fill with real orange juice dripped from a tethered helium-filled "orange." Indeed, so pleased was Leigh with his drinking-glass motif that he proposed several more, all filling regularly with bubbly beverages. And, reprising one of his greatest prewar hits, he found room for another giant steaming coffee cup.

As things turned out, Times Square was spared all this dripping, bubbling, and rosy plastic glow. Most of what Leigh proposed never got built. However, if the failure to plasticize Times Square so long ago disappoints you, don't blame him. He tried. And we can applaud the uniquely American boldness of his vision, if not his taste.

Times Square in those days was a symphony in light, color, and jazz—and people. Well-dressed crowds swirled through the streets at all hours. It was at night, though, that the neighborhood really came alive. "The excitement, the sense of revelry, the sex in the air, were palpable," remembers one New Yorker. "It was a mecca, especially for singles and college students." Great entertainment was inexpensive. Fifty-second Street was lined with jazz clubs. For seventy-five cents one could sit at the bar at Birdland all night and nurse a beer, and listen to Ella Fitzgerald. Or Louis Armstrong, or Billy Eckstine, or Lionel Hampton—all living legends. The Square was one of the few American places at the time that was racially integrated—on both sides of the orchestra. This may have been partly thanks to the pervasiveness of the music, but more, perhaps, to the sense of plenty.

Many advertising dreamers honed in military intelligence brought their postwar visions to Times Square. Showmanship met Salesman-

**Signs of the times in the mid-1930s:**
Times Square looking north.
*Postcard, Collection of Artkraft Strauss*


**"Steadies the Nerves":**
Wrigley's 1936 Times Square neon classic used a soothing aquatic motif.
Ride out the Depression calmly, it said, with refreshing Wrigley's gum.
*Postcard, Collection of Artkraft Strauss*

**Times Square** on a sunny morning in 1956.
*Postcard, Collection of Artkraft Strauss*

**The 1964 Coca-Cola display** on the north tower would be
the only new spectacular built in Times Square until the 1980s.
*Collection of Artkraft Strauss*

**Spectacular sex:**
Pornography hit the street in the
1970s. The neon-bedecked Pussycat
enticed passersby with the promise
of visual thrills.
*Collection of Artkraft Strauss*

**Tradition:**
The Artkraft Strauss crew lowers
the New Year's Eve Ball the old,
punctual way—by hand.
*Collection of Artkraft Strauss*

**Joe Camel,** where Wrigley's fish once swam. This spectacular smoker departed in 1994. *Collection of Artkraft Strauss*

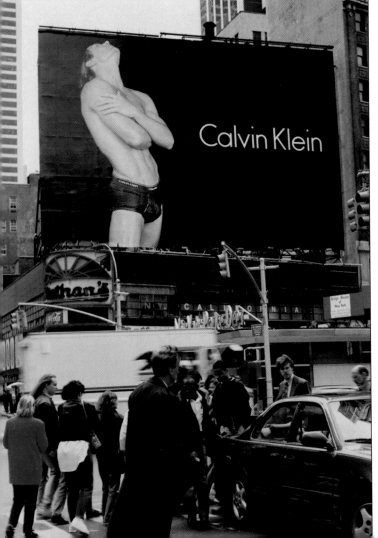

**Pushing the envelope:** Calvin Klein's controversial underwear ads often made news in the 1990s. *Collection of Artkraft Strauss*

**Tower of signs:** By 1990, when Artkraft Strauss built these mammoth spectaculars on One Times Square, the rebirth of the Crossroads of the World was well under way.

*Photo by Peter B. Kaplan, all rights reserved*

**The building is the sign:**
Real-time financial information, a living sign.
*Photo by Scott Humbert*

**The half-size scale model** of British Airways' Concorde, ready to take off . . .
*Photo by Scott Humbert*

. . . up, up, and away . . .
*Photo by Scott Humbert*

. . . landing gracefully on its perch at the south end of Times Square.
*Photo by Scott Humbert*

**The Coca-Cola spectacular**
anchoring the north end of Times Square
since 1992 is a technological marvel that
even has its own phone number . . .
*Collection of Artkraft Strauss*

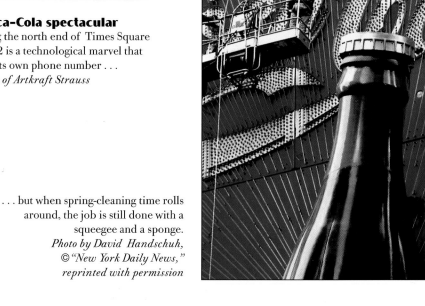

. . . but when spring-cleaning time rolls
around, the job is still done with a
squeegee and a sponge.
*Photo by David Handschuh,*
*© "New York Daily News,"*
*reprinted with permission*

**Times Square today:** The more it changes, the more it remains the same.
*Photo by Scott Humbert*

ship in a time of creative and entrepreneurial fervor not known since the early days of electric lighting. There was no room for small ideas, small ambitions, or small budgets. The decade and a half following World War II was a period of unparalleled achievement in the creation of spectaculars. The displays were triumphs of both imagination and technology that celebrated country as well as company.

A new sense of corporate citizenship emerged too. Every sign had a traveling message center to greet visitors, caution against drunk driving, encourage workplace safety, endorse charitable giving, salute veterans and high school scholars and other Winners—and, in passing, to sell theater tickets, perfume, and meals.

Advertising was becoming a sophisticated art form. The industry—like the new TV industry with which it cross-fertilized—attracted some of the brightest, wittiest writers and idea men of the day. Advertising saw itself as a fundamental cog in the American postwar industrial machine—building markets, creating employment, bringing down prices by stimulating mass production, supporting quality standards, informing people about products and educating them about the great and growing marketplace of which they were a part. Communicating such profound ideas demanded whimsy and the light touch—as well as sheer creativity.

And my father, Mel Starr, soon to become the next Lamplighter of Broadway, was in the middle of all this imaginative hustle-bustle. He and the environment of postwar Times Square were a perfect fit. In a sense, they created each other.

The Sign Man, the Advertising Man, and the Customer huddled in fashionable Manhattan clubs and did deals to the tinkling accompaniment of a cocktail piano, or the cool/hot sounds of brassy jazz. Signs were designed on place mats and contracts written on napkins. Big money was on the table, and there was plenty more where it came from.

Every sign was a message, and a message about the message: We are a great American company, each proclaimed. What you see before you—this giant steaming Silex iron, this huge neon-striped box of multicolored tissues, this glowing five-story stein of sudsy beer—is an all-American symbol of success.

# The Neon Lady with the Great Gams

*Fashion advertising didn't move* into Times Square on a grand scale until the late 1980s, when vinyl capable of being computer-printed with photographic images and installed in a matter of hours made billboards almost as easy to change as costumes. But earlier fashion spectaculars had considerable charm. Among the most captivating was Miss Youth Form.

She was, as the guys would have said then, a *big* dame—a perfect size 14 (the equivalent of today's size 10) and all of 60 feet tall—who sashayed in neon across a 100-foot-wide sign atop the Brill Building at Broadway and 49th Street for five years beginning in 1947. Wearing tasteful black pumps, a slip, a coquettish half-smile, and a perfect 1940s neck-bun hairdo with pompadour, her daytime incarnation—in paint on plywood—was an alluring presence too.

Youth Form was, the sign told us, "The Aristocrat of Slips." When the flashing message changed to "Cannot 'Ride-Up,'" Miss Youth Form began her stately stroll. In a series of neon overlays, she ambled elegantly on the perfect legs of an Eleanor Powell. It was a movie star walk, stylishly brisk yet unhurried. She did the pivot-and-sit—which, believe it or not, all girls practiced in those days, balancing dictionaries on their heads—and, sure enough, her slip never rode up.

Chances are the actual model was a secretary or receptionist at the Youth Form company in the Garment District just south of the Square. Then as now, Garment District models often doubled as clerical workers until the buyers walked in, when they dropped their steno pads and ran into dressing rooms to change. Why not pose for a spectacular too? Raven-haired, pink-cheeked, and wholesome, she had the perky sex appeal of the pinups that kept many of these men company during the war. Refined but inviting, she was the kind of girl every man in uniform yearned to come home to.

Artkraft Strauss built 300 miniature versions of the sign to be used as point-of-purchase displays in stores. A Tinkerbell-sized Miss Youth Form marched across many lingerie counters after that. I wonder how many slips she sold.

The company she represented eventually went out of business. Even a veteran official of the Amalgamated Clothing & Textile Workers Union doesn't remember it. In American industrial history, fifty years might as well be fifty thousand.

## Niagara Comes to Times Square

*Leigh didn't have to wait* long to make one of his grand ideas a reality. He envisioned a real waterfall on the roof of a Times Square building and sold the idea to Bond Clothing, the superstore of the day. Jake and Kerwer figured out how to make it work without flooding the Bond showroom underneath. Artkraft Strauss built it, and in June of 1948, after nearly four years of planning and construction, the water began to pour.

Bond was located on the east side of Times Square between 44th and 45th streets, a squat, block-long building reminiscent of the early Las Vegas casinos. Its roof was perfect for towering displays, and indeed had contained some of the great ones, most notably the endearing Wrigley's chewing gum spectacular of 1936.

The store—called "the cathedral of clothing" by its owners when they opened there in 1940—was a Times Square fixture, the proud sartorial standard-bearer for men and women on a budget who wanted to step out in style. Thus attired, those men and women might meet in Times Square and fall in love with one another. The code of the day permitted only one proper recourse to those so afflicted—a wedding and a train ride to Niagara Falls, the sexiest spot in North America.

Just to make sure everyone made the connection between Niagara and sex—the inevitable reward for those who shopped at Bond—Leigh flanked his bubbling cataract with 70-foot nude statues: a man on the right above a sign proclaiming "Clothes for the Man," a woman on the left above "Apparel for the Woman." In the center, suspended above the waterfall, was a round Bond logo containing a forward-looking digital clock and the compelling information that "Every Hour 3,490 People Buy at Bond."

Beneath the waterfall and wrapping the corners was a 278-foot-long traveling message center with moving letters six feet high—de rigueur for a Times Square spectacular in the modern 1950s—made by Trans-Lux, then the General Motors of the message center industry. Leigh sold advertising time on the message center, slipping ads into a "news" service called "Baedeker of Broadway," an hour of tips on where to go and what to see around the Big Apple, repeated 14 times a day at a speed of 40 words per minute.

Placing a working waterfall on a roof was an idea that harked back to the late-nineteenth-century theater's love of spectacle and to the early-twentieth-century lightbulb images of fountains and cascades that characterized the first spectaculars. Modern technology and sophisticated engineering made possible the reality. We built the block-long 225-by-85-foot-high display in huge pieces that were then lifted onto the site. At the base of the 132-foot-wide falls was a trough holding 10,000 gallons of water (and, in winter, glycerine-based antifreeze). The twenty-three 10-horsepower recirculating pumps that churned the water over the falls at 800 gallons per minute—48,000 gallons per hour—were concealed within the trough. A complex cam-driven flasher system made 23,000 incandescent lamps and nearly two miles of neon whirl, rotate, blink, and flutter.

The block letters spelling BOND, suspended in midair, appeared to float in front of the falls. Lamps on their sides enabled them to be lit in silhouette, and lamps on their backs added luminescence to the flowing water.

The 27-foot-tall face of the falls, made of expanded metal, was elaborately rippled—to create realistic-looking turbulence and, more important, to create a series of hidden pockets that the onrushing water turned into mini-vacuums holding the liquid in place even in high winds. Many experiments, conducted on the roof of Artkraft Strauss beside the windswept Hudson River, made this possible. The waterfall's authentic-looking rocky facade was painted by Bob Everhart, one of the finest billboard artists of the day.

The seven-story-tall faux Deco nude figures, weighing six and a half tons each, were built by sculptors Rochette & Parzini, over steel skeletons that we provided to them, in one of the Long Island City marble works that even today offer Old World–quality craftsmanship. The figures were made in six sections—feet to knees, knees to hips, hips to waist, etc.—and lifted and stacked into place. The artisans used the same lava-concrete and plaster compound they'd used in the Statue of Liberty and the Iwo Jima statue they'd built for us during

World War II. The two figures, described at the time as perfectly proportioned, were the Brobdingnagian equivalent of a 40 long (the man) and a size 14 long (the woman). No Schwarzeneggers or anorexic supermodels these. Perfectly proportioned meant something quite different then.

The Artkraft Strauss workforce of 250 built and installed every inch of the display in a matter of months. Jake was very proud of that job. New York had a record snowfall during the winter of 1947, but his troops, like Patton's plowing across Europe in the bitter winter three years earlier, managed to get the nudes up there with the water flowing on time and within budget. A herculean achievement, for a Hercules-size display.

Times Square lore has it that the nude statues drew the ire of some proper and well-connected ladies staying at the Astor Hotel across the street, and that the see-through gold neon robes the statues wore were added to appease them. In reality, the statues were intended to be robed in neon from the beginning; proper and well-connected ladies could hardly be expected to spot the neon housings built into the statues and look away demurely until the construction was completed. In any case, the neon togas had to be formed by tube benders on-site, as the elaborate compound curves that were required baffled the draftsmen, who in the days before computers were restricted to two dimensions. Every tube bender we had who wasn't afraid of heights was hoisted in a bosun's chair and employed as a made-to-measure tailor.

The wonderfully kitschy Bond waterfall plashed away soothingly, wafting a hint of cool mist over the street below on windy days (Leigh got to spritz people after all) until 1955. That year we transformed it into the Pepsi-Cola waterfall, removing the statues and replacing them with a pair of five-story-tall porcelain enamel Pepsi-Cola bottles, and replacing the clock with a 50-foot-diameter Pepsi-Cola bottle cap paved with 15,000 twinkling red, white, and blue lightbulbs forming the Pepsi logo. By then, the million-watt display was being heralded everywhere as the "Biggest 3-D Spectacular Ever." Borrowing an idea from the Lagoon of Nations, a vestige of the 1939 World's Fair at Flushing Meadow, Leigh had Artkraft Strauss install an illumination system that shone multicolored beams of light up through the cascading water, playing out a light show that ended in a great flashing white climax. Then it really did look like Niagara Falls at night.

The waterfall came down for good in 1960 to make way for less expensive, more conventional billboards. Signs of change were already appearing down below. Stepping out in Times Square was soon to become a very different experience.

## Postwar Prosperity

*As the 1940s closed, Times Square* was the apotheosis of America's vision of itself. That it produced in the visitor the feeling that all was right with the world was not accidental. Though no formal Right with the World commission ever convened, there was a consensus among the ad hoc fraternity of like-minded men of business who staked claims to slices of the American pie, a shared understanding of What People Want and How Things Worked.

That understanding is traceable to the earliest days of outdoor advertising in America. But it came to its full realization in the decade of the 1950s. The proof of the vision of American dominance in all fields was everywhere then, and celebrated nightly in Times Square. Bigger, bolder, and more modern were the watchwords of the day—bigger Hollywood epics filling wider screen canvases, bolder fins on automobiles with awesome horsepower churning under their hoods, more modern work-saving electric appliances and plastic materials to replace the tired domestic implements of the prewar world.

Times Square of 1950 was a bridge between the past and the future. The old signs were back in business, blowing smoke rings, regaling the public with animated cartoon shows, twinkling like frosty beverage bottles, the very sight of which are unavoidably thirst-inducing. The new technical marvel of the Bond waterfall sold a celebration of style and sex appeal that was grandly operatic even by Times Square standards.

And the rest of the Square looked like it might have been designed by the Happy Hour committee—Rupperts Beer from a tap, filling a mug with golden brew topped with a white electric head; a chilled long-neck bottle of Budweiser resting in pure mountain greenery, circled by a real model train; Kinsey, Schenley's, and Four Roses, names vying to be spoken across the bar to the man in the white shirt and bow tie; Johnnie Walker, his long mechanical legs completing twenty strides per minute, a small smile on his face, ambulating eternally toward Miss Youth Form but, alas, never getting there.

The party was under way. And the best was yet to come—especially for my family. In the 1950s and '60s, Artkraft Strauss would come to dominate the outdoor advertising and sign manufacturing business in Times Square—and all of New York City.

# 6. *The Fabulous Fifties*

## ELECTION NIGHT

lthough I had worked the Magic Motograph before, I had never worked on it on election night.

The air seemed sparkly with excitement as Mel and I

tooled down Broadway in our new Buick Skylark convertible, black as patent-leather Mary Janes, with a white canvas top and red leather seats. It was not only my own elation—I'm going to work! And I'm going to get paid! Mel promised me a dollar an hour and a new type-writer ribbon!—but the entire city seemed filled with a sense of fes-tivity and anticipation.

It was November 6, 1956. Adlai Stevenson, the former governor of Illinois, was running for the second time against the incumbent, wildly popular war hero General Dwight D. ("Ike") Eisenhower. I was in the fifth grade, and I was going to get to stay up very late, perhaps even until midnight, when the final results came in. I felt like an im-portant person because I was about to do an important job: provid-ing up-to-the-minute election results over the traveling message signs to the watching crowd in Times Square.

Stevenson was my mother's candidate. She was passionate about him. As the election drew near, many young Upper West Side matrons like herself, including many of my friends' mothers, sported campaign buttons bearing the slogan "I'd lay for Adlai." My mother skipped that one, but she did wear a button with the Stevenson logo—a shoe with a hole in the sole, after a famous news photograph of him with his feet up on his desk. But even the most ardent champions of the un-derdog acknowledged the uphill battle in the Stevenson-Eisenhower challenge. Stevenson, they conceded, was "too intellectual" to win. (Mel, however, always steadfastly refused to reveal any preference in political candidates.)

Mel left the Skylark in the competent brown hands of Sunny, the garage operator on 45th Street west of Broadway. To get to the Palace Theater on the east side of Broadway at 47th Street, where our Broad-way office and control room were housed, we had to cross the elab-orate intersection: both Broadway and Seventh Avenue, which come together in the great X that forms the center of Times Square, were still two-way streets. A small but animated crowd was already assem-bled, chatting, laughing, and wagering, both men and women wear-ing fashionable hats and gloves despite the mild late autumn weather.

Mel was dapper as always in his snappy fedora. (Grandpa, more conservative, always wore a homburg.) The air reeked of Shalimar. Winking from the shoulders of the ladies' fall suits were looped scarves consisting of pointy-nosed, glass-eyed pelts—stone marten, baum marten, mink, or even sable—with tails and little feet hanging down, munching one another's hindquarters with spring-clip jaws. Every man, woman, and child, of every ethnic and economic group, dressed up to go downtown in those days, whether your downtown was Dallas, Dayton, or Times Square. Dressing properly was serious, so everyone suited up to attend an event like election night in Times Square.

I was wearing my best school outfit: a gray circle skirt appliquéd with a pink poodle on a chain; a stiffly starched white cotton blouse; bobby socks with pink plaid laces X-ing up the sides; and brand-new penny loafers. My coiffure was bangs and a proper teenage ponytail, which had to be up so tight it stretched one's eyebrows into a look of perpetual surprise. More significantly, I knew how to type, which is why I had the job.

## INFORMATION AS CELEBRATION

*The tradition of public gatherings* in Times Square to commemorate breaking events went back more than half a century, to New Year's Eve 1904–5, when the *New York Times* inaugurated its brand-new skyscraper—at 24 stories, it reigned briefly as the tallest building in the world—by thrilling a crowd that they estimated at more than 200,000 with a fabulous fireworks display to mark the turning of the year. As communications technologies improved and audiences became more educated and demanding, the ability to read breaking news "live" and on a massive scale amplified the public experience, combining animation, instant information, and entertainment in new and exciting ways.

In 1912 and again in 1913, the *Times* unveiled a state-of-the-art "electric scoreboard" which depicted, in real time, the titanic World Series struggles being waged between the Giants and their adversaries at the Polo Grounds. These dramatic displays were cheered by more than 15,000 viewers, not counting the hundreds of clerical workers who laid down their fountain pens to crane their necks from office windows or the thousands of schoolboys who augmented the street crowd when school let out during the fifth inning. On October

8, 1913, the *Times* modestly reported about its "new and improved" display: "On every side, it was conceded to be the last word in automatic baseball portrayal contrivances. Electric bulbs mark the positions of the players in the field. In the centre of the diamond the letter 'P' signifies the pitcher and 'C' the catcher in his natural position.... Directly in front of the catcher is an electric bulb which, when lighted, shows that the batter is at the plate...."

The first traveling message sign, or motograph—subsequently named the "news zipper" by some anonymous person with a tin ear—encircling the base of the Times Tower, was completed in time to broadcast the results of the Herbert Hoover–Al Smith election of 1928. As the crowd below cheered and jeered, technicians wearing headphones that connected them directly to Western Union in Washington translated the Morse code results into headlines, and passed their scribbled notes to workers who stood by to load the machines.

The fonts consisted of individual Bakelite panels, with bronze letters or numbers inlaid in a seven-high, five-wide pattern of dots—the same economical alphanumeric lamp matrix we use today. The panels were stacked manually, letter by letter, into a chain-driven mechanism that carried them up over a roller, and then down past a series of metal brushes, each of which was wired to a lamp in the sign. Wherever a metal brush made contact with a bronze dot, the corresponding lamp would light, and the message seemed magically to "travel" along the lamp bank. Information in motion! Everybody caught the drama: the nature of information is to be renewable, to change all the time. Those early traveling message technicians monitored two machines simultaneously, one running the motorized message while the other was being loaded with a fresh set of letters.

By the mid-1930s, nearly a dozen motographs ringed the Square. Advertisers, broadcasters, politicians, and news purveyors used them as state-of-the-art attention-getters and emotional focal points. Before TV, they gave people the opportunity to "see" and react to the news as it was breaking. Harking back to the days when newspaper publishers posted fresh front pages in their windows for everyone to read, receiving the news was a social event whether the news was good, bad, or merely morale-boosting. In the late 1930s, President Roosevelt used the motographs as a visual enhancement to his Fireside Chats, which he broadcast live nationwide, using the other young medium, radio, to help boost the spirits of a Depression-weary populace.

We would receive an advance copy of the Chats (marked "WARN-ING: Do Not Release until 7:00 PM, EDT"'), and the attendant in charge would prepare the paper tapes for the motographs. At the designated time, he'd hit the switches and start all the machines. Cabdrivers would pull over to the curb, doors agape and radios on full blast, so the gathered crowd could listen to the President's inspiring words while reading them, larger than life, in the sky overhead. The effect was like that of a chorus, as all the message centers echoed the same text in a sensory surround.

This was the first true multimedia event. Movietone News, in its weekly wrap-up of public events, played and replayed films of the Times Square public, reading, listening, and reacting, in movie theaters from Maine to California, and around the world.

The same thing happened at Roosevelt's death and throughout World War II. The news itself was important, of course, but people's reaction to the news was also important—so important in fact that it too became news.

Even satellite TV and the Internet, which have made live news and information available to everyone twenty-four hours a day, have not made obsolete the attraction of sharing emotion en masse in America's traditional town square. In recent times, small crowds gathered to watch the O. J. Simpson verdicts and to read the news of the death of Diana, the Princess of Wales. Experiencing news as a communal event—sharing emotion in public—gives it additional dimension: on many levels, it gives the individual a place to stand.

From 1932 until 1978 we operated all the travelers—except the one on the Times Tower, which was operated by Times technicians from inside the building—from our office on the fourth floor of the Palace Theater building.

The office was old-fashioned and dusty, and looked out on the alley behind the Palace. Its centerpiece was Grandpa's curved desk in the style that would now be called Art Deco. It was subsequently my father's desk, then my brother's, and now it's mine. Against the wall stood a matching walnut bar that opened to reveal an incomplete set of shot glasses, an ice bucket that was never filled because there was no ice, and a dusty bottle of rye whiskey that evaporated faster than it was consumed. In the hall outside the office was an ancient, cracked brown leather couch that was said to be Grandpa's friend Flo Ziegfeld's own personal casting couch and was the subject of many jokes.

The windowless control room occupied the Broadway side of the narrow building, behind the Palace Theater sign. Dominating its east wall were a pair of man-sized UPI Wire machines (one in case the other broke down) that looked like Robbie the Robot. Massive-shouldered and impassive, they clattered out the news as it was transmitted from UPI, spewing out miles of palely printed ticker tape that poured into large wastebaskets and overflowed onto the floor. This tape could be cut apart and pasted onto paper, like a telegram, for a permanent record or souvenir.

The operator's job was to read the ticker tape and type the relevant news into a "translator." The translator converted the characters into a five-dot code, something like braille, and punched the resulting message into a second, electrically insulated tape. The five holes, punched in various combinations, represented letters that the sign-driver machine could read and project onto the sign.

The operator would run the punched tape through yet another machine, a proofreader, that translated the pattern of holes back into English to be checked against the original UPI tape for errors. The importance of this step was impressed upon me as critical. I understood that the appearance on a Times Square traveler of a message containing even the most minor mistake would result in consequences so dire as to be unspeakable.

Satisfied that the coded tape was error-free, the operator would connect the ends of the tape together into a loop, install the loop into the "Play" machine—and at just the right time, hit the "Do" button. This was to be my job on that election night.

The machines never went unattended, either because of mechanical unreliability, fear of practical jokes, or some combination of the two. In the 1950s the sitter was usually an electrician, sometimes doubling as the Night Rider who checks the signs for outages. Before that, it was a job for students, particularly medical students, who could be relied on to stay awake all night while they hit the books.

During the 1930s, when Mel was still in school, he sometimes took the job. He and my mother were dating then, and she would take the subway up from Wall Street when she got off work to keep him company. This had to be love. "How dreary it was there!" she remembers. "It was dark and dusty, and the clacking of the machines was deafening." But to me it was a magical place.

## INSIDE THE PALACE

*Mel took my hand and* we headed for the Palace. He greeted a police captain he knew, and I got to pet a friendly police horse. The police cavalry were assembled on the side streets, not deployed along the avenues as in times past. The avenues were open to traffic, and would remain so all evening.

Nobody knew it then, but this was one of the last election nights that would attract anything like a big crowd to Times Square to celebrate the occasion and cheer or mourn the results. The advent of radio, and then TV, changed the nature of the event and slashed personal participation in it with stunning suddenness. In the late 1940s, commentators prophesied "the death of a tradition," attributing it both to the arrival of the new media and to the passing of the peculiar organizations and personality types that made up the old cast of performers. "The man who could shout himself hoarse when the old Fourth Ward rang up four extra votes for the Tammany choice for coroner, or go bug-eyed in frenzied joy at a Tammany assemblyman's little triumphs, was not in last night's assemblage," wrote a reporter for the Newspaper of Record in his 1949 postmortem.

In earlier decades, election night was on an equal footing with New Year's Eve as a mass jamboree, complete with special audio, visual, and gustatory effects. Peddlers, relegated to the side streets by police in order not to impede the parading throngs, did a brisk business in tin horns, cowbells, confetti, political party hats, popcorn, peanuts, candy, apples, ice cream, mechanical toys and novelties, and postcards of all sorts, some of them quite scurrilous. Hundreds of uniformed officers, stationed five feet apart, lined the curbs, attempting to restrict the crowds to the sidewalk; hundreds more, in mufti, mingled with the multitudes. Dozens of mounted police paraded majestically up and down the avenues, ready for anything.

As the 1949 reporter described, people in the 1920s and '30s were nuts. The mood was a mix of patriotism, partisanship, jubilation, and mass ecstasy. Storekeepers boarded up their windows. Estimates of the size of the crowd ranged into the stratosphere: 100,000; 250,000; 300,000. It was impossible to tell, since the routine was for people to keep moving, creating what was called a "floating crowd." Yielding to this impulse, the police allowed pedestrians to circumambulate the Square, designating the sidewalk on the east for northbound foot traffic and the sidewalk on the west for southbound. Anticipating later permanent traffic regulations, they also made vehicular traffic one-way through the Square when they didn't close it altogether: northbound on the east and southbound on the west.

But all this was before my time.

Once inside the Palace, we ascended to the fourth floor in the creaky elevator. Every Times Square elevator in those days was apparently run by a failed comedian, and you, the passenger, were expected to be the straight man.

"How's life, Joe?"

"Up and down, up and down."

"Got any interesting tips lately?"

"Yeah. Don't invest in the stock market."

"Ha, ha."

"I got a million of 'em! A million of 'em! Ever hear of Bob Hope?"

"Sure."

"Well, I'm his brudda. No Hope."

Mel gave the man a dollar in appreciation of these jokes that he'd doubtless heard countless times before.

We greeted the electrician on duty that night, Nat Winthrop, and settled down to go to work. Nat was quiet and sandy-colored, and Artkraft Strauss was the center of his existence. He achieved the pinnacle of his career in 1954, when the *New York Journal-American* ran a feature story on him, with heroic color photographs of him as the fearless and philosophical Night Rider, climbing the Broadway signs to check for outages. (As if anybody really climbs signs in the middle of the night. What the Night Rider really does is study the signs from the street and fill out a service report, so the service electricians can do the repairs the following day.) Thereafter he styled himself "Broadway Nat," and his fedora barely fit on his head. His son Warren telephoned me in 1989 to tell me that Nat had recently passed away at the age of ninety and that spread around him on his hospital bed at the end, for his final enjoyment, were his souvenirs of his life at Artkraft Strauss, especially the 1954 newspaper story.

"Hi, Nat! I'm going to work! This is my job tonight!" I announced.

Nat winked at me. *"Kenst machen a leben fun dus?"* he asked— "From this you can make a living?"—the classic question of Yiddish-speaking parents to offspring who declare their intention to become poets or polo players. (Joe the Elevator Man was not the only comedian on the premises.) Then Nat donned his fedora and set out to inspect the signs. Mel settled himself into Mr. Ziegfeld's couch and pretended to read a *Fantasy and Science Fiction* magazine he was carrying in his pocket, so I could pretend I was doing my important job unsupervised.

I sat down at the electrician's desk, a slab of plywood balanced on a pair of broken-down metal two-drawer file cabinets, and started to read the tapes. The early results were coming in, and even to a child it was evident that it was a rout.

Despite the Democratic Party leaders' confident forecasts of a last-minute swing that would carry Stevenson to the White House, and although the Democrats retained control of both houses of Congress, the election results all evening were neither mysterious nor suspenseful. Alas for my mother, who was doubtless hoping for a last-minute upset like Truman's over Dewey in 1948—the memorable photo and collective memory depicts a grinning, victorious Truman brandishing a prematurely printed headline screaming, "Dewey Wins!"—an upset was not in the cards.

By ten-thirty it was all over, and Mel said it was time to go home. The General had beaten the Professor by nearly 10 million votes out of a total of 61 million—the most spectacular presidential victory since Roosevelt demolished Landon by the same margin twenty years earlier, and the largest margin ever given to a Republican candidate up to that time. Sorry, Mom.

Down on the street, the "election thermometer" on the Times

Tower, inaugurated in 1952 and again in 1956, perhaps in the hope of reinvigorating attendance, announced the Eisenhower victory, and the searchlight at the top of the Tower pointed steadily north, indicating the same thing to those who couldn't read but somehow knew the code.

## BROADWAY MELODIES

*Leaving the Palace to mingle* with the after-theater throng, we passed under the marquee and portrait covering the entire facade of the theater that promised: "Tonight—In Person—Last 6 Weeks—Judy Garland & All-Star Variety Show." The election and its audience now history—they'd repaired to their bars and political clubs to digest the results and discuss the what-ifs—the new crowd, well-dressed theater- and moviegoers, laughed and talked animatedly about what they'd just seen. The illuminated marquees and twinkling chaser lights blended with the endlessly cycling, flashing neon to rinse the streets, the buildings, the people, and their memories of an extraordinary evening, in lapping waves of glow.

If our signs tell us who we are, then our marquees that year told us in no uncertain terms that we were people who loved fine theater and great performances. A snapshot of the menu of plays and movies available on Broadway that night reveals a smorgasbord of choices unimaginable today.

If a musical that sent you out of the theater humming unforgettable songs suited your mood, your cheerful choices included the original productions of *My Fair Lady*, with Rex Harrison and Julie Andrews; *Bells Are Ringing*, starring Judy Holliday; *Happy Hunting*, with Ethel Merman and Fernando Lamas; and *The Pajama Game*, about union organizing and romance in a pajama factory—as well as *Li'l Abner, Fanny, Show Boat, The Most Happy Fella, Mr. Wonderful*, starring Sammy Davis, Jr., and Kurt Weill's *Threepenny Opera*, with Lotte Lenya, the star of the original German production, as Jenny Diver, and Bea Arthur as the tenor-voiced Mrs. Peachum, completing its third sold-out year at the Theater de Lys.

If comedy was your shtick, you could catch Rosalind Russell in

*Auntie Mame,* Charlton Heston and Orson Bean in *Mister Roberts* (tickets only $3.80 at City Center), Ruth Gordon in Thornton Wilder's *The Matchmaker,* Alfred Lunt and Lynn Fontanne in *The Great Sebastians, No Time for Sergeants,* later the basis for a movie and a TV series—or any of half a dozen others.

If you were in the mood for serious drama, your choices that season included the original productions of Tennessee Williams's *Cat on a Hot Tin Roof, The Diary of Anne Frank* with Susan Strasberg, *Inherit the Wind* with Paul Muni, Edward G. Robinson in Paddy Chayefsky's *Middle of the Night,* Julie Harris and Boris Karloff in Jean Anouilh's *The Lark,* Bert Lahr's stunning performance in Samuel Beckett's *Waiting for Godot,* Agatha Christie's *Witness for the Prosecution,* and Eugene O'Neill's *Long Day's Journey into Night* (and, at another theater, *The Iceman Cometh*). Or you could choose from among the classics: Shaw's *Major Barbara, Arms and the Man,* and three other plays, at various theaters; plays by Gogol, Chekhov, Ibsen, and Strindberg; or, at the Winter Garden, the Old Vic's performances of *Macbeth* alternating with *Romeo and Juliet.*

And these were only the prize winners! There weren't enough nights in the week to see them all. No wonder the grown-ups were constantly, tiresomely, talking about theater: what they'd just seen, what they were going to see, who was better in which role, the politics of casting and awards, who had invested in what, who was or wasn't paying their bills. Even then I had the impression that the real drama in the theater takes place behind the scenes.

## Movie Giants

*In 1956, 288 major motion* pictures were distributed by leading companies, a high-water mark. They included *The Ten Commandments,* with Charlton Heston as Moses, one of the highest-grossing films of all time; *The King and I,* starring Yul Brynner, based on the hit Broadway show; *Moby Dick,* with Gregory Peck as the tormented Captain Ahab; and *Around the World in Eighty Days,* also to this day among the highest-grossing movies of all time. All of them enjoyed an exclusive "first run" on Broadway, and each required a spectacular display of its own. The movie studios were some of Artkraft's best—and steadiest—customers.

Some of the spectaculars we created for the studios were merely paints, but they were spectacular paints. The precocious Baby Doll, a precursor to Lolita, sprawled across the front of the Astor-Victoria Theater, 200 feet wide, 40 feet high, and pouting and heaving to beat the band. My cousin Gene says it was a chore to persuade the painters to climb out of her cleavage and declare the job done.

*Baby Doll* was declared too "racy" for children ("Why?" I asked, when the movie was obviously about one), so I never did get to see it. But it was my good fortune, like Florence Strauss before me, as the daughter of the man who built the signs, to attend some of the openings—glamorous affairs with everyone in formal finery. Outside the theater, the surrounding buildings and sky were lit by cones of swirling light emitted by huge skytrackers mounted on flatbed trucks—a magical effect that spelled excitement. Movie stars emerged from limousines onto ruby-red carpets that lined the sidewalk while paparazzi and pop-eyed commoners behind police barricades elbowed one another for a glimpse of them. At the opening of *The Ten Commandments* at the Criterion Theater, I walked just *this far* behind Charlton Heston, who looked even taller than he did on the screen.

I wasn't the only child who was intrigued by movie-opening spotlights. A friend, artist and author Alicia Bay Laurel, grew up in Hancock Park, just south of the glitziest part of Los Angeles, during the 1950s. "There were constant openings and previews then," she remembers, "just about every night it seemed, on Hollywood Boulevard and Sunset Boulevard, right near my house. As a child I believed the searchlights were natural phenomena, like the moon and the stars. They were brighter than the stars, in fact, those moving columns of light twisting back and forth across the sky. The moon was often difficult to distinguish, and the stars usually were too. They tended to blend into the city lights: just part of the generalized glow. The searchlights, though! They were far more real, exciting and magical—quite worth watching because, after all, they moved.

"I remember how astonished I was—I must have been about five—when I was riding in a car along Hollywood Boulevard and we passed one of those searchlights, and I realized that the effect was not part of nature at all, but came out of a giant lamp that was obviously built by people. In a way, that made it even more mysterious and exciting."

The early 1950s saw the advent of new and exciting cinema technologies, each of which was predicted to revolutionize the movie industry and make all the others obsolete. 3-D, Cinerama, Cinema-Scope, VistaVision, Todd-AO. All produced some stunning visual effects, especially when used in connection with the mythic epics with their "casts of thousands."

All of these productions required new marquee displays and signs that had to hold their own against the dazzling spectaculars that ringed the Square in those years. Light and hype, strategic components of the spectacular advertising arsenal, had a natural affinity for the cinematographer's art, especially when it came to bringing that art out onto the street. The display for *The Vikings*, for example, on the block-wide Astor-Victoria site, featured a Viking ship with immense oars that rowed through the air. *Annie Get Your Gun* depicted Annie Oakley tall as a four-story building firing lightbulb bullets across the width of a building. *Joan of Arc*, fifty feet tall, burned at the stake, consumed every night by flickering neon flames; by day, her pyre emitted smoke.

As stunning as these theatrical dream-images writ large in light may have been, however, they had to row uphill to match the new, high-tech glamour of their advertising competitors.

## ELECTRONIC TURN-ONS

*During the 1950s, television transformed* communications, its impact felt in every facet of American life. In 1946, virtually no American homes had TV sets. By 1948, 350,000 sets were in use; by 1960, more than 50 million. Nearly all of these sets were made in America by American workers employed by companies like Motorola, Zenith, Westinghouse, and Admiral. The signs of this proud, booming postwar business appeared quickly in Times Square.

For ten years, starting in 1952, Admiral occupied a prime location in the middle of the "tower" of spectaculars at the Square's north end, dramatizing its new presence in American life by staging a ballet that expressed change, excitement, and power through multilayered animation sequences that awed as well as dazzled.

The 50-foot-square spectacular performed its dance against a background of brilliant sky-blue porcelain enamel. Its 1,500 separate circuits and 300 miles of wire made the animation capabilities of its 12,000 lamps and mile and a half of neon tubing virtually limitless. The idea, Mel explained to me, was that the customer could have a completely "new" sign just by changing the animation sequence. All the possibilities were pre-wired in. This versatility was Mel's hallmark during his years as the Square's premier designer-salesman..

The word "Admiral" was composed of prismatic letters 11 and 16 feet tall and 2 feet deep, filled with red, gold, and blue (horizontal) and white (vertical) neon, and outlined front and back with channels of orange-amber lamps. The sloping sides of the letters were packed with white lamps wired to twinkle, chase, or burn steady. Beneath the company name were the words "TELEVISION" and "APPLIANCES" in 8-foot channel letters filled with concentric rows of gold and white double-intensity fluorescent tubing, wired to "breathe"—that is, to grow larger and smaller.

There was also a border of green tubing and gold lamps, wired to chase in a ropey sort of pattern, to do the same thing in reverse, or to burn steady. Along the bottom was a seven-foot motograph that ran the time and weather. The initial animation sequence, which included spelling "Admiral" in a variety of combinations of lamps and tubing, went through 52 different changes and lasted more than a minute and a half without repeating itself.

By the time the sign was turned on in April of 1952, the arrival of a new spectacular in Times Square was routinely covered by the press as news. Press agents happily fed the public appetite for hoopla with ever bigger, and sometimes ever more antic, events.

"You've got to be a little bit pixie in this business," Mel told an interviewer around that time. However serious the big signs might be—involving serious money, serious technology, serious construction, and corporate image—the atmosphere surrounding them never lost its sense of fun.

Since the early days of the spectacular, signs had been ceremonially "lighted" by celebrities and corporate bigwigs who, at the climactic moment, pushed a button or threw a switch or joined a pair of hawser-sized "wires" together, creating a fountain of Frankensteinish sparks. What was really happening, of course, was that someone near the celeb was giving a cue—visual in the early days, later by walkie-talkie—to nimble electricians up in the sign.

So numerous were these staged events that Mel designed a prop: a knife switch that looked like it could activate the turbines at Con Edison. On the back was a cluster of flashbulbs connected to a battery. At the turn-on moment, Mr. CEO would heave the switch, the flashbulbs would go *poppity-pop!* and emit a puff of smoke, the crowd would go "oooh" and "aaah," and the sign would blaze into action.

The flashbulbs had a practical, as well as a cosmetic, function. Early walkie-talkies were unreliable—so if the electricians missed the audio or waving-handkerchief cue, they could respond to the glare of the flashbulbs, visible from the roof.

We still use a switch similar to that one today, although we've substituted a seven-foot replica of an ordinary wall switch, like one from a giant's castle. In recent years we've also tried using a mammoth computer mouse, complete with a sidewalk-filling mousepad and laser flashlight "cursor." I'm still amazed by how many people think these surreal switches actually work.

Admiral's p.r. men went over the technological edge with the Admiral turn-on. Having a little nervous fun with the specter of nuclear annihilation, they set up an archery target in Duffy Square across the street from the sign and armed the celebrity of the hour, Manhattan Borough President (later Mayor) Robert F. Wagner, Jr., with what looked like an air pistol.

What it really was, the gathering was solemnly told, was a neutron gun. And the target, continued the story, was an atomic target. Wagner took careful aim at the atomic target and squeezed off a round.

*Radio & Television Weekly* reported what happened next with a perfectly straight face: "The stream of neutrons from the pistol struck the Geiger counter in the bull's-eye of the target to start a chain reaction, which touched off a small magnesium bomb and illuminated the sign for the first time."

Take that, you Russkies! Betcha don't have anything like THIS in Red Square!

That wasn't the only time the Cold War was exploited for a sign turn-on. In 1960 we built a display, on our factory roof next to the West Side Highway, for King's Ransom Scotch. For the turn-on, my cousin Phil Marshall gave a riveting space-age performance as he tapped into the mysterious power of Sputnik to illuminate the display. (The tie-in was that King's Ransom's slogan was "The Round-the-World Scotch," and its symbol a jet plane orbiting the earth like an electron.)

An accomplished prestidigitator and amateur actor, Phil, wearing a massive set of earphones, kept up a running commentary as he twiddled the dials on a huge, battle-scarred tube radio. He was "tuning in" Sputnik, the first Russian satellite, as its orbit carried it over the Hudson River and across West 57th Street. A series of beeps and blips and unidentifiable outer-space sounds emanated from the radio, proving that the satellite was steady on the approach path.

"Here she comes!" Phil announced. "Almost . . . almost. . . . Uh-oh . . . we lost it," he declared, heightening the suspense. "Ahh, there we are, got the signal back. Here she comes. Nearer and nearer and nearer, and it's overhead . . . right . . . now!" And the sign flashed on. Everyone was appropriately thrilled to be part of the modern age, including the King's Ransom execs and the winking reporters.

## "Say C.C."

*Admiral's closest neighbor—spatially,* chronologically, and technically—was the Canadian Club classic directly above it, which we installed only three months later. And its turn-on ceremony was of a completely different order of dignity and class than those I've just described.

For Hiram Walker & Sons, Mel came up with an elaborately layered interpretation of the Canadian Club logo that expressed elegance and sophistication in a particularly splendid way. Along with its equally distinctive upstairs neighbor, it is still remembered by connoisseurs of the craft as the crowning achievement of what was called "skywriting" in the early days of electrical art.

The sign was 48 feet high by 62 feet wide, with the elegant-script

Canadian Club signature in letters 12 to 22 feet tall. The letters were massive prisms, 36 inches deep but only 4 inches wide at their narrowest point, widening to 12 to 26 inches at their backs. This was said to be the first use of prismatic script letters, and if you consider the geometry of a prism, you can see why. You might break your brain trying to figure out how to connect the compound curves.

The bright red letters were suspended a foot away from the elaborate gold neon background on concealed supports, so they seemed to be floating in midair in front of the sign. ("We had to use a pirate's plank—not just an ordinary scaffold—to reach behind the letters," remembers Bobby Dianuzzo, Artkraft Strauss' electrical foreman, who serviced the aging sign as a maintenance electrician in the 1970s.) The letters were packed with 30,000 lamps, not only on their faces and beveled sides, but on their backs as well, so there was a constant dialogue and interplay, in the animation sequences, between the letters and the background.

Perhaps the most stunning of the sign's 28 initial animated effects was the "writing-on" and "writing-off," in languid but perfectly timed and spaced Spencerian script, of the signature Canadian Club logo. The desired effect, as Mel put it, was as if it were "penned by a giant brush dipped in light." A single side-by-side row of 1,500 75-watt PAR 38 lamps, set into a channel so their faces were flush with the edge of the metal, were individually wired to create this effect.

The letters were also outlined, both front and back, with a double row of double-intensity ruby-red neon, so that when the clear lamps on the faces of the prisms did their graceful "writing-off" trick, the shapes of the letters remained knife-sharp. (An inviolable rule is that at no time, even for an instant, is the customer's name to go dark.) The letters filled and emptied using different combinations of the red neon outlines, the clear lamps on the faces, orange-amber lamps on the prism sides, and white backlights throwing a glowing halo onto the background. The design made great use of black—wherever the light wasn't—as a powerful color.

The gold neon background, which contained over a mile of tubing, was wired in 108 sections, so it could perform all kinds of patterns of sweeps, wipes, curtains, checkerboards, and even herringbones that appeared to be racing in opposite directions. There was also an animated border containing 2,000 lamps (a composition like that had to be "contained," Mel said), and, oh yes, 8-foot-tall animated letters—they could twinkle, spell on, or burn solid—across the bottom that spelled "IMPORTED WHISKY."

If Admiral and Canadian Club sound somewhat similar in my description, it is because describing their components is like describing the components of a symphony orchestra. The difference is in what they played. And Mel, during his tenure as the "Lamplighter of Broadway," was the composer, arranger, and conductor.

I can remember him sitting at his desk at home on weekends with the giant pieces of graph paper in front of him that he used to "score" the animation. It was like writing a symphony in light, he explained. Everything had to do with harmony, rhythm, and mood.

He would list the various sign elements—including each individual letter—down the side of the page, with time increments in quarters of a second across the top. Various symbols indicated the animation techniques, and the length of the lines indicated their duration. A bunch of little dots, for example, meant twinkling. A straight line was a steady burn, and a series of stair steps, of course, meant a step-on. A squiggly line was an on-and-off flash, with the size of the squiggles denoting the frequency. A spiral was a bombardment, where the entire sign, or the entire background, flashes on and off. Our electrical department could read these sheets, and used them to design the wiring and to give instructions to the cam cutter.

Our cam cutter was Harry Trackman, who worked out of a little upstairs shop near Times Square, on West 43rd Street. Cam cutting was a skilled profession in those days, like watchmaking. Until the mid-1970s, when electromechanical switching gave way to electronics, all of the switching that turned lights on and off was done with cams. And every single cam, thousands and thousands of them, was precisely cut by hand.

A cam is a device that mechanically changes the direction of energy. A sign cam was a little disk made of nonconducting Bakelite, with notches in it, that rode on a shaft that turned like an axle. The notch, when it came around, engaged a roller bearing attached to a copper "finger." The finger closed a relay, making a contact, so a light turned on. Each lamp had its own cam, and the size and spacing of the notches determined the intervals of on-time or off-time for that lamp. The cams were "stacked" on their axles like doughnuts on a stick.

This was some elegant machinery. The machine that ran the 1,500 lamps spelling "Canadian Club," for example, contained five parallel rows of cams, all connected to a master camshaft. "When you looked down a row," remembers Bobby, "you could see the spiral that showed you how fast the lamps would turn on. It was really quite beautiful."

Harry the cam cutter was even more enthusiastic. I once ran into him in the roof hut that housed the machinery for the Anheuser-Busch display, which featured animated neon Clydesdale horses. The clatter and click of thousands of relays makes a sound that is both literally and figuratively electrifying, and Harry was just sitting there, listening in ecstasy.

"Listen! Listen!" he cried when he saw me. "You can hear the horses galloping!" He didn't mean that the sound was *like* that of horses galloping. He could actually distinguish the different parts of the animation sequence by the sounds the switches made. Any spectacular electrical expert with a good ear can do that. If you were to blindfold Bobby and put him inside an electrical hut, not only could he tell you which sign he was inside the machinery of, he could also tell you if something was misfiring—and which part of the display it was. He says he used to mystify his elder brother, Mike, our previous foreman, with this trick.

The Canadian Club spectacular took its first bow on a warm night in June of 1952, in an elaborate ritual befitting the arrival of royalty. Hiram Walker threw a party in the restaurant on the roof of the Astor Hotel, the vantage point of choice for sign-lighting events in those days. The unusual view from above, in the words of Virginia Sebastian, who covered Broadway sign doings for *Signs of the Times* magazine, was "breathtaking—you feel so close to those great blazing animated shafts of light pouring up at you."

Several hundred revelers, provided with a generous supply of Hiram Walker's product, paused at the appointed hour as Ross Corbit, the president of the company, placed his hand on the tasteful little tabletop switch that would illuminate the sign. My cousin Gene Kornberg, then Artkraft Strauss' general manager, remembers that turn-on: "We did this so often, we really had it down to a science. Canadian Club, however, was a little more complicated than most. It required just a little more choreography because all the other signs were involved."

Gene is being just a little too modest. He was the stage manager of a novel production number that was easily as elaborate as anything taking place on any of the nearby stages—and more difficult, as our stage was twelve city blocks in size.

As Mr. Corbit waited in gleeful dignity for his cue, all the other signs in Times Square, cued by Gene, simultaneously went dark. Ms. Sebastian reported that the blackout lasted fifteen minutes "to allow this newest beauty to make her debut." Down on the street, people were confused. Times Square had suddenly been plunged into darkness. A power failure? Had the Russians landed? Traffic stopped, and people got out of their cars and taxis. Restaurants and shops emptied as the Square filled with anxious citizens. Police, who apparently hadn't been let in on the plan, arrived quickly to keep order and investigate.

With Gene at the parapet of the Astor roof discreetly flashing signals to his men, the show began. First, a single theatrical spotlight picked the sign out of the darkness. Then Mr. Corbit hit the switch with a flourish and the sign came on in all its splendor, the great invisible brush writing "Canadian Club" for the first time in flowing script that seemed to hang in the night air. Then the other elements, one by one, were added. The crowd in the Square and the gathering on the roof watched in awed silence as the spectacular went through its 28 changes several times.

Then, one by one, the other signs—each manned by an electrician following Gene's script and taking flashlight cues—came back on, their own light sequences weaving fuguelike counterpoint to Canadian Club's melody. Viewers looking at the sign head-on saw that it was framed by the familiar Chevrolet logos, running up and down the sides and dancing merrily across the top. The Admiral sign, immediately below, spoke first through its traveling message center: "Admiral Welcomes Canadian Club to Times Square." The others followed suit, a chorus of gracious neighborly voices—even those of competitors—saluting the new arrival.

The crowd in the Square cheered. The policemen smiled, grateful they didn't have to fight the Russians that night. On the roof, Mr. Corbit and his Hiram Walker entourage gathered around Jake and Mel in a flurry of handshakes and backslaps. Then they distributed gold "Special Edition" Anniversary bottles of Canadian Club all around. (Gene still has his.) At the edge of the celebration, Gene breathed a sigh of relief and turned off his flashlight.

## THE EAGLE SOARS

*One early spring day in* 1952, a pair of panel trucks delivered Mel, a team of men, and a pile of equipment to the front door of the 69th Regiment Armory on Lexington Avenue and 25th Street. The principal item of cargo was a large covered cage, carried gingerly up to the front door by two men.

Inside, the armory's great central hall had been emptied and closed to the curious. One of the men set up a tripod. Others unloaded a 16-millimeter motion picture camera, strung electrical cable, and mounted lights. The covered cage was placed carefully in an out-of-the-way corner, where one of the men sat cross-legged on the floor and spoke quietly to it. Except for an occasional flapping sound, what was in the cage was a silent, unseen, but clearly felt presence.

Mel never talked much about his work. In fact, he didn't talk much at all; and when he did, it was often in Zen-like aphorisms. But this is one memory that always brought a twinkle of amusement to his eye: the day we flew the eagle in the armory.

This was an early part of the design phase of what was to be one of Artkraft Strauss' widest-reaching creations, a display for Anheuser-Busch on the Brill Building, at 49th Street and Broadway, where Miss Youth Form's reign was about to come to an end. We were to re-create the central feature of this particular spectacular—the Flying A and Eagle—over the next fifteen years on advertising locations and on the roofs of Anheuser-Busch breweries throughout the country. One of these eagles still wings its way over the Newark brewery, across the New Jersey Turnpike from Newark Airport, nearly fifty years later.

Budweiser had first planted its flag on New York's Great White Way in 1905, on the west side of Broadway near 38th Street, and maintained a continuous presence until Prohibition. In 1933, they had a big sign in place ready to meet Repeal—replacing the word "Malt" with the word "Beer" literally hours after the Eighteenth Amendment was overturned.

After World War II, Budweiser reasserted its presence with a huge and entertaining display on the southeast corner of 43rd Street and Broadway. The entire roof of Toffenetti's restaurant, a three-story building, was transformed into a diorama ten stories high, in which a frosty 90-foot bottle of Budweiser nestled at an angle in a mountain of thirst-provoking ice, surrounded by a piney mountain scene. Around the edge of this tableau, through a tunnel in the mountains and out again, ran a realistic model train. The engine and cars were 5 feet tall, and their windows were lighted at night. Passersby were inevitably reminded of the little trains they found running around their trees on Christmas morning.

The mountain railway served a dual purpose. It associated the King of Beers with western vitality and the purity of a mountain wilderness, and alluded to its national reach. At the same time, the train helped pay for the display by serving as an advertisement within an advertisement and a cross-promotional vehicle.

In 1946, when the sign was built, there were still twenty-three passenger railroads in the United States, some serving the whole country, some operating regionally. It was a splendid idea, cooked up by Mel along with Bob Flood, Budweiser's account manager at their ad agency, D'Arcy of St. Louis, to turn the model train into the Railroad of the Month. For a small fee, the Santa Fe or the Union Pacific or the Knoxville & Jacksonville could have the model transformed into a miniature replica of its flagship train. Every few months (Railroads of the Month tended to stay for several months), we received a package from D'Arcy containing the new sponsor's timetables, advertising brochures, color samples, and photographs of its trains in action. Artkraft Strauss workers, accustomed to odd assignments, climbed up into the diorama to repaint the model and add such embellishments as observation domes, railroad logos, distinctive lighting, and striping. At the same time, the Railroad of the Month featured the Beverage of the Month—guess what that was—in all of its club cars.

Alas, Budweiser's train, like Woody Guthrie's City of New Orleans, suffered the disappearing-railroad blues. By the early 1950s, America's romance with the automobile was in full swing, and air travel was quickly becoming the long-distance transportation of choice. And Anheuser-Busch, as eager as any company to avoid seeming behind the times (perhaps more so, considering their 150-year history) needed something that would dramatize both their modernity and their stability—a technological wonder that said, "Budweiser is America."

This, then, is what brought Mel and his film crew to the old armory on that early spring day.

When the camera was in place, the man who had been babysitting the cage removed the cover, lifted the side wall, reached in with two heavily leather-clad crossed arms and withdrew them—with a solemn American bald eagle perched on top. Slowly the animal's handler raised his arms, clicked a signal with his tongue, and the eagle leaped into flight with a flap of its wings.

The eagle glided slowly and effortlessly around the great hall of the armory near the ceiling, banking neatly at the corners and leveling out again, its wings billowing gracefully and efficiently to maintain altitude. It weighed nearly seventy-five pounds, and its real-life wingspan was over six and a half feet. This was before wildlife films were readily available, so the only way to get film of an eagle in flight was to rent an eagle and film it. As Mel watched, the camera rolled, and a man standing beside Mel made charcoal sketches on a large manila pad, his hand moving with the delicacy of a surgeon's.

The artist was a Disney-trained animator named Bunny Rabbit (an inevitable nickname: his real first name was Byron). Bunny was to combine the film with his sketches and make this eagle fly in neon.

Neon animation of the kind that reached its apogee in the 1950s is a lot like cartooning. It's accomplished by means of overlays. Outlines of the figure in different stages of motion are superimposed over one another and lit in sequence. Designing the overlays carefully and lighting them with just the right timing can create a smooth appearance of continuous motion.

Bunny had to accomplish this with only six positions. The neon eagle was to fly in place, and if neon tubes are too close together, the high voltage can arc between them and short them out. The layer of neon farthest from the sign face, where the supports were, was 34 inches away. That is quite a span for a cantilever made of lightweight glass tubing, especially in the wind, and it took moxie even to try it.

Ultimately, the Times Square eagle—six superimposed eagles, actually—had a wingspan of over 60 feet, and were limned in a mile and a half of ruby-red neon tubing. The bird's motion was sublimely graceful. When its wings rose, the feathers curved down, and when its wings descended, the feathers, momentarily stationary at their tips, arced up. Our shop was filled with thousands of individual neon eagle feathers—two, three, four, five, and six feet long.

This eagle had plenty of personality. Its head extended and retracted like a reptile's, its piercing eyes blinked, its talons clutched and released, and its tail feathers stirred up and down—all in coordination with the beating wings.

The majestic bird flying solo against the night sky created an awesome effect. It seemed lifelike, the grace and power of the national bird in flight captured in just the right flare of wing, stretch of neck, and jut of beak. At the end of the sequence it froze, wings fully outspread, while the fat Roman A, its prismatic sides paved with real gold leaf, ran through its twinkling, cam-driven animation sequence.

The A and Eagle comprised the sign's crowning image, but it wasn't the whole show. Across the bottom of the display, above a message center, Anheuser-Busch's trademark Clydesdale horses pulled their monster load, the lumbering beer wagon—its wheels turning, the driver's animated whip flying. The gait of the eight horses, their heads bobbing, their backs straining, 32 fringed hooves stomping in a harmonious flow—Bunny captured it all, in sky-size dimensions. The horses—48 of them in six neon overlays each—were nine times life size.

Between the eagle and the horses, the sign spelled "Budweiser" in three-dimensional, animated letters. The dot on the "i" was 4 feet in diameter, weighed 200 pounds, and contained 80 feet of neon as well as several hundred lamps.

The trademark A and Eagle was repeated across the country; but, sadly, most of these spectacular signatures came down in the mid-1970s, along with other classic supersigns, victims of the purported energy crisis. I'm glad there's at least one member of this endangered species—the one in Newark—still alive to tell the tale.

The sign was lit up for the first time at 11:15 P.M. on November 6, 1952. The ceremony was timed to coincide with the finale of the weeklong National Horse Show at Madison Square Garden, which traditionally ended with a parade around the inside of the Garden led by the famous Clydesdales and their beer wagon. This time, the finale took a novel turn.

Under the direction of Bob Flood of D'Arcy, the Astor roof had been decorated as a designer stable—saddles, bridles, and other tack on the walls; a layer of fresh straw on the floor; table centerpieces composed of nosegays of fragrant green oats, apples, and multicolored ears of corn. The equine motif extended even to the glassware, napery, and silver. One imagines that Flood thought this up to please his most important clients, and that when the Busches saw it they were indeed pleased. (One also imagines that when the guests saw it, they were tempted to make jokes about "putting on the feed bag.")

At the end of the parade at the Garden, the team of Clydesdales hauling their wagon clip-clopped out the door and headed down Broadway to Times Square. In a masterpiece of coordination—especially considering that the theaters were letting out at the same time—they arrived on schedule and halted at the south end of Duffy Square for the kind of photo op that was their reason for life on earth.

August Busch, Jr., accompanied by Mrs. Busch and the mayor of New York, Vincent Impellitteri, descended from the wagon—for an occasion like this, Mr. Busch drove the team himself, of course—and stepped into the waiting Astor elevator. On arriving at the roof, Mr. Busch and the mayor threw the big switch. The great sign came on, going through its sequence of 30 animated paces while a message of welcome to the mayor, Mr. Busch, and his colleagues, sent from our control room in the Palace Theater building, coursed across the motograph in letters 10 feet high.

Down on the street, the equine octet posed serenely in front of their trotting neon portrait while flashbulbs popped, riling the big animals not a whit. Even for them, the best was yet to come.

Soon the lead horse was unhitched from its right front position in the team and led toward the Astor Hotel. The press waited, not knowing what was going on. And they would never know. For, in supervention of who knows how many city ordinances, the 2,000-pound animal was taken to the delivery entrance of the hotel, walked into the freight elevator, and conveyed to the roof. There it was escorted into the ballroom, where it made the grandest of entrances and joined the party.

The celebrants rejoiced at this wonderful fraternity stunt. The crowd on the roof was euphoric. Only the horses were unimpressed.

## LEAPIN' LITTLE LULU

*Little Lulu was the chief* doll in my collection. She wasn't the oldest or the biggest or the prettiest, but she was the smartest—the soul sister I always wanted. I followed her comic book adventures, and I figured that she operated just the way I did.

Lulu was a merry little girl with a secret sense of irony who always knew a lot more than anyone gave her credit for. Without ever losing her cheerful composure, this perennial eleven-year-old managed to extricate not only herself but also her dumb boyfriend Tubby from one tough spot after another. She was more than a match for the other denizens of my collection—the elegant Madame Alexanders, grandes dames of princesses in their exquisitely hand-sewn gowns; gregarious Ginny, with her vast wardrobe; the sedate Teddys (Papa, Mama, and Baby) from my crib days, and even Wednesday, my beloved counterpart from the macabre Addams Family. By 1955, my days of playing with dolls were nearing an end, and the gang spent most of its time arranged neatly on the top of my bookcase. I liked having them around for company even as I looked forward with unalloyed enthusiasm to the teen years on the far distant horizon.

Mel and the men provided me with a wonderful last blast of childhood that year—they built a monument to my secret best friend. Little Lulu was the star of one of the most charming spectaculars ever built in Times Square. Of course, the customer, Kleenex tissues' Kimberly-Clark, believed the sign was put there to advertise its product. But all they did was pay for it. I knew Mel built it for me.

The seven-and-a-half-story-high Kleenex spectacular, which wrapped 180 feet around the corner of 43rd Street and Broadway, was a monument to the art of pictorial neon animation. The sign's story was a lesson in both Kleenex's new "pop-up" technology and the product's new multicolor availability. The sheets were folded into one another so that when one was pulled through the opening slit in the box, the one below it automatically popped up. My exuberant alter ego, 20 feet tall, served as our guide and teacher.

She began by jumping from a swinging trapeze to the 16-foot letter K of the word Kleenex at the top of the sign. Then she skipped from letter to letter in a wonderful acrobatic sequence, spelling on each twinkling letter as she landed on it. This was my favorite part of the sign, the Little Lulu I loved. She cavorted, gamboled, and frolicked, skipping and turning cartwheels at just the right playful speed, landing on each letter in a different pose. She was a masterpiece of neon animation. At the letter X she jumped onto a huge sheet of Kleenex billowing up from the 50-foot-long box below, and slid down its curved length, finally winding up at the bottom of the sign, where she waved a teacher's pointer to call our attention to the amazing new box—"The Only Tissue That Pops Up," the sign told us in 10-foot letters.

Then something scary happened. A 40-foot neon woman's hand, big enough to squash a little girl like a bug, appeared above the box and plucked out a tissue. This always made me nervous. But when Little Lulu reappeared swinging on her trapeze to start the whole show again, I felt better. Pop-up was for sure the way to go. Why fish around in the oval opening of an old-fashioned tissue box and come up with an annoying handful when you could grab just one soothing Kleenex on the fly and save gosh knows how many precious seconds? Little Lulu was right, as always.

Each Little Lulu, of course, was a separate neon overlay, and there were dozens for the whole sequence. The woman's hand alone also required six positions, each crafted with the same care Mel invested in the flying Anheuser-Busch eagle to create realistic motion.

The sign was further distinguished by its use of color and its flexibility in color change. Neon craftsmanship was at its peak in the mid-1950s, and Artkraft Strauss' artisans created for the sign the full range of Kleenex's new pastel hues—yellow, pink, green, and blue, as well as white. Each color featured on the box and in the pop-up tissue sequence had its own complete set of neon tubes: five parallel sets in all. Behind the sign, five cam machines were necessary to drive just this sequence.

The sign began its life in the first nationally televised turn-on ceremony ever. A public relations man—the only one Jake ever hired—arranged to have the event broadcast live on NBC's *America After Dark*, the forerunner of *The Tonight Show*. The event was a great success. With the whole country watching, all the Times Square spectaculars did their neighborly number. On its message center, Budweiser flashed "Budweiser Salutes 'America After Dark' and Welcomes Little Lulu." Admiral, TWA, and the others offered similar greetings. Kleenex replied on its message center, "Little Lulu Thanks Broadway for Warm Welcome." Nobody was happier than the public relations man—except, perhaps, Little Lulu and her equally feisty creator, Marjorie Henderson Buell, who had negotiated for herself a royalty worthy of a princess for the use of her spunky character.

The Little Lulu Kleenex spectacular, which was modified and rebuilt twice before it finally came down in 1965, was a demonstration of the neon animator's art at its best—not merely because of its engineering complexity but even more because of its charm and entertainment value. It was an expression of pure joy. Little Lulu didn't know, of course, that the decline of pictorial neon animation was just a few years away. But even if she had known, I'm sure it wouldn't have dampened her exuberance one little bit.

## Hurtling into the Future

*The TWA sign that replaced* the Budweiser railroad display on Toffenetti's roof in 1955 was of a different artistic order than its witty and elegant neighbors. Built for speed and hard sell, the eight-story behemoth embodied the "Everything for everybody—right now!" sensibility that drove American consumerism and the advertising that fueled it in the mid-1950s.

Designed by TWA's art director Rex Werner, who built the model for it in his home workshop in Darien, Connecticut, the sign was a baroque extravaganza that incorporated every display technique known to man—and a few innovations too. Just as air travel now made it possible to "see 21 European cities in 17 days," the sign's barrage of messages created in viewers the dazed synesthesia often experienced by survivors of those seventeen-day jaunts.

It was surmounted by a two-fifths-size scale model of the Lockheed Super Constellation, the leading passenger airline of the day, complete with spinning propellers, blinking running lights, a cabin full of dummy passengers, and pastel gel lights playing across its belly to create the illusion of speeding through the stratosphere. It boasted two separate information-packed lamp banks, one stationary and one traveling, and a 30-by-20-foot tri-vision they called a "Scenearama," depicting changeable, rotating scenes of TWA destinations. The first set oddly juxtaposed California, Paris, and Arizona.

Underscoring the 45-foot plane was the message "FLY TWA," with TWA letters 20 feet tall, that spelled on at a normal speed, then spelled off a little faster, then spelled on even faster, off faster, on faster, faster and faster until it developed into a wiping effect, then a chasing motion—as if you were really taking off, with your heart in your throat.

Beneath that, "breathing" neon letters proclaimed "USA ★ Europe ★ Africa ★ Asia." And stretching 100 feet across the bottom of the sign was an elaborate blue-and-white neon-and-lamp logo consisting of a "breathing" multilayered five-pointed star, an aerodynamic wing, and the words "Lockheed Super Constellation" in a combination of italic caps and script. This logo was also wired to animate at ever-increasing speeds, the climax of the sequence being a blinding flash of light that started as a pinpoint at the tip of the wing and traveled along the wing into the center of the star, setting off a flash of sixty photo floods.

It wasn't exactly a beautiful sign, perhaps, but it was arresting. Like the decade itself, it seemed to be hurtling toward a faster, slicker, more technologically complex future. The shining model airplane that flew in ghostly solitude above the sign's pyrotechnics reminded us that the world was getting smaller every day.

I doubt, however, that "smaller" as a concept was getting much play on the Astor roof on the hot June night in 1955 when the sign was turned on. In a coup that must have assured their careers, the publicity department at TWA had secured the switch-throwing services of mega-celebrity Jayne Mansfield, a larger, puffier, gaudier version of Marilyn Monroe, the 1950s male ideal of womanhood. Mansfield's vaunted statistics were 40-21-35½-163—the last figure being her reported IQ. History has been kind to Monroe, and perhaps someday Mansfield too will rate another look. But at the time, she was just a female version of a new car with bigger fins than last year's model.

Mansfield was then wowing audiences with her acting skills in the Broadway play *Will Success Spoil Rock Hunter?* and witnesses report that at the turn-on ceremony, stuffed precariously into a black sausage-skin-tight evening gown with a white feather boa, she played her one-note role to the hilt. The dummy switch for the occasion was designed to resemble an aircraft throttle. All eyes were riveted on the way Ms. Mansfield's hand caressed this throttle while she made her speech. (Afterward, nobody remembered the speech.) Then, at the signal, she grasped the throttle and gave it a heave, there was an explosion of light, and giant engines—the sound of an actual Constellation, recorded earlier that day at Idlewild Airport—roared into action.

Whether or not anyone noticed, something happened that night. Glamour became glitz. Art became special effects. Celebrity replaced personality. And marketing replaced soul.

None of this was absolute, of course. The world doesn't change all at once just because one bosomy blonde flips a throttle. The Canadian Club signature, for example, continued to pen its elegant way across Times Square's night sky until 1975, and the graceful Anheuser-Busch eagle soared for almost as long. But if there was one defining moment when the art and aspirations embodied in the American spectacular of the 1920s and 1930s were transformed into an entirely different aesthetic, it was here, at the midpoint of the golden decade that was the midpoint of the electric century.

TWA's sensational sentinel was clearly a sign of the future—and very popular too. It was repeated on Randolph Street in Chicago and replicated throughout the country. Its multimedia approach foreshadowed the Sunkist Smell-O-Ramas in New York and Los Angeles, which provided olfactory as well as visual stimulation. And its daring, futuristic approach may have inspired some other companies—such as Citgo in Boston, now a landmark—to brave the unfamiliar terrain of spectacularity.

But for the most part, by the end of the 1950s, the great age of the advertising spectacular in the rest of America was coming to an end. And things were starting to change in Times Square as well. The great smoking Camel sign came down in 1966, the same year that Sony, the first Japanese sign, went up—truly a symbol of the Changing of the Guard.

## 7. *Out with the Old, In with the New*

T he Times Square of the teens through the fifties that we are

so drawn to now is the one we turned away from in the two

decades that followed.

The "Triumph of Youth Culture" that everybody was talking about in the 1960s necessarily implied the defeat of Old Culture. Compromise is a gift of middle age—and nobody then was, or would admit to being, *there.*

While decrying, for the record, the flamboyant "sex, drugs, and rock 'n' roll" agenda of Youth, matrons donned miniskirts, and workadaddies sported Nehru jackets, beaded necklaces, and side-burned Beatles hairstyles at business meetings. Everything seemed sexualized, and carried a hint of high. Even Republican politicians, in an attempt to appear "with it," uttered phrases like "cool," "groovy," and "turn me on." The cultural hegemony of youth, without a conspiracy, a business plan, or a press agent, was engaging in some spectacular marketing of its own.

Out with the Old, In with the New. Down with the downtown, up with the Mall. Old music, old art, old cities—all were passé.

Nothing epitomized this like the demise of old buildings, as irreplaceable vaulted theaters, sports arenas, and transportation hubs met the wrecking ball. We couldn't tear them down fast enough. It was a nationwide craze.

New York's Penn Station, McKim, Mead & White's 1910 Beaux-Arts masterpiece in cream travertine and pink granite modeled after the Baths of Caracalla, was demolished in 1966. In Chicago, the Old Stock Exchange, Adler & Sullivan's classic creation that had adorned the Loop since 1895, fell to the wrecking ball in 1971. More than half of the extraordinary buildings designed by Frank Furness, Philadelphia's master of the Victorian extravaganza, were destroyed by 1973—and many of the rest were mangled beyond recognition.

Detroit's magnificent City Hall, built in 1871, succumbed to the bulldozer in 1961 to make way for an underground parking garage identified in an increasingly forlorn urban landscape by a forbidding concrete bunker—and its splendid Michigan Theater, one of the city's great entertainment palaces of the 1920s, was razed for parking too. All but one of Dayton's historic theaters—the entire district—fell like dominoes. In New Orleans, the wholesale destruction of the city's historic commercial downtown—with the singular exception of the landmark-protected French Quarter—was locally dubbed the "demolition derby."

This orgy of destruction—prosecuted over the objections of critics and preservationists, whose concerns were deemed eccentric and trivial—was a conscious abandonment of the past. In many cases, the demolitions occurred, not for the purpose of building something new, but merely to save the owners the burdens of maintenance and tax money. The period marked a pinnacle of parking-lot production in the United States.

## NAXON

*One dubious renovation was the* stripping of the Times Tower down to its steel bones by the Allied Chemical Corporation in the brief hope of establishing Allied Chemical as a permanent, futuristic presence. The idea was to create a "Showcase of Chemistry" celebrating Allied's leadership in the world of plastics, fibers, building materials, and chemicals. Allied's tenure lasted barely three years, but in that time it managed to replace the building's elaborately hand-carved granite and terra-cotta Beaux-Arts facade of 1904, once favorably compared with Giotto's Campanile, with slabs of dull white marble.

There was a bright spot in this desecration, however. In connection with the renovation of the famous motograph that encircles the base of the building, Allied had Artkraft Strauss install one of the last great electromechanical sign controllers, named the Naxon after its now otherwise anonymous inventor.

Everybody loved the Naxon. It is everyone's all-time favorite machine. And the more knowledgeable one is about machinery, the more ingenious it appears to be.

This room-sized wonder attracted so many admirers that it was placed behind a glass-windowed wall. Visitors, as captivated as cats, would stand watching—and listening, and sniffing the ozone—as thousands of ball bearings rolled down an inclined plane, onto a set of twisting worm gears, past a series of electrical contacts, and then, through a set of copper tubes, back up to the top to go around again. Meanwhile, on the outside of the building, a message in 6-foot-tall capital letters "traveled" around and around the tower, bringing people the headlines of the hour. How did it work?

The Naxon machine was actually seven machines in parallel, one for each row of a seven-dot-high letter. (All of the alphanumeric characters in the English alphabet can be created on a matrix that is seven dots high and five dots wide.)

The message started out as a tape, with the shapes of letters punched out perpendicular to the length of the tape. Each hole represented an "on" lightbulb. The tape was spliced end to end, creating a continuous loop, and threaded into a mechanical reader that drove the tape along while "reading" it by means of seven plunger-type fingers. When a finger encountered a hole, it completed a circuit that closed a relay that de-energized a coil that dropped a ball bearing. The intervals between the ball bearings determined the spaces between the "on" lightbulbs.

The seven 5-foot worm gears were like screws turning in place. As they rotated, the balls were driven along the worm gears' length, flipping the 12,400 individual switches that turned each of the lamps on and off. The balls traveling along the parallel worm gears created the illusion that the letters were "traveling" around the building. At the end of their journey, the balls were fed into copper tubes, where they pushed one another up and along to start the cycle over again.

Watching this machine was a multisensory experience. Besides the clickety-click-click of the tumbling metal balls and the cricketlike, sparky whir of more than 12,000 switches switching, the smell of ozone filled the air—trillions of positive ions created by all that flying electricity, as in the country after a storm.

Amazingly, this machine survives—it is stored in a warehouse outside of Dallas. No one knows how it got there. One of these days, industrial nostalgia will reach the point where someone finds it viable to resurrect this relic of the electromechanical age and put it back into operation.

## Pop Goes the Billboard

*Pop Art burst onto the* scene during the 1960s, cheerfully and brazenly mining the common commercial culture for images. A reaction against Abstract Expressionism with its cerebral lack of surface, Pop Art found tackiness in the sublime—and vice versa. Paradox and irony were in play, big time.

While advertising had long been denigrated by the sophisticated art world as a mere running dog of capitalist imperialism, Pop Art acknowledged advertising as the transcendent expression of American cultural values. Andy Warhol's meticulously rendered soup cans and soap cartons; Roy Lichtenstein's surreally magnified comic strip frames; Claes Oldenburg's droopy, outsized sculptures of objects such as bathroom fixtures, typewriters, and hamburgers—all elevated ordinary commercial images to the level of high art. Pop Art acknowledged the dominance of image over reality in the American psyche—an endorsement of form over substance that went beyond Marshall McLuhan's 1960 dictum that "the medium *is* the message."

Pop mirrored America's obsession with image and gave it new meaning. It played with the paradox between cynicism and celebration that is not only the hallmark of advertising art but also the essence of America's ambivalence toward art and culture.

Many of the new Pop artists came out of the world of commercial art. Hyperrealist James Rosenquist started his career in the early 1950s painting barns, silos, and gas stations in Iowa, Wisconsin, and North Dakota (not pictures of those things, the things themselves), and then worked for General Outdoor as a billboard painter. Moving to New York in 1956, he worked briefly at Artkraft Strauss, where his nickname was Rosie.

"Rosie was a great artist, but not a particularly good billboard artist," remembers my cousin Gene. "He kept painting things the way he thought they should look, rather than the way the customers wanted them to look." Luckily for Rosie, he was soon discovered by the galleries, and his real career took off.

Because of this common heritage—and also just as a sign of the times—billboard art and Pop Art enjoyed a productive symbiosis, inspiring each other to new heights. Hand-painted billboard art—soon to be replaced by computer-produced vinyls—reached its pinnacle during the 1960s and became the leading sign form.

Los Angeles's Sunset Strip epitomized this golden age with its images of supersized celebrities reigning like deities, decontextualized, in midair. Marilyn, Ringo, Groucho, Cher, Santana—as well as celebs who required two names for name recognition—inhabited billboards with cutouts that took their portraits beyond the restrictions of the frame. Op Art and psychedelic art too stretched the boundaries of billboard reality, employing dazzling colors and dizzying optical effects to capture the eyes, and, more important, the minds, of viewers.

Taking a cue from the 1954 Jack Lemmon–Judy Holliday movie, *It Should Happen to You,* one aspiring starlet, Mamie Van Doren, owed her start to an appearance on Sunset's boards. Her press agent spent their entire marketing budget renting four of them, and had them embellished with an outline of the big blonde's voluptuous figure and the provocative question "Where's Mamie?" This led to Mamie's Big Break and several movie roles—including her trademark star turn in *Sex Kittens Go to College*—before the actress faded back into obscurity. (Advertising is powerful, but it can't accomplish miracles.)

The billboard art of the period has been extensively documented elsewhere, but it is worth noting that the movement of the center of sign art from the East Coast to the West parallels the westward migration of the "soul" of TV. As our culture became less cerebral and more visual, New York took a back seat to Hollywood in the control of what Americans see. As what we see—in movies, on TV, and now in the universe of computers—started to become more important than what we read, Hollywood asserted itself as the center of the entertainment industry, and its imagery became predominant.

In Times Square, the movie displays of the early 1960s still retained the spectacular character of the 1950s. *Cast a Giant Shadow,* for example, starring Kirk Douglas, Frank Sinatra, Yul Brynner, and John Wayne, did indeed cast a giant shadow, as a 57-foot-tall Kirk Douglas towered over the 6-foot-high heads of his co-stars. At the same time, the new artistic sensibility had arrived. Pictorial billboard art by then had achieved portrait quality, thanks largely to the fine artists entering the field. It had lost the flat, idealized, animated-cartoon effect it had possessed since the days of Maxfield Parrish, and was approaching the photo-realism it would shortly achieve in reality. Close-ups of the paintings of the cast of *Cast* show every pore and follicle rendered in uncompromising, three-dimensional detail.

Reprising the aesthetic of the 1950s could place a producer on the cutting edge of decadence. *Cleopatra,* with megastars Elizabeth Taylor, Richard Burton, and Rex Harrison, commanded an immense supersign of a hectic and confused lushness that matched the values of the production itself. The megamillion-dollar extravaganza—which still, after accounting for inflation, is said to hold the title of Most Expensive Movie Ever Made—was a fabulous flop. In 1963 it heralded the beginning of the end of the overwrought, over-budget Hollywood spectacle—just as it marked the beginning of the end of the Times Square cinematic supersign.

## Neon Goes Baroque

*The neon art of* Times Square, which had enjoyed a golden age in the 1950s, was still thriving in the 1960s, despite the apparent triumph of billboard art—but it was coasting on past glories rather than demonstrating true innovation. Classical neon is fundamentally incompatible with Pop Art anyway, since neon—clear, bright, hot, and happy—essentially lacks irony.

In 1964 Coca-Cola moved into its present position at the north end of Times Square with the 45-foot "Disc," a curvilinear interpretation of their famous logo. They would rebuild it into the "Wave" spectacular in 1969 when their upstairs neighbor, Canadian Club, rebuilt its reconceived logo also.

Douglas Leigh, still active, riffed on his popular "smoking" Camel sign by designing the "Gigantic Presto Spray-Steam Iron" at 45th Street, which, boasted Leigh, "puffs out three varieties of steam on a nonstop basis." He also designed a big Scripto pen, a million times larger than life, augmented by the somewhat retro image of rotating "atoms," an homage to the once-futuristic atomic age.

By the mid-1960s, the art of Times Square had become self-referential. The hype was there, and even the sincerity, but the true novelty and grandeur had faded. Leigh and Artkraft competed to see who could make the most extravagant claims about displays that were, all in all, pedestrian. In 1966, Leigh, promising signs that would be "bigger, flashier, and more spectacular" than ever, confided to a reporter that plans were under way "to create the greatest sign extravaganza yet known to sign-dizzy Times Square." What was it? An 80-foot-long Gordon's Gin bottle—nothing but a painted plywood cutout, really—pouring "a steady flow of neon gin" into a painted plywood martini glass. (As it turned out, the neon never materialized.) This, on the site once occupied by the 132-foot-long Bond waterfall, with its superhuman, neoclassical, neon-togaed nudes.

The claims of Artkraft were no less silly. We told the same reporter, writing for the *New York Herald Tribune,* that a display for Cue, a new Colgate-Palmolive brand that soon sank without a trace, represented "the world's largest toothpaste tube" (as if anyone went around measuring toothpaste tubes); and that Braniff Airlines' new motograph, at 100 feet long and 20 feet high, with 7,000 lamps, was "the world's largest [tallest, actually] moving-message sign." (This may have been true, but it was still just another moving-message sign.)

What is clear from these communiqués that, at a generation's remove, seem tinged with desperation is that Times Square in those days was a tough sell. With the rarest of exceptions, never, even in the darkest days, has anyone seen a Times Square advertising space that says "For Rent." This is partly due to the nature of the medium. Because any message planted in the Square takes on the aura of spectacularity, placing "Space Available" on an empty location is like proclaiming failure from the rooftops—and makes the space even harder to sell.

But even as the Square began to lose its luster in the eyes of its traditional customer base, big changes were brewing. The most striking symbol of the Changing of the Guard was the occurrence of two almost simultaneous events: the removal of the famous Camel smoker, who puffed his last puff on January 3, 1966, and the installation of Sony, the forerunner of what has been called the Japanese Invasion, on 1600 Broadway—atop the "cascade" of signs at the north end of the Square. This is the much-photographed high spot once occupied by such American stalwarts as Chevrolet, Four Roses, and Firestone.

Another two decades would pass before the Asians arrived in full force—and another decade more before the Americans fully returned. The old Times Square, of Ziegfeld, Damon Runyon, and O. J. Gude, had had its day.

# Ring-a-Ding-Ding!

*Meanwhile, in keeping with the* westward momentum of image making, Las Vegas was on a roll.

By the 1960s it had outgrown Glitter Gulch—Las Vegas's original downtown—and was spreading south into the desert. The Strip, America's new boulevard of dreams, was starting to reach dizzying new heights in the marketing of itself.

No place on earth has reinvented itself as flamboyantly and as often as Las Vegas. The city exists in layers, like ancient civilizations stacked atop each other to the delectation of archaeologists. We can see remnants of the old beneath the new, and remnants of the even older beneath the old. But we must look quickly, because in Las Vegas, nothing is built for the ages.

Today's top layer is the newest and most ambitious Las Vegas ever, a multibillion-dollar architectural hash of pretend Wonders of the World—a great black pyramid with a mighty beam of light streaming straight up from its point guarded by a Sphinx the size of a ten-story building; a working volcano, spewing smoke and flame high enough to look like a real emergency to the arriving air traveler who doesn't know better; the skyline of New York City in half-size, complete with the Chrysler and Empire State buildings and World Trade Center all jammed together in exuberant disregard of the actual geography. All this and more is packed along the Strip in what looks like the Everything in the World Theme Park. The whole sprawl looks like a movie set where the filming never stops. And there's precious little neon to be seen. Indeed, almost the only actual signs are the big electronic menu boards that tout blackjack odds and buffet prices. The buildings themselves *are* the signs. The architecture is the statement.

The second layer is what's left of the 1960s and 1970s, the older casino hotels that still depend on neon extravaganzas towering above the traffic. The Stardust, the Frontier, and Circus Circus are among the survivors, their impact muted by the clamorous crowding around them.

The third layer is actually better preserved than the second, and stands a better chance of surviving. It's old Glitter Gulch, once the downtown heart of Las Vegas, now rejuvenated and preserved beneath the canopy of the fabulous Fremont Street Experience—which we'll visit in a later chapter.

The original builders of Glitter Gulch in the 1930s and 1940s had shown the world how to embellish simple, low-rise buildings with elaborate, high-rise, dazzlingly animated displays. These neon-encrusted facades converted humble structures into seductive pleasure palaces that, in traditional Old West style, seemed to be larger than they actually were.

In the 1950s and 1960s, the architects of the Strip reached higher and even higher. They designed sprawling hotel-casino-entertainment complexes that were every bit as big as they looked—worlds unto themselves—and heralded them at curbside by means of colossal, pyrotechnical towers. These amazing light sculptures, taking advantage of the desert's luxury of space, were freestanding and three-dimensional—ingeniously engineered to support immense weight and intricate electromechanical effects. Built to be viewed from long distances, way out in the desert on the approaching highway or from the air—unlike Times Square spectaculars—these pylons stood alone in the landscape like separate sentinels, the identifying towers of self-contained city-states within Las Vegas-land.

The first of these literally *was* a tower—the Flamingo's Champagne Tower, a cylinder 80 feet high and 20 feet in diameter, covered entirely with giant neon champagne bubbles. Built in 1953, it effervesced through the 1960s. Its contemporary, the Dunes' one-sultan welcoming committee—a dashing, bearded, turbaned figure who might have stepped out of a gargantuan production of *Kismet*—was so big, a real chorus girl in Frederick's of Hollywood-style harem lingerie standing alongside him in a publicity shot barely reached his ankle. In 1964, he found a new home alongside a Los Angeles freeway.

The sultan's replacement at the entrance to the fabled entertainment mecca—an abstract, three-dimensional pylon proclaiming "The Dunes"—stood an awesome eighteen stories high and boasted 17,000 linear feet—more than three miles—of neon tubing and 7,200 incandescent bulbs. This 1964 display, the work of the Los Angeles Division of Federal Sign, became the pacesetter, according to Charles F. Barnard in his beautiful photographic study of Las Vegas displays,

*The Magic Sign.* It established the inverted-pyramid format—enormous permanent "heraldry" at the top designed for long-range viewing; decoration running up, down, and between the stanchions; and changeable information panels at the bottom, growing smaller near eye level—that later Strip signs largely followed.

The Stardust's new display, two years later and, at eight feet taller, briefly the world's tallest freestanding electrical sign, featured an ethereal burst of shimmering diamond shapes in neon and enough incandescent bulbs to cast a glimmering glow over a huge chunk of the night Stripscape—a shower of electric stardust, the visual equivalent, though in transcendent size, of Hoagy Carmichael's romantic standard. Not to be outdone, the Frontier next door opted for its name in mammoth western-style letters on a pair of pylons 200 feet high. And Circus Circus, Las Vegas's first bid for the family trade, beckoned its constituency starting in 1968 with a jolly clown 100 feet tall, bursting in bright stripes and swirls of red, pink, and yellow, brandishing a pinwheel-spiraling lollipop. Each of his floppy red-and-yellow shoes is bigger than a locomotive.

Words fail at the prospect of describing the sheer size of these constructions. Each one is larger than any building most of the people in the world have ever seen. And they are covered with light! All have built-in elevators for servicing from the inside, and most also conceal internal maintenance rooms, where spare parts are stored and computer controllers—the "brains" of the displays—hum away.

Even Tom Wolfe, rarely at a loss for words, threw up his hands when confronting Las Vegas. "But such signs!" he wrote in *The Kandy-Kolored Tangerine-Flake Streamline Baby* in 1965. "They tower. They revolve, they oscillate, they soar in shapes before which the existing vocabulary of art history is helpless. I can only attempt to supply names—Boomerang Modern, Palette Curvilinear, Flash Gordon Ming-Alert Spiral, McDonald's Hamburger Parabola, Mint Casino Elliptical, Miami Beach Kidney."

There was no precedent for the Las Vegas spectacular. The companies that created it, in all its permutations over more than sixty years, were equipped only with hardware, engineering ingenuity, and imaginations as vast as the West itself. The customers were America's high rollers, armed with bankrolls almost big enough to buy the sun, moon, and stars. As we know from our visit here in the 1930s, the Young Electric Sign Company started it all, and dominated the electric flowering of Las Vegas until the 1960s. The work of YESCO designers Kermit Wayne, Jack Larsen, Sr., Ben Mitchem, and Hermon Boernge, acclaimed by Tom Wolfe as "the designer-sculptor geniuses of Las Vegas," deserves to be ranked with the greatest American commercial art.

While YESCO remains a dominant player, the 1960s boom brought other companies to the gaming table, including Federal, Heath, and aggressive young AD-ART. "We brought a new sense of graphic design and the use of new materials, an appreciation of plastics and electronics," says Terry Long, the president of AD-ART. "These elements became increasingly important in the coming years as neon started to fall out of favor throughout the country."

As the 1960s progressed, the heroic, freestanding pylons marking the entrances to the pleasure palaces gradually yielded in importance as the porte cocheres of the complexes, and eventually the architecture itself, began to dominate. Starting with Caesars Palace in 1966, in a trend that would not reach New York for another twenty-five years, the signs became, not signs associated with, or affixed onto, buildings, but architectural features incorporated into the buildings themselves. The buildings *became* the signs. And the insides of the buildings expressed themselves on the outsides: the experience moved out onto the street. By the 1990s, vast new hotel-entertainment-gambling complexes such as New York, New York; Luxor; and the MGM Grand, while dazzlingly illuminated, no longer had identification signs separate from the buildings themselves.

In their landmark 1972 thesis, *Learning from Las Vegas,* architects Robert Venturi, Denise Scott Brown, and Steven Izenour analyzed Las Vegas's built environment as a cultural expression worthy of serious study. Route 95 through Las Vegas, they wrote, is "the archetype of the commercial strip, the phenomenon at its purest and most intense. We believe a careful documentation and analysis of its physical form is as important to architects and urbanists today as were the studies of medieval Europe and ancient Rome and Greece to earlier generations."

They were not the first architects, they admitted, to attempt to gain insight from the existing landscape—as opposed to the more autocratic, top-down approach of simply tearing it down and replacing it, as Le Corbusier suggested doing with Paris in the 1920s. But their nonjudgmental "learning from everything" approach was more open-eyed and open-minded than most. And by questioning how we look at the commonplace, they bestowed intellectual legitimacy on the commercial landscape, as well as giving people a new way of thinking and speaking about it—with far-reaching consequences, including, perhaps, the Municipal Art Society of New York's successful commitment to "Save Times Square" in the 1980s.

The unique and still unparalleled development of Las Vegas displays was possible because of their singular purpose. Unlike Times Square, which is traditionally an advertising theme park, promoting everything from smokes to cabarets to fashion to automobiles, Las Vegas has only one product to sell: itself. The vast majority of its signs are on-premise business signs, not third-party advertising signs. And the "self" it sells is an environment: places where things happen, places where *you* may become lucky! It makes perfect sense for the signs to be incorporated into the shells of these fantasy environments. When you enter into the display, you simultaneously enter into the fantasy.

## OH, THEM SILVER SLIPPERS!

*The biggest sign graveyard in* the world is in Las Vegas. Owned and operated by YESCO, the Boneyard, as sign people call it, is the final resting place for hundreds of dead signs, the commercial archaeologist's ultimate dig.

Lined up neatly on the raked gravel inside the chain-link fence that encloses the grounds of YESCO's spotless Las Vegas factory are the faded relics of the city's fabled past, row after row of them, all packed in tightly with stacks of younger plastic castoffs from Las Vegas's perpetually rebuilding commercial landscape.

Here's Toyota, its bright red logo spray-painted and baked onto a rectangle of heat-formed translucent plastic. And NatWest Bank, a big plastic box with rounded corners and raised plastic letters, one of a thousand once internally illuminated by fluorescent lamps and mounted on a pole alongside a convenient drive-through branch. And a generic Bar-B-Que, also in heat-formed, robot-painted plastic, its artificially charred black letters contrasting with a peeling, burnt orange background. Efficient, practical, cost-effective, easily replaceable—and lifeless. Whatever spirit they had is long departed.

In welcome contrast, the battered old-timers are a joy to behold.

The 1956 Golden Nugget Casino sign—its red face washed dull by the sun, its scalloped border and Old West lettering outlined in black holes once occupied by white and golden lamps—commands a regal position in a corner of the yard. A jumbo golf ball, a roadside invitation to some putt-putt course of yore, stands alongside like a faithful, stumpy sidekick.

The original Silver Slipper—its lustrous surface peeling, stripped of the myriad of small white lamps that once made it glitter as it revolved on a pole above the entrance to the casino that bore its name—has been placed carefully away from traffic in the yard. It seems to invite a tender, consoling touch. This old lady was once a debutante who could dance all night.

A rusty blue vertical sign that says, simply, MOTEL, still attached to the braces that held it to a pole on a pre-interstate thoroughfare where it served as a beacon for tourists of a bygone day, pokes through the tidy piles of metal, plastic, glass, and wire.

Even higher above the organized clutter is the double-sided Hacienda Hotel caballero, tall and resplendent atop a rearing golden palomino with a once-snowy white mane. He was the principal greeter and sentinel at a quintessentially 1950s establishment on the outskirts of town that became an early casualty of the city's rapid expansion.

"This was a fine piece of work," says my host, the CEO of YESCO, Thomas Young, Jr., pausing on our tour to admire the cheery horseman, drawn almost crudely, as if by a high-spirited child, in metal, paint, and electric lamps.

"See"—he points—"a pole-mounted sconce went right up through the horse and rider, and the whole thing rotated. Clever in its day. The builder had to be resourceful. Each of these pictorial signs posed a slightly different problem. The customer would say, 'I want a sign that has a dashing caballero on a horse, and I want it to turn and light up, and I want him to wave his hand, and I want it to be the biggest thing seen by people driving in from way out in the desert. Can you do that?' The answer, of course, is 'Of course.'"

Tom, a grandfatherly gentleman who with the addition of a white beard would make a perfect Santa Claus in *Miracle on 34th Street,* is the son of YESCO founder Thomas Young, Sr. As such, he's more than a CEO. He's the chief trustee of a company that is widely regarded as an institution. And being an institution is not always easy.

With 500 employees and plants in six western cities, YESCO is one of the largest sign companies in the world. Yet, to many, what YESCO is all about is contained right here in this Boneyard. Venturi, Brown, Izenour, and their army of industrious Yale graduate students discovered the yard in 1968 with the enthusiasm of archaeologists cracking the tomb of Tutankhamen. On its publication their study drew scores of scholars and journalists and photographers to the Boneyard, and today the stream of visitors continues unabated.

"This isn't a museum," Tom says, a bit wearily. "It's a working scrap yard. Signs come in and they go out. Sometimes they fall apart here. We try to take care of them, but there's weather and high wind. We get an occasional twister through here. I suppose it's so popular because it's the closest thing we have to a real neon museum. It's not even open to the public, but we hate to turn anyone away."

The Boneyard stays busy even at night. Many of the signs are wired together and can be lit, giving a temporary new burst of life to the enfeebled relics. The night scene is a photographer's feast, all ghostly flickers and portentous shadows. Many of the movies and TV shows that shoot in Las Vegas find a way to write in a Boneyard scene, just because it's so nifty. Countless rock-and-rollers have filmed music videos here.

*GQ* magazine had a party in the Boneyard, wining and dining classy fashion advertisers amid the glowing sign corpses. The magazine sent in crews to lay red carpet on the paths between the rows of signs and set up a tent housing a bar, buffet table, and band. At sundown the limos began to arrive, depositing their chic passengers at the end of the carpet runway.

The Boneyard even has the distinction of having served as the setting for a porn movie. "It wasn't our idea," Tom hastens to explain. "An employee sneaked a crew in here one night. Security caught them, and now that employee is an ex-employee."

I look around at all the rusty, jagged metal edges, broken glass, and coarse gravel. "But, how did they, uh..."

"The mind of man," says Tom. "You tell me."

## MARKETING WITH A BIG STICK

*Back in New York,* the 1964–65 World's Fair, on the 646-acre site at Flushing Meadow in Queens formerly occupied by the fabled 1939 World's Fair, was a bonanza for the local construction industry. Billions were spent by American corporations eager to strut their stuff. For local sign businesses, it happily took up the slack caused by advertising deflation and the decline of the art of neon.

Under the aegis of Robert Moses, the omnipotent demolition-and-construction czar who had also masterminded the 1939 Fair, the 1964–65 World's Fair celebrated two rather disjunctive themes. One was the commemoration of the 300th anniversary of British forces under the command of the Duke of York wresting control of the city of New Amsterdam from the Dutch in 1664; and the other was the dawning of the space age. The Fair's confusing, and weirdly intimidating, slogan was "Peace Through Understanding: Man in a Shrinking Globe in an Expanding Universe."

One of the Fair's problems was that it wasn't sanctioned by the Bureau of International Expositions, so most European countries, as well as the entire Communist bloc, boycotted it. Nonetheless, some thirty-six countries in Asia, South America, the Middle East, and Africa were represented. But it was U.S. industry, led by General Electric, Ford, General Motors, Chrysler, IBM, Bell Telephone, U.S. Steel, Pepsi-Cola, Du Pont, RCA, and Westinghouse, that spent lavishly, erecting nearly 100 mammoth pavilions stuffed with "edutainment" that they hoped would boost their consumer image.

IBM, believing (erroneously, as it turned out) that it had a lock on the future of the computer, offered a mundane exhibit on the similarities between the mechanical and the human brain. Ford offered a ride in a new convertible on a track through Disney-created dioramas depicting clichéd images of the dawn of life and the coming Space Age. General Electric too used Disney "audio-animatronic" characters to dramatize the glories of Progressland—an extensive display of GE products—under its bulging 200-foot-diameter lighted dome. AT&T showcased the videophone, breathlessly promising it would imminently be the communications medium of choice. Du Pont cutely used live actors and dancers to demonstrate chemical reactions.

Perhaps I shouldn't criticize this Fair, because at the time it helped pay my tuition. Artkraft Strauss built virtually all the Fair's spectacular signs and many of its huge sculptural displays, under the direction of the customers' corporate image design teams. For nearly two years our shop was crammed with sections of lighted extravaganzas and huge metal objects, pieces of a giant puzzle that would be assembled on-site at Flushing Meadow. And every piece, it seemed, was studded with corporate logos. We were awash in logos—big ones, little ones, shiny ones, brightly painted ones, richly burnished ones, and dazzlingly illuminated ones—all icons America had grown up with. Now, I am second to none in my appreciation of the American corporate logo and all the magic and promise it implies. But the 1964 World's Fair, it seemed to me, wasn't about anything *but* logos—a monumental exercise in ham-fisted marketing.

The 1939 World's Fair is remembered and cherished because it had a genuine vision of the future—a naive vision, perhaps, but a vision nonetheless. It had personality, imagination, energy, whimsy. It looked to a world beyond the war everyone knew was coming, and found a renewed sense of community. Most people experienced a sense of awe and wonder. And in memory, it still has a glow.

David Gelernter, in his comprehensive *1939: The Lost World of the Fair*, writes: "In that small slice of time and space, the city and its vast visiting crowds enjoyed what might be the best gift of all—to glimpse and not yet possess the promised land." The 1939 Fair, he writes, "was a credo in stucco and steel."

Historian Alan Anderson, who maintains a Web site on the 1939 Fair, writes: "To go to this Fair was to have your life changed forever. It was there that I was amazed by a device that measured the thickness of my hair, by a General Motors vision of 1960 (I asked my parents whether I'd still be alive at that distant time in the future), by mighty Railroads on Parade and Railroads at Work, by climbing up to look into the cockpit of a real airplane, by witnessing for the first time something called television; and I was chilled by the sight of a gas mask, as if I realized that here was a sign of what soon would dash or delay many of the hopes that THE FAIR expressed. . . . I have never forgotten THE FAIR. I think it has given me a better perspective on human beings as dreamers, aspirers, hopers, and builders than I could have had if there were not somewhere in me memories of THE FAIR."

The difference in public affect between the 1939 and 1964 Fairs is stellar. As Thomas Hine notes in *Populuxe*, a cultural history of the 1950s and 1960s, the 1964 World's Fair felt tired. "There was clearly not the kind of overwhelming enthusiasm for such a grand excursion into the future that might have been found only a few years before," he writes. "Americans seemed to be getting a bit jaded about the future; it had been around for too long a time."

I attended the 1964 Fair as a teenager, and I wasn't even born in 1939. But, in yet another example of image overwhelming reality, my "memory" of the 1939 GM "Futurama" ride, with its sweeping, visionary vistas, is more vivid than my impressions of the 1964 Fair, which seemed, more than anything, pompous and *large*—emblematic of everything wrong with the adult world.

Exhibit buildings celebrated their own girth and sprawl, bragged of the weight of their metal and electricity consumption, and touted their forests of ribs, buttresses, and toothy spires. If leadership were measured in tonnage, American business as represented in the 1964 World's Fair was truly the master of the industrial universe.

But that 1950s view of the world was already becoming obsolete. The dominance of American corporations in such fields as auto manufacturing and electronics would be openly challenged by the end of the decade. And signs of the coming economic earthquake were evident in 1964—to anyone who could read them.

The Volkswagen Beetle was already a fixture in the landscape, and Datsuns and Toyotas were multiplying on California streets. Complacent Detroit auto executives were blind to this as they piloted their boatlike gas-guzzlers through the streams of Pontiacs, Dodges, and

Mercs that filled Michigan freeways. Big engines, big power, and speed were the watchwords. "Little GTO, you're really lookin' fine," enthused a popular song of the day. "Three deuces and a four-speed, and a three-eighty-nine." Ronnie and the Daytonas spoke for Detroit.

Americans still bought hi-fi and television sets made in Pennsylvania and Delaware, and wore clothing made in North Carolina from fabric woven in Georgia. Pittsburgh steel—not Korean steel—was America's steel, and millions of miles of wire and cable were still extruded from it in old New England factories.

But the label "Made in Japan," a guarantee of lightweight quality and fragility in the 1950s, wasn't laughable anymore. The inexpensive transistor radios that flooded the country, enabling young people to take imported Beatlemania to the beach with them along with the Beach Boys, came from overseas. The suburban "discount" stores that would soon change American retailing forever already offered knockoffs of American products side by side with the real thing. Two decades later, many of those knockoffs would *be* the real thing. As early as 1965, anyone who hadn't heard the name Sony needed only go to Times Square and look up.

At the Fair, however, the modest, environmentally sensitive House of Japan was as threatening as a teahouse compared with the General Motors "Futurama"—a self-referential knockoff of its successful 1939 "Futurama"—a colossal barn with a cantilevered face that looked like a great maw taking a bite out of the earth.

Ford boasted the largest monograph sign at the Fair, a signature almost three stories high in dark blue plastic, spreading 188 feet across the side of a complex that contained a rotunda ringed by great curved teeth. Seven-Up went for sheer height with a tower almost eleven stories high, bearing a bulbous fiberglass logo. And IBM topped its pavilion with a gargantuan, slightly squashed "egg," emblazoned with more than a thousand .080 butyrate plastic logos, that was said to represent the company's bouncing Selectric typewriter ball.

A maze of rectangular prisms and scaffoldlike structures made up the Tower of Light, sponsored by 140 investor-owned power companies. This "Brightest Show on Earth" certainly lived up to its name. More than a hundred 1,500-watt quartz-iodine floodlights, with multicolored rotating gels, illuminated the base alone—which climbed to nine roof levels, each featuring a separate set of lighting technology and timers. The whole shebang was topped off by a *12 billion* candlepower beam, produced by twelve 5-kilowatt xenon bulbs of 1.08 billion candlepower each, pointed directly at the sky. But such a display of electrical muscle—the celebration of electricity for its own sake—was hardly as remarkable a theme in 1964 as it was in 1894.

As an exercise in spectacular marketing, the 1964 World's Fair was a spectacular flop. Its 50 million visitors (compared with 1939's profitable 45 million) were not enough to pay off its debts or finish Flushing Meadow Park in the glorious Promised Land fashion envisioned by Robert Moses. While the 1939 version has found a place in our folklore and in our collective memory of the way we felt about the world, the 1964 Fair, emotionally and spiritually empty as it was, has left few traces of its time on earth.

Part of the site is now home to the corporate logo-encrusted World Tennis Center, home of the U.S. Open. The Fair's welcoming symbol, the Unisphere, officially declared a landmark in 1995, survives as a symbol of the noble borough of Queens. And the eight-story-tall U.S. Royal Tire, which once boasted a real ferris wheel running around its circumference, long ago found a new home alongside a Detroit freeway.

Not surprisingly, the giant tire—an oversized toy that unfailingly makes the viewer smile—was the most popular display at the Fair. It had charm, wit, and charisma, the kind of touchability that endears us to big toys. It survives today—in an environment that is far more natural to it than the Fairgrounds—as a sentinel at the gateway of America's Motor City.

Today, the same American corporations that marketed themselves so ponderously in 1964 are the envy of the world. American workers are the most productive, and American corporations are the most efficient. Du Pont, AT&T, Ford, GM, GE, IBM, and the rest have rejuvenated themselves in the face of competition, and express a new dynamism in both their technological and their marketing skills.

But in any case, the day of the future-glorifying World's Fair seems to be over. In the 45 years following the 1894 Chicago Exposition, culminating in 1939, North America hosted fifteen World's Fairs. The next 60 years saw only six more—starting with the 1962 Seattle Century 21 Exposition ("Man in the Space Age") and ending in 1984 with the Louisiana World Exposition ("The World of Rivers"). The whole notion of Futurama is dwindling, or gone—perhaps because the future, as it has classically been conceived, is here now.

What the 1964–65 Fair, for all its self-congratulatory zeal, failed to foresee was the *real* future just in store.

# 8. *Information, My Boy!*

**M**y brother, Jonathan, came to work at Artkraft Strauss in 1976, shortly after Jake died. People thought the gruff, warmhearted, self-taught techno-whiz was a reincarnated version of the old man—only built to more modern, more generous, specifications.

"Frankly it was a boring era, signwise," Jonathan recalls. "Plastic-faced fluorescence was king. The earlier animated signs were much livelier. They used just paper tape and relays, but achieved lots more color and movement. Somehow the seventies were architecturally and designwise a rebellion 'back' from the wild sixties. 'Taste' was more important than interest or excitement."

It was the pure polyester period. Blasé and barely beige. The new American suburb, including its industrial parks, eschewed signs for shrubbery, with six-inch corporate identifications, installed at knee height, cowering behind the bushes. No more shouting from the rooftops for us, Corporate America seemed to be saying. Someone might get the wrong idea.

"This was when zoning codes started to prohibit neon and animation," remembers Jonathan, "and Plexiglas became strong and flexible enough to use for sign faces without blowing out. The on-premise identity sign switched from neon or animated lamps or interesting paint to plain Plexi logos. The stencil-cut and especially the difficult push-through plastic letter techniques came into common use. Also, aluminum became the material of choice for sign boxes, affordable as a common material for the first time. Pole signs abounded, but usually with boring round or oval or square Plexi faces instead of the earlier 'floating objects.'"

Materials triumphed over labor—"things" over craft. Earlier sign structures, with their delicate tracery of spiderweblike bolted or welded small steel—still to be seen in the Far East—are emblematic of a time when labor was cheap and materials expensive. The new single-pole structures, shop-fabricated and quickly lifted into place with large cranes, mark a change in the Point of Diminishing Returns. Labor became expensive and materials cheap.

The 1970s also saw the advent of computer-printed vinyl, a method of applying photographic images directly onto enormous fabric sheets that can be mounted onto billboards in a matter of hours—as compared with the weeks, and sometimes even months, required for artisans with rollers and brushes to transform a billboard or wall. This invention was destined to transform the face of fashion advertising. For the first time, advertisers were able to change their displays almost as easily as fashion models change their outfits.

But as interesting as plastics may be, it is hard to feel as much enthusiasm for new materials as for design vitality, creativity, and skill—the visible marks of the human hand.

Neon signs were still manufactured in the polyester period. But the glowing tubes in their traditional troughs were frequently concealed behind routed plastic faces in aluminum-track extrusions. Neon artisans gnashed their teeth to see their fine work hidden as if it were something shameful.

And in a way it was. Since it is always easier to attack the symbol than the reality, city planners, feeling helpless against the tide of pornography and honky-tonk that arose out of the darker side of the sexual revolution of the 1960s, went after the flashing signs they associated with it. A proliferation of zoning laws throughout the country banned direct display lighting in favor of Plexiglas coverings and cute carved wood. The number of aspiring neon apprentices shrank to just about zero—as if, in a mere fifty years, an exciting and promising art form had peaked early and then died.

"We tried to sell bright neon and got laughed at for being tacky and passé," recalls Jonathan. "People thought neon was strictly for the birds."

And this was especially true in Times Square.

## FLYING FROM THE LIGHT

*Times Square in the early* 1970s belonged to the pigeons—both the feathered variety in great gray flocks that nested in the empty sign structures and the human "marks" who crept along the walls of grimy pleasure emporia at all hours to purchase glimpses of bump-and-grind nudity, moments of ersatz affection, or mind-altering drugs that often as not turned out to be stove-blackened oregano.

New Yorkers despise pigeons. We consider them meta-vermin, flying rats infested with lice, symbolic of everything that is filthy and parasitical. We are horrified to learn that some people actually keep them as pets. "Why not keep mosquitoes?" we ask.

In the gritty dawn, when the breeze picks up, the avian flocks would whir awake and arise en masse from their steel perches to spend the day swirling around the Square, uncannily resembling the blowing newspapers that accompanied them.

This was Times Square's nadir—the bottom of a pit from which the only escape seemed to be a subway ride into a black hole. It seemed utterly laughable that in 1809 Washington Irving had once described the area as "a sweet rural valley, beautiful with many a bright flower, refreshed by many a pure streamlet, and enlivened here and there by a delectable Dutch cottage, sheltered under some sloping hill; and almost buried in embowering trees." Irving's embowering trees had long ago been chopped down to make wagon wheels, and most decent folk, both pedestrians and advertisers, had hopped on those wagons and fled.

Apart from a few diehards at the north end, such as Coca-Cola and Canadian Club (both rebuilt in 1969), most of the signs that were not blanked out with a pale gray cover coat were plywood painted in various shades of vulgarity.

There was the one we called the "tushy" sign—a large wraparound on the southwest corner of 46th Street and Broadway, featuring, on the 46th Street side, an ad for Desenex, the cure for diaper rash, and on the Broadway side, an ad for Coppertone, in which an ebony cocker spaniel playfully pulled down the drawers of an adorably abashed female tot, revealing her white, dimpled bottom—above the slogan "Don't Be a Paleface." (Just try an ad like that today! A politically incorrect quadruple-header invoking kiddie porn, animal-companion exploitation, racism, and ultraviolet radiation.)

Three other locations, paid for in theater tickets, were occupied by towel-clad cuties hawking the self-conscious topless-bottomless revue *Oh! Calcutta!* At the south end of the Square, on 42nd Street, the 200-foot Rialto theater wraparound wall and 60-foot tower were dedicated in desperation to the Public Art Fund, which covered them with flat, stylized, multiracial faces. A 30-foot painted bottle of St. Joseph's aspirin was an ongoing presence, the cure for a major headache.

Never did our signs tell us more about who we are than when they were empty. The answer was—quite literally—Blowing in the Wind.

## Energy Crisis, Anyone?

*Just as the cheerful prosperity* of the 1950s was created by a combination of forces, so too was the civic bleakness of the 1970s. Divided by the Vietnam War, dispirited by knavery in high places (President Nixon resigned in 1974 rather than face impeachment over the Watergate scandal), hung over from the thrilling excesses and unfulfilled promises of the 1960s, the American public was in a dark mood. It was ready for a takeover by the Crisis Industry.

A reassertion of the puritanism that always lurks beneath the surface of the American psyche proclaimed Doomsday at Hand. Guilty consumers must pay for past profligacy, we were told. The rivers were dying, the Great Lakes dead, the topsoil choked with poison. Toxic waste would soon engulf the Rockies.

On the other hand, as the joke goes, the cities were even worse. The Great Society proclaimed by President Johnson—who weirdly believed that without raising taxes we could simultaneously fight a land war in Asia and end poverty at home—had failed, as witnessed by soaring crime, the breakdown of the nuclear family, and rioting by the War on Poverty's intended beneficiaries, the urban ghetto dwellers. The white middle class was fleeing to the suburbs with the grim dedication of refugees—and an unprecedented number of their offspring were repairing to communes or foreign climes to escape this fractious confusion and live a simpler life.

Urban tax bases were shrinking, as a result partly of "white flight" and partly of the wholesale demolition of old, but taxpaying, buildings. New York City, facing the probability of a disastrous default on its bonds, appealed to the President for help, and received the reply that inspired the famous *New York Post* headline: "Ford to City: Drop Dead!" Pundits predicted a premature demise for the American Century.

**Swank on a swing:**
Florenz Ziegfeld glorified one of his All-American Girls by donating her services as the model for Pepsodent's 1929 extravaganza.
*Museum of the City of New York, The Gottscho-Schleisner Collection (88.1.4.720)*

**Welcome back, brew:**
On the day Prohibition ended in 1933, the "Malt" in the lower right corner of this Times Square spectacular changed to "Beer."
© *Collection of the New-York Historical Society*

**Catching the light:**
Millions of tiny mirrors that reflected ambient light filled the faces of
Times Square spectaculars during the World War II dimout.
*Collection of Artkraft Strauss*

**World's most famous sign:**
From 1941 to 1966, the Camel man blew smoke rings
made of steam across Times Square.
*Collection of Artkraft Strauss*

**Lyman Clardy, a nonsmoker,**
posed for this photo in 1941 and became the first Camel man.
*Collection of Lyman W. Clardy*

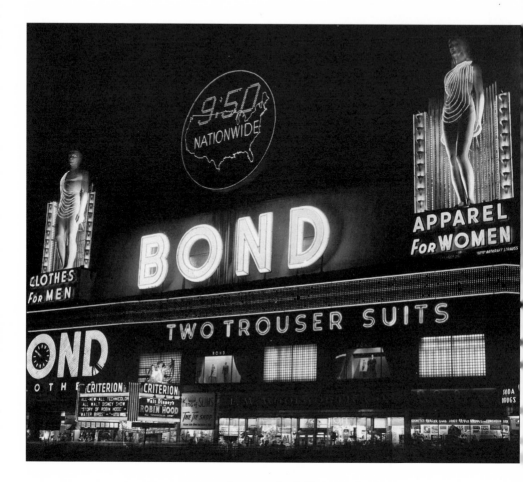

**Sexy waterfall:**
Neon-togaed statues of a man and a woman flanked
a real working mini-Niagara on the roof of
Times Square's Bond Building starting in 1947.
*Collection of Artkraft Strauss*

**Traveling torso:**
A section of the Bond man en route to his new home.
*Collection of Artkraft Strauss*

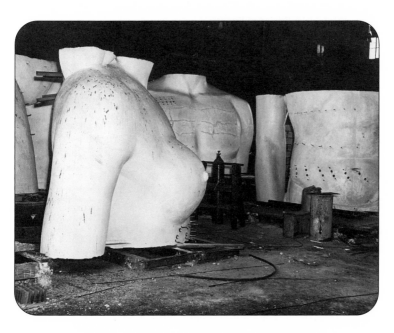

**The Bond lady's forma divina circa 1947:**
Anorexic supermodels weren't even born yet.
*Collection of Artkraft Strauss*

**A midtown bank**
gives its all for the war effort.
*Collection of Artkraft Strauss*

**"When the lights come on again . . .":** The dimout
ended in 1945, and by 1946 Times Square was aglow again.
Broadway looking north from 45th Street in the early 1950s.
© *Collection of the New-York Historical Society*

**Charm afoot:**
Miss Youth Form, 70 feet tall and every inch a lady, sashayed across this spec-
tacular, pivoted, and sat down millions of times—and her slip never rode up.
*Collection of Artkraft Strauss*

**Miss Youth Form** on her way to the top in 1947.
*Collection of Artkraft Strauss*

**Goodbye, neon nudes:**
In 1956, the Bond waterfall became the Pepsi waterfall,
with 50-foot bottles as sentinels.
*Collection of Artkraft Strauss*

**We Liked Ike:**
On election night 1952, Eisenhower's landslide victory over
Stevenson was charted on the face of the Times Tower.
© *"The New York Times"*

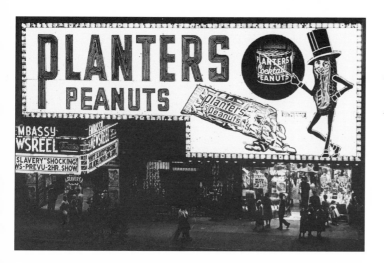

**Salty stuff:**
Mr. Peanut, monocled
aristocrat of snacks,
as he appeared in
Times Square in 1952.
*Collection of
Artkraft Strauss*

**The ever-changing gallery:**
Times Square in 1958.
*Collection of Artkraft Strauss*

**Disappearing railroad blues:**
A model train, repainted monthly to portray different sponsoring railroads,
chugged around this Times Square spectacular from 1947 into the 1950s.
*Collection of Artkraft Strauss*

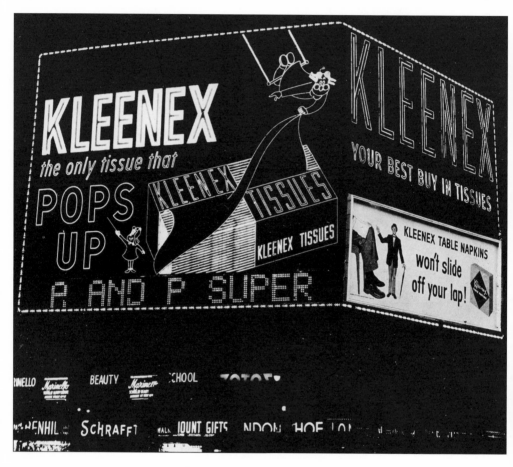

**Little Lulu on Broadway:**
The prefeminist cartoon heroine, the smart little girl
who always came out on top, introduced new colored tissue
in this popular 1956 spectacular.
*Collection of Artkraft Strauss*

**Hubba-hubba:**
Blond bombshell Jayne
Mansfield turns on TWA in 1956.
*Collection of Artkraft Strauss*

**Sign of the times:**
The ultramodern 1956 TWA spectacular, replacing
the Budweiser railroad, attacked the viewer with
every kind of technical razzle-dazzle known at the time.
*Collection of Artkraft Strauss*

**Times Square movie advertising,**
always a big show in itself, grew even bigger in the 1950s.
*Collection of Artkraft Strauss*

**Round-the-clock martyrdom:**
Ingrid Bergman's Joan of Arc burned at the stake nonstop in
Times Square—flaming by day, smoking by night.
*Collection of Artkraft Strauss*

**The end is nigh:**
Seen through the wreckage of the Astor Hotel
in the declining 1960s, a plywood gin bottle replaced
neon fish and waterfalls on the Bond Building.
*Photo by Ned Harris*

**Ball's eye view:** What the New Year's Eve Ball saw just before midnight, December 31, 1987. Spread below is the "new" Times Square, its renaissance under way.

© *Photo by Laura Mueller*

But while these grim prognostications contained elements of truth, they also contained the seeds of their own redemption. No one in the 1970s could have predicted that a mere twenty years later, commercial fishing would once again be a major industry on the Great Lakes, that the air in New York City would be cleaner than it had been at any time since before the coal-burning era, or that the rising expectations of the civil rights and feminist movements would so rapidly integrate businesses, universities, and the professions. Nor could anyone have predicted the comeback of the bison or that great man-made ecological miracle, the reforestation of the Northeast. There is something comforting about the Doomsday Scenario—at least one knows how the story ends—and since it has spawned an entire Doomsday Industry, complete with accredited experts and consultants, it is unlikely to take its rightful place in the landfill of history at any time soon.

More than any other event—or, more accurately, non-event—of the 1970s, the "energy crisis" of 1973–74 combined all the themes of group guilt and shame, bad economics, worse history, central planning gone awry, political correctness, and management by press release in a way that the signs themselves, by their very absence, illuminated in stunning relief.

When the Arab oil embargo in early 1973 drove the price of oil up from 30 cents a gallon to over a dollar, and the government responded by instituting rationing, the public responded by hoarding— an unconscious collusion between two mutually mistrusting entities that was bound to turn a minor problem into a disaster. It is generally agreed now that there never actually was an "energy crisis." There were spot fuel shortages, but they were caused more by people persistently keeping their tanks topped off than by an actual lack of supply. There was plenty of heating oil, motor oil, diesel fuel, and gasoline—but it was all in cans in people's garages or in tanks in their yards. The fear of the crisis *was* the crisis.

One proof that the "energy crisis" was a manufactured illusion is that there never was an "energy crisis" in Canada, which shares fuel supply sources with the United States. At Christmas 1973, when the Nixon White House celebrated the national malaise by illuminating the usually resplendent White House Christmas tree with a single flickering 15-watt plastic star, people in dimmed-out Detroit gazed wistfully across the Detroit River to Windsor, Ontario, which was gaily ablaze with seasonal decorations—and then hopped into their cars, using their precious, rationed teaspoonfuls of gasoline to drive across the Ambassador Bridge to Canada to do their Christmas shopping. The same kind of traffic jammed the bridges and highways between Sault Ste. Marie, Michigan, and Sault Ste. Marie, Ontario; Seattle/Tacoma and Victoria, British Columbia; Buffalo and Fort Erie; Duluth and Thunder Bay; Plattsburgh and Montreal. At no time was there a shortage of Christmas treats and gifts to buy in the United States. It was only the dearth of Christmas lights that prevented people from gathering and shopping. Darkness is death to downtowns.

Neon's gaudy effusion was decidedly out of style. The very visibility of signs and identifications which makes them so effective when information is in favor, makes them uniquely vulnerable when self-expression is out. Advertisers, lacking a meaningful response to a "crisis" that had no cause, opted for the public relations gesture and canceled their displays. Landmark signs across America, including a dozen Flying A and Eagles on Anheuser-Busch's breweries, were demolished and sent to the dump—even though high-voltage, low-amperage neon is highly efficient. The energy consumption of even the largest corporate logo was minuscule compared with that of its owner's new sealed skyscraper, which required heating and air conditioning around the clock. But the movement against neon was part of a larger picture, a general turning away from the light.

Tom Young of YESCO says that that period was the only time in the history of Las Vegas when the casino industry lost money. "People stopped coming here simply because the lights were out," he says. "The odds were the same, the entertainment was the same, the shows, the restaurants. . . . Nothing had essentially changed. Everything was open. And there was no problem with transportation. If people didn't want to bring their cars, well, they never had to. Trains, buses, and planes still ran, as they always have."

But each casino, which people were accustomed to seeing piercing the sky with watts and cheer, was permitted to display only one small-town-type on-premise business sign. "It almost killed us," Young admits. And the same was true in cities throughout the country. In Salt Lake City, Los Angeles, and Denver, people stopped shopping for more than necessities. Retail plummeted in the dark. The manufactured "crisis" had a devastating effect on the American economy.

There was a ripple effect as attendance at entertainment events declined. In Chicago, where the Loop was deserted, poor attendance at theaters, restaurants, and cinemas forced them to close—and to be demolished in hopes of better times. In Cleveland, two major department stores and nine out of ten downtown theaters closed, and the buildings sat empty, inviting desolation and graffiti. Across America, downtown business and theater districts, already ailing, closed up shop, taking many custom sign companies with them—and suburbanites Went to the Mall, which was safe, plastic, and white.

Nobody ever made money in the dark—at least not legally. Human beings are apparently hard-wired to seek the light and shun the darkness. This goes back to our cave-dwelling days, when we knew, without having to think about it, that it was smarter to stick close by the cave entrance, with its campfire, than to chance the dark, with its potential potholes and predators.

But, in a reprise of World War II, the government invited us to ignore the darkening of the light and continue our normal behavior. This was just not to be.

## WHAT'S NEW? PUSSYCAT!

*Even today, when some people* think of Times Square, they think of peeps. There are still a few venues where one can catch an eyeful of activities that are normally visible only to a camera's prurient eye—and, as far as about half the population is concerned, are better altogether left unseen.

Personally, I'm left cold by X-rated movies. They remind me of industrial documentaries about hydraulics. In 1973 I was thrown out of the big X-rated movie theater on Market Street in San Francisco, along with my boyfriend—for laughing out loud at the dialogue. (Thirty-year-old actress: "Hi, Uncle Harry!" Harry Reems: "Hi, little girl. Wanna play with my lollipop?")

Today's Times Square is essentially G-rated. The few surviving topless-bottomless bars and peep shows have been marginalized to the point of obscurity. But in the 1970s, with the commodification of sex, Sin and Times Square were synonymous.

"This wasn't entirely fair," points out Professor Eric Sandeen, director of the internationally recognized School of American Studies at the University of Wyoming at Laramie. I'm indebted to Professor Sandeen for the notion of reading Times Square as a text—a storybook of the American psyche.

"Any place can be read as a text," says Professor Sandeen. "But Times Square is the epitome of the American place. The way ultimate issues are negotiated is the same everywhere. It's all about how citizens assert power, and how a civilization remembers its past. If you can read Wyoming, you can read Times Square. The similarity is masked by differences of landscape—but what it all comes down to, in the end, is Land Use."

Through the 1970s and 1980s, Professor Sandeen led his graduate students on field trips to New York, where they created—and updated—the most comprehensive survey of street-level commercial uses within the Theater District, from 43rd to 52nd Street and from Sixth to Eighth Avenue, that had ever been done.

"There was never as much porn as people said there was," says Sandeen. Of 643 commercial establishments, he found, just 26, or 4 percent, were sex-related. "The demonization of porn, though, was real," he says. "It was being used to prepare the way for massive redevelopment. There was also a confusion between Times Square and 42nd Street—two quite different environments—in some cases willfully promulgated by the same forces that favored massive redevelopment."

Richie Basciano, the proprietor of X-rated Show World, agrees. "Why do you think there was so much crime on 42nd Street in those days?" he asks rhetorically. "The police went away. The real estate developers *sent* them away. They *wanted* more crime, to justify their condemnation of properties for real estate development."

But no matter. Image overrides Reality anytime, and in the 1970s sex became known as the Square's major industry—along with the unsinkable Broadway theater.

Legitimate theater owners carried the torch of "cleaning up"

Times Square—and ultimately they succeeded. But this is not without its touch of irony, since historically, the theater was rarely considered respectable. And Broadway itself always had a sort of raffish charm—the hint of the forbidden, the whiff of spice—as in Damon Runyon's charming tales of lovable hoods and their molls, dramatized in the perennially appealing musical *Guys and Dolls.*

The association of commercial sex with the theater—and concomitant public outrage and calls for official crackdowns—goes back to the 1820s. "By midcentury," reports Timothy J. Gilfoyle in his fascinating historical study *City of Eros,* "New York had become the carnal showcase of the Western world for native-born Americans and foreign visitors alike." Playhouses often shared premises with brothels, and in the notorious curtained-off "third tier" of theater balconies, "sporting men" noisily enjoyed pleasures with professional ladies of the night while the play went on in the theater below.

In the 1840s, naked performers posed as "classical nudes" on revolving stages (turned by stagehands belowdecks, evidently, as electricity was not yet available), and theaters featuring lewd *tableaux vivants* were common. In 1847 the *Tribune* reported that at Palmo's Opera House, women danced the polka—and, incredibly enough, the minuet—naked, with "their gross sights displayed." Men and boys stood in the doorway of the theater "distributing prints of naked women to the immense throng of people in Broadway"—until Mayor Fernando Wood, celebrating his 1855 election in one of the city's first staged press events, raided the place, parading the performers and their "gross sights" along Broadway all the way to City Hall.

The tradition continued into the 1920s, when Broadway's numerous speakeasies featured scantily clad dancing girls—both amateur and professional—who would "date" for a price. And burlesque, vaudeville's raunchy heir, of which Minsky's Burlesque was the most famous, was all about sex. Dirty-joke monologuists alternated with strippers, and racy skits, packed with double entendres, depicted humorous if improbable sexual situations. Wink, wink, leer, leer. Sex was something naughty to have fun with. (Meanwhile, family-values dramas like *Life with Father* and *I Remember Mama* were playing their umpteenth performances right around the corner.)

In the 1930s and '40s, Mike Todd, the King of T&A and later one of Elizabeth Taylor's husbands, carried on the burlesque tradition with a series of forgettable productions featuring goofy baggy-pants comedians and a stage groaning under the weight of a smorgasbord of female pulchritude—the kind of women the word "babes" was invented for—as undressed as the law would allow.

In the 1970s, this tradition achieved a new dimension—or low point, depending on one's point of view. Paradoxically, once sex was out in the open—under the banner of "letting it all hang out"—what was once thrilling titillation took on the unmistakable odor of sleaze. To paraphrase Charles de Gaulle, there is no eroticism without mystery.

It was probably the level of vulgarity, more than its sheer quantity, that was so unnerving. Every shade of the hitherto taboo—all the forms of "love that dare not speak its name"—seemed to be in one's face, all over the place. Posters for movies with titles like *Hot, Wet and Nasty* seemed to leap from every wall. Clubs offered an unimaginable selection of kink. It was nearly impossible to walk down the street without being offered an incredible variety of sexual transactions—by males, females, and a staggering variety of in-betweens.

The entrance to a roof where Artkraft Strauss maintained several signs was through a window on the shabby landing of a narrow staircase that led up to a second-floor entertainment that billed itself as the *Hunk-O-Mat All-Male Revue*. This staircase was typically lined with Hunk-O-Mat patrons, who viewed intruders on their turf with spidery curiosity.

The Artkraft Strauss painters, electricians, and metalmen were all terrified of the Hunk-O-Mat and its scary staircase. Courageous survivors of the horrors of Vietnam, innumerable barroom brawls, and windblown, frostbitten, rope-suspended scaffolds 500 feet above the ground begged to switch duty when assigned to the Hunk-O-Mat roof.

They'd creep up the stairs in a huddle, like B-movie G-men, eyes wide, brandishing tools such as socket wrenches, hammers, and wire cutters in their fists. What I'm sure they didn't realize is that with their tough physiques, workmen's garb (boots and all), and interesting tools, they must have attracted more attention as sex objects than they would have if they hadn't behaved so melodramatically.

In any case, once sex became a public product, it had to be publicly marketed; and anything that's publicly marketed has got to have signs.

Sealing the association of neon with the tawdry and the fallen, in many central cities, peep shows, hot-sheet hotels, and sex-toy stores became neon's only customers during that signally dismal period. Purveyors of sin had no problems with the implications of flash. We should be grateful to those long-gone customers today, because, almost single-handed, they kept the skills of the neon trade alive.

Broadway's most spectacular neon display in those days—apart from the dignified and immortal Coca-Cola and Canadian Club—cascaded across the entire front of what was once a Trans-Lux theater, on Broadway between 48th and 49th streets, now, in the 1970s, a peep show called the Pussycat Lounge and Cinema. In what I used to describe to members of the press, with a straight face, as "a perfect example of the Bauhaus ideal of form following function," the main part of the display consisted of an immense, ruby-red neon curtain that opened and closed, opened and closed, opened and closed. "What better dramatization," I asked rhetorically, "of the business inside?"

I'm doubtless giving Mickey Zaffarano, the Pussycat's proprietor, more intellectual credit than he would ever dream of in his wildest imagination, wild as that was. But in truth, he was the first New York business operator to bring the spirit of his enterprise out onto the street in a bright and spectacular way—a practice that was already becoming common in Las Vegas but wouldn't hit our village until nearly ten years later.

Eventually, though, the Pussycat had to go. X-rated businesses were declining of their own accord with the advent of AIDS and the home VCR. More importantly, the Pussycat was occupying prime real estate in a changing marketplace.

In 1986, Bill Zeckendorf, Jr., the developer who planned to erect the Holiday Inn Crowne Plaza Hotel on the site, conducted a grand photo op to inaugurate the ground-breaking. Only it was a marquee-breaking. Accompanied by the mayor and a squadron of p.r. men—all of them, as is customary at such events, wearing construction worker's hard hats emblazoned with the new project's name—he tugged on a giant hawser fastened to the marquee. And the marquee, with its Pussycat logos and neon curtain motif matching the big wall sign, came crashing to the ground with a mighty *crunch!* and a great spray of glass. (Artkraft Strauss workers had disconnected the wires and cut the bolts earlier that morning, so the marquee was hanging by a thread—a couple of steel cables, actually—suspended from the roof. It was the old walkie-talkie trick again.)

That event marked the end of the sex industry's dominance of Times Square. It was to be another decade, and more, before the G-rated forces achieved total control. But the risqué days of Burley-cue were numbered.

## THE ELECTRONIC G-$POT

*If the reader is not* yet exhausted from all this titillation, I would like to confess to an extraordinarily intimate—and quintessentially seventies—experience.

I myself, personally, have penetrated into the heart, the pulsating center, the very beating matrix, of the X-rated industry. That is, the place where sex, money, and information intersect. (It is not located where you might think—I leave that to political investigative reporters within the Beltway.)

The place I visited was Control Central at the Supermarket of Peeps—the "brain" of Show World, the weirdly jolly, circus-themed smut emporium. Since 1971, Show World, on 42nd Street and Eighth Avenue, has offered one-stop shopping for the prurient eye—"looks" at live sex objects, video booths with more of the same, and a souvenir shop stuffed with libidinous books, gadgets, and toys.

Show World is a labyrinth of galleries, throbbing with disco, brightly lit and immaculately clean. The Man with the Mop is a constant presence. Neon and mirrors, carousel horses, and kiddie-car colors create the disorienting ambience of a funhouse.

There is *no touching* at Show World. This rule is ironhandedly enforced. Touching and the rest are completely different enterprises within the sex industry, and no smart peep-show operator risks trifling with the law—not if he wants to stay in business.

At peeps, the money is in the miles of tape, the minutes they are viewed, and the minutes the metal shades are up that uncover the viewing windows, apparently made of bulletproof glass, separating patron and performer.

Long before ordinary businesses enjoyed sophisticated, instantaneous marketing feedback, Show World, with its hundreds of booths, boasted a state-of-the-art hard-wired computer system that fed continuous usage information back to Control. It was the Wal-Mart of its universe. By the mid-1970s, the entire operation was more mechanized than Horn & Hardart's Automat Cafeteria—which the constantly sliding up and down windows and insertion of coins does bring to mind—in its heyday.

The business works like this. At the door, customers buy stacks of specially stamped metal coins, like customers in gaming establishments buying chips. The coins are good only on the premises—they make great souvenirs, though; I have one on my key chain—and come in various sizes and denominations: 25¢, $1, $5.

Like slot machines, peeps are a solo vice. The customer enters a booth, closes the door, and feeds coins into an insatiable machine. He (rarely, she) may choose among two dozen movies, with previews instantly available at the push of a bank of user-friendly buttons. The customer—only one is allowed in a booth at any one time—may stay inside the booth as long as he wishes—Show World is open twenty-four hours a day—and the whole time, his viewing choices are being monitored up at Control Center.

Not, it must be said, for the purpose of learning anything personal about him. Nobody cares. Management is spectacularly uninterested. The customer, like the activities he views, is strictly a commodity. He isn't even using his credit card—only the site-specific, cash-purchased coins. The purpose of monitoring his selections is to update them for tomorrow's customer. And apparently it works, because he keeps coming back.

"See?" Show World's clean-cut operations manager, who looked like a regional manager for Winn-Dixie, pointed to a row of video monitors displaying spreadsheets of data. We were inside the hot, narrow room where the info was collated. Neat bundles of wires ran up and down the walls and across the ceiling. "Booth #76 has been occupied by the same customer for forty-one minutes, and he has viewed tapes #3, #11, and #19 for more than twenty seconds each. (Less than twenty seconds is a preview, and doesn't count.)

"Now see here." He punched some buttons, and the spreadsheets changed. "Tape #19 has been viewed by thirty-three customers for a total of 276 minutes during the past week, while"—he punched more buttons—"tape #17 has been viewed by only four customers during the same period, for a total of nine minutes. Tape #17 has got to go." Other data compilations reflected viewers' preferences for particular themes, actors, and production companies. This was how the manager determined the new lineup for the coming week.

I couldn't help noticing from the titles that the selection of videos in every booth reflected every kind of taste. "Why aren't the booths specialized?" I asked.

"You'd be surprised," the manager told me, "how many ordinary folks like to see something different from the everyday. A lot of married guys, for example, are into gay fantasies. But they don't want to admit it. So we just let them choose."

As I watched, the spreadsheets changed, blossoming with data. And all that data meant the dropping of coins—which were automatically collected, rolled into stacks, and restocked at the entrance counter. No employee could steal, because every slug was accounted for. The music I heard, drowning out even the earsplitting ambient disco noise, was the ding-ding-ding whir kerchunk! of the money machine.

## Comes the (Real) Revolution

We heard a lot of flaming revolutionary rhetoric in the 1970s, but the most significant revolution of all was cool and quiet. And we can read it clearly in the signs if only we look behind their surfaces.

While neon took a breather, its counterparts and counterweights—computer controllers, new and more efficient light sources, new technologies, and even new customers—had the chance to catch up. By no means were all of the social and technological upheavals of the 1970s, as we read them in the signs, negative.

An invisible transformation was taking place. The solid-state revolution transformed signs from mechanical devices into electronic ones—just as the computer has transformed all our lives.

The earliest modern computers—ENIAC (1946), BINAC (1949),

UNIVAC (1951), and the rest—relied on tens of thousands of vacuum tubes to act as *logic gates:* switches, amplifiers, voltage regulators. A room the size of a barn, its walls banked with tubes from floor to ceiling, was dedicated to one of these computers, and its teams of attendants, bundled in sweaters and earmuffs against the chill required to prolong the life of the hot, unstable tubes, moved around inside it, plugging and unplugging the connections of this giant, three-dimensional switchboard to make it perform its calculations. (ENIAC was capable of 7,500 calculations per second. By contrast, 1997's Janus, the first teraflop machine, performs one *trillion* calculations per second, a 133-million-fold increase in speed.)

More teams of full-time technicians, equipped with well-stocked wheeled carts, were dedicated to replacing the tubes—18,000 of them in the case of ENIAC—which were constantly burning out from thermal fatigue. Anyone who has ever tried to maintain a lamp bank with, say, even a thousand lightbulbs, understands the problem. It is almost impossible to keep them all working at once.

People knew then that computers would become faster, but hardly anyone imagined that they would become so small, and so inexpensive and ubiquitous that hundreds of millions of people would own them, often without even knowing it. It was widely believed then that eventually there would be only two computers on the planet: one in Washington, with all the Free World's information on it, and the other in Moscow. Primarily, the new calculating machine was considered a military appliance. It was unthinkable that ordinary people, even if they could afford it, would ever be entrusted with so powerful a tool.

Three immense breakthroughs shrank these clunky monsters into the dandy desktop devices and electronic controllers we use today.

The first was the transistor, invented in 1947 and developed through the 1950s. Made of a purified crystalline material called a semiconductor, it did the same job as a vacuum tube, but it was much smaller, far cheaper to produce and operate, and about a million times more reliable.

The next leap in efficiency was the integrated circuit (IC), which combined an array of transistors and other devices onto a single chip. By 1970, a single IC chip an eighth of an inch square contained up to 1,000 electronic components and cost no more to produce than a single transistor.

Then, in 1971, along came the microprocessor, the self-contained "brain" that operates your programmable microwave oven, telephone answering machine, self-focusing camera, and home security system—as well as your stand-alone computer. Today, a "large" microprocessor contains tens of millions of transistors on a single tiny silicon chip.

Each of these advances was put to work for electric signs just as soon as sign makers could get their hands on it.

Essentially, all an electric sign does is switch lamps on and off—just as it did in the 1890s, when someone manually flipped a knife switch up and down. These electronic devices, with their ability to perform millions of switching operations almost instantly, and their ability to be easily and quickly reprogrammed to perform different millions of switching operations, added an immeasurable dimension—the fine-tuning of time—to the concept of electrical animation. "In the early days, people just turned lamps on and off," says Bobby Dianuzzo, Artkraft Strauss' electrical foreman. "Today, we really make 'em dance!"

Early transistor switches were called flip-flops. A flip-flop consists of two transistors working together: one turns the signal on and the other turns it off—an electronic teeter-totter. The earliest spectacular in New York to use flip-flops was the rebuilt Canadian Club motograph in 1969. Banks of transistors were wired onto boards measuring two feet by four feet. A dozen or more of these boards operated each row. Each row—seven in the case of CC—had its own set of boards, a hierarchy similar to that of the motor-driven cams. But the programming was still cumbersome, and by modern standards these machines still had too many parts.

Sign people point to the advent of the triac, which replaced the flip-flop in the mid-1970s, as a defining moment, because it made possible the switching of AC power directly, by means of a digital signal, without having first to rectify it into DC. This eliminated a lot of gadgetry and inefficiency. Triacs are still used today to turn lightbulbs on and off instantly.

The integrated circuit enabled gangs of transistors and other devices to be incorporated onto a single chip. And the e-prom, or Electronic Programmable Read-Only Memory, which came along at about the same time, enabled designer-engineers to control the look and feel of a display without the traditional rolls of paper or Mylar tape.

The e-prom was erasable. The sequence and timing of the lamps that made up the lamp bank was "burned" into the chip. "Burn me a new chip!" the boss would demand after spending an evening with the customer and determining that the display was running a mite too slow or too fast. And back would go the chip to the laboratory. The accurate scoring, in advance, of an elaborate display like a piece of music was as important as it ever was.

The microprocessor allowed the use of software. Taking instructions not only from e-proms but also from other external devices, such as a keyboard, computer disk, or telephone signal, it controls many, many bits of essentially simple information ("on or off?") in a highly organized way.

"It's all about switches. That's all it's about," says Dr. Aelred Kurtenbach, the founder of Daktronics, the electronic display manufacturer in Brookings, South Dakota. "They just get finer and finer, and faster and faster." Today's high-rate animation controllers can refresh an entire screen, no matter how large it is, thirty times a second, just like a TV set. That is faster than the eye can see. Even color values—shades of gray—are determined by how long, in milliseconds, a light stays on, rather than by the amplitude, or intensity, of the light itself.

These advances in switching technology added up, not only to finer and more flexible controls for traditional displays, but to new kinds of displays altogether.

## TAKE ME TO YOUR LEDER

From the sign maker's point of view, one of the most exciting developments rooted in the 1970s is optoelectronics. This sexy new field of science studies the fundamental relationship between light and electrical energy, and its applied results have yielded such promising breakthrough display techniques as LEDs, LCDs, lasers, fiber optics, and holograms.

None of these technologies has yet fully flowered. Years would elapse before even the first of them could be applied outdoors on a large scale. But ideas, like plants, germinate in the dark; and these illuminating innovations of the 1970s are lighting the way to the next century.

The term LED, or light-emitting diode, was coined in 1968 to describe a semiconductor diode that emits light under the influence of electricity. These chemically sophisticated little widgets are formed by combining elements from column III of the periodic table—such as aluminum, gallium, and indium—with those from column V—such as phosphorus, arsenic, and antimony. These so-called III-V compounds with tongue-twisting names—like aluminum indium arsenide and indium gallium phosphide—emit photons, little quanta of light, when tiny voltages are applied. Goodbye, incandescence (light created by heat), hello luminescence (light created by electronic excitation). The meaning of this, in a word, is efficiency. LEDs use but a fraction of the power required by traditional light sources, and outlast them by tens of thousands of hours.

For the first quarter century of their existence, LEDs were available only in a spectrum ranging from red, through amber, to green. The Holy Grail of LEDs has been blue, which would fill in the rest of the rainbow, including white. Finally, in 1994, blue-emitting LEDs based on silicon carbide became available, and although still expensive, they were immediately put to use in large video-type displays.

The laser is yet another intriguing device lighting the path to the future. A laser is essentially a light amplifier. It is a device containing a liquid, a crystal, or a gas whose atoms have been "fooled" by artificial excitement into emitting a more powerful, intense, and coherent beam of light than they ordinarily would.

The word "laser" is an acronym for "light amplification by stimulated emission of radiation." Einstein was aware of stimulated emission in 1917, but the first laser, using a rod of ruby, wasn't built until 1960. Today lasers are used for a multitude of purposes: to drill holes in diamonds, for example, to perform microsurgery on chromosomes, bounce signals off the moon, and measure stratospheric dust particles and continental drift. It may seem fatuous to use so powerful a tool to sell soft drinks and cigarettes, but doing so is quite consistent with the twentieth-century history of power.

The brightness and coherence of laser light makes it especially suitable for use in holography: a photographic technique that simulates three-dimensional depth. Simply put, a hologram is a three-dimensional image formed by combining two optical interference patterns recorded by lasers. Full-color holograms can be created by recording three holograms simultaneously—one red, one green, and one blue. The applications of holography to display are obvious—life-size, three-dimensional images of Marilyn Monroe, Michael Jackson, and Elvis behind show windows already greet arrivals at the Las Vegas airport—but this art is still in its infancy.

Lasers can also be used for communication. In principle, one laser beam can carry as much information as all existing radio and TV channels combined. The problem is that laser light can be blocked by rain, fog, or snow, so it needs to be contained. And so the first narrow-frequency light "containers," fiber-optic cables, came along during this period as well.

Fiber-optic cables—resembling nylon fishing twine and often thinner than a human hair—perform the amazing feat of "bending" light, which throughout history was believed to be capable of traveling only in a straight line. The flexible strands contain a central glass core in which the light travels, and an outer cladding made of glass of a different chemical formulation, with a lower optical index of refraction. This causes the light to be "bounced" from the cladding back into the core as it travels along. Light applied to one end of the fiber comes out the other, even if the fiber is tied in knots.

Scientists found that if the fiber core has the same diameter as the wavelength of the light traveling in it (about one micrometer, or .000039 inch), the light remains coherent even over long distances. By 1993, optical fibers were capable of carrying light signals more than 135 miles.

Since they are essentially carrying information—most telephone and video cable installations now use fiber optics instead of conventional wire—it is more than likely that these smart cables will eventually replace other electrical switching devices. ("Light transistors" have been built experimentally, but at the moment they are still as large as ENIAC.) And it is also probable that light itself, which is clean, cool, fast-moving, and takes up no space, will be used to perform computations now being done by computers, which, by comparison, are starting to look like horses and buggies.

All optoelectronic devices—light-emitting diodes, semiconductor lasers, optical fibers, optical-fiber amplifiers, and the rest—deal with the conversion between light and energy. One final group of these futuristic tools should be mentioned: the photodetectors and solar cells that convert photons into electrical current. How long will it be until Tesla's dream is realized and large-scale energy is transmitted over long-distances without wires? No one knows. It's easy to predict *what* will happen; more difficult to predict *when*. In the 1970s, large-scale, full-color holography—realistic, three-dimensional images leaping off billboards—appeared to be imminent. Meanwhile, the New York Museum of Holography has closed. But other optoelectronic surprises are doubtless in store.

## What Counts in the Age of Information

*Americans are endlessly fascinated with* keeping score. How much did that cost? Who had the highest r.b.i. in the National League last year? How many watts per channel? How many BTUs? How many horsepower? This preoccupation with data goes back a long time, but it began its public crescendo with the advent of reasonably priced counting clocks.

The origins of these popular clocks can be traced to the time-and-temperature units—displaying two attention-getting items of interest to practically everybody—that are now ubiquitous at banks and shopping centers across America.

Luke Williams (1923–96), co-founder of the American Sign & Indicator Company in Spokane, Washington, pioneered the development of these displays. Luke was a real old-time sign man, and his success story is about as all-American as they come.

Luke and his brother Chuck grew up on a stump farm in Washington State, the sons of an itinerant sign painter. "Dad'd give a farmer five dollars and paint an advertisement on the side of his barn," Luke told me many years later. "Didn't make much money, though."

World War II sent Chuck to England and Luke to the Pacific.

"After the war," said Luke, "we took the six hundred dollars I'd saved, plus a little more we'd won at poker, and started our own sign company. We bought a used truck and used Dad's ladders and worked out of Mom's garage, with her tellin' us every day to go get *real* jobs or we'd end up just like Dad.

"But there was money to be made, we could see that. The war had stopped any neon work, so everybody needed signs built or repaired. Shoot, we even built brand-new signs for the three bordellos in Wallace, Idaho."

In 1951, according to Luke, Chuck came up with the idea of making time-and-temperature signs. "There were a few in existence, but none would do what ours would do—flash the time and temperature in the same spot alternately, to look better and attract more attention and save electricity all at the same time.

"Doesn't sound like much now, I know. But it sure turned out to be the right idea at the right time. The first one we built was for the Spokane and Eastern Branch of the First National Bank of Seattle. A crowd gathered to watch us turn it on, and then the crowd just grew bigger. No one knew how interested people were in time and temperature until that darn sign went up. It just about set the town on fire!"

So they patented their invention and founded American Sign & Indicator, and started making the signs for banks all over the country. "We leased our signs instead of selling them—the lease included maintenance, and often the bank that was our customer would even finance it for us, so it didn't cost us anything. And we cornered the market."

From banks they went on to electronic stadium scoreboards. "We bought the rights to the Unix Dot Matrix sign, a computer-controlled magic slate invented by the English. We also started doing information signs in airports. In 1975 we built the Spectacolor sign for the old New York Times building in Times Square, with animated advertisements in seventeen shades of red, white, blue, and green." That display, with its intriguing cartoon graphics and complete video editing facility, was installed by Calvano Erectors for West Side Neon of New York, later both Artkraft Strauss companies. "We built the Golden Nugget casino sign in Las Vegas," Luke continued. "And we also provided the scoring and information system for the 1980 Summer Olympics in Los Angeles.

"By 1980 we were the largest electronic sign maker in the world, with $46 million in sales, 8,000 time-and-temperature leases, and 300 stadium scoreboards, 250 of them in colleges and universities.

"Pretty good for a couple of guys who grew up on a stump farm and couldn't even catch a goat. We always wanted one. First we built a cart, then we tried to catch some wild goats. We couldn't get within a half mile of them!"

## TOUCHDOWN!

*Scoreboards made a big hit* in the 1970s. Like other displays intended to entertain while they inform, they present a show that appears smooth and seamless to the viewer, but behind the scenes is a show that is even more complex and exciting than the one on the surface.

According to Dr. Kurtenbach of Daktronics, a scoreboard operator performs a ballet in real time that is nearly as elaborate as that performed by players on the field. Following a script with a limited outcome but much adventure along the way, the operator must coordinate the selection and switching of display elements with the announcer's commentary and other audio effects as well as with the action on the field—and, most important, with the mood swings of the spectators.

"The most important thing is to play to the fans," says Dr. Kurtenbach. "The audience is there to cheer, and they expect as good a show in the stadium as they get on TV at home. If there is bad coordination between the scoreboard and the action or the announcer, the fans become uneasy, and they don't know why. This might ultimately affect the players." What an intriguing implication! Uneasy players might blow the game, and sacrifice the championship, and jeopardize the franchise—costing the city millions. So artful scoreboard operation is crucial.

"Scoreboards in the 1970s often had a message center or a matrix center," says Dr. Kurtenbach. "The operator had a library of, say, a hundred items. Touchdown. Fumble. Field goal. Broken tackle. Good catch! Time out. And biographies of the players. Statistics. Sports trivia: If he makes this catch, it will be his hundredth catch. These were all made in advance and grouped in batches of ten. The operator had to select them with not more than three keystrokes.

"In the early electronic days, stadium scoreboards often had female operators," remembers Dr. Kurtenbach. "I don't know why this was. But they had to be good improvisers and deal with many different elements at once while the play was going on, with all its surprises. In many ways, what these women did in those days was more difficult than putting on a theatrical production, which is at least rehearsed." I might wonder whether this combination of multitracking, improvisational abilities reflects some inherited, evolution-driven quality in the female brain, but Dr. Kurtenbach is an electrical engineer, not a biologist, so I didn't ask him to speculate.

Jonathan, more cynical, has a different explanation for the early entry of women into the scoreboard operating profession. "The original scoreboards," he says, "used number turners, like Vanna White, who were dressed like cheerleaders. In the 1970s, when electronics came along, they were just put behind walls and punched buttons."

Throughout the 1950s and 1960s, as major league sports grew into big entertainment, scoreboards became more elaborate, often celebrating home team points with special crowd-pleasing effects. The scoreboard at Comiskey Park in Chicago was one of the first to do this, marking White Sox homers by shooting off fireworks. At Busch Memorial Stadium in St. Louis, a neon-overlay cardinal flew ecstatic figure eights all around the scoreboard, emitting amplified chirps, whenever a Cardinal hit a homer. Mel designed this delightful display in 1965 under the personal direction of Mr. Busch.

But I'm a little less entranced with Artkraft Strauss' 1971 creation at Veterans Stadium in Philadelphia, which celebrated Philly home runs with a display that today would get people arrested. The team's mascots were a pair of round-bellied, plump-cheeked dwarfs in 1776-style patriotic garb, appropriately named Philadelphia Phil and Philadelphia Phyllis. When a Philly swatted one over the fence, mechanically animated Phil swung his bat and lobbed a fast one straight across the scoreboard, thwacking Phyllis in the fanny. She jumped into the air in round-eyed surprise. Cute, boys, real cute.

"Scoreboards became advertising media for the first time on a large scale in the 1970s," recalls Jonathan. "They were paid for by sponsors, with sign companies acting as middlemen. The exciting, earlier 'payoff' effects that fans like Gussie Busch created in the 1950s and 1960s were replaced with large ad panels, painted or backlit, that played better for the television cameras, which had become the *real* audience."

Large-screen TVs started to take the field—but only, at first, as cheerleaders for the advertisements. "The early Diamond Visions were much smaller than the paint panels surrounding them," says Jonathan. "They were 'teasers' aimed at attracting the cameras to the paint copy. They were hard to see in daylight by the fans, and at first they weren't allowed to show live field action or replays that might lead to criticism of the umpires."

## Jumbo Vision

*By the end of the decade,* large-screen TVs were cropping up in sports arenas throughout the country—the only venues that could support them financially. Costing millions of dollars and weighing many tons, these leviathans also required plenty of care and feeding, with their elephant-size appetite for electricity, high maintenance requirements, and back-office support consisting of full-on video editing facilities with all the associated technical personnel. By the early 1980s, they were bringing to stadium audiences the instant-replay, close-up, and entertainment features the audience at home had grown used to.

After a brief flirtation with black-and-white displays—which failed to overwhelm at a time when a majority of Americans already had color sets in their homes—the earliest big-time entrant into the big-TV field was Mitsubishi, with its Diamond Vision. This fascinating technology was essentially holographic. Each pixel (dot) was a separate CRT tube (TV screen), so each dot contained the entire image. Sony became a big player in the 1980s with their Jumbotron; Jumbotrons replaced Diamond Visions at Shea Stadium, Yankee Stadium, and other stadiums across the country.

It was not until twenty years after their introduction that the big TVs made a major debut outside of arenas. The reason is economics. From the beginning of full-screen technology—dating all the way back to Douglas Leigh's Epok photocell sign of 1938 and Artkraft Strauss' four-color Wondersign of 1939—entrepreneurs have sought to finance these expensive installations in public places by selling display time on them, the way TV advertising is sold. The concept harks all the way back to the "Leaders of the World" "talking sign" of 1910—and it is such a brilliant idea, someday someone may actually make money from it.

But with the singular exception of hardware manufacturers, whose core business is selling TVs, not vending advertising time on them, no one, to my knowledge, has yet made a killing with this concept (although some operators in Asia and South America claim to have done so.). Hardly a month goes by that every sign or outdoor advertising company of any size doesn't get a call from someone—either a display manufacturer or a real estate operator—with the Big Idea: "Hey, we'll make a fortune! You [sign company] put up a [multimillion-dollar] video display at your expense, sell the time on it, and we'll split the money!" Yeah, sure, is the usual reply.

The reason for this spectacular lack of enthusiasm is that moving images and moving audiences don't seem to mix. A TV audience tends to be sedentary, so an advertisement conceived as a thirty-second microdrama has the opportunity to make an impact. Billboards and signs, conversely, stand still while viewers move past them. In both cases there is the opportunity for repetition, which is the essence of advertising.

But outdoor advertisers expect exclusivity and continuity for their money. Your customer who buys a twenty-second spot on an outdoor video screen, then has his view of it cut off by a passing bus, and then has to stand around for eleven minutes and forty seconds in the rain or snow, waiting for it to come around again, may be irritated rather than entranced. For this reason, most outdoor advertising people say they'd rather sell space than time, anytime.

Another problem is that unlike a spectacular sign, whose image and message transcend the medium, the screen itself still tends to be the icon. People look at the medium itself—Golly! Look at the big TV!—rather than at what is on the TV, the way people used to do in the early 1950s, when TV was a novelty, or in the 1920s, when people listened to the radio no matter what was on it.

For a medium to be meaningful, it must become transparent—

carrying content that transcends the medium and deals with problems of context: in this case, visual competition and lack of sound. The first successful step in this direction was ITT's 1996 screen at the top of One Times Square, with its hypnotic image of a massive, spinning disk. Ordinary TV programming—such as "talking heads"—doesn't seem to rate much of a glance from passersby, who conclude that they can see better TV, with sound, at home. Outdoor TV must be radically more compelling than indoor TV to succeed as a spectacular medium. The key to this success is in the content, not the hardware.

## THE JAPANESE INVASION

*"The Japanese Invasion" was a* term used with some hostility by America's beleaguered automobile and electronics industries, which failed to see the Asians coming and felt they'd been blindsided. But to the outdoor advertising community, especially in Times Square, the coming of the Japanese was not an invasion, but a liberation. We welcomed these "invaders" with open arms.

Sony. Canon. Panasonic. Maxell. JVC. TDK. Seiko. Fuji. Casio. Minolta. Mitsubishi. Citizen. Brother. Olympus. Ricoh. Sanyo. Aiwa. Konika. Yashika. Mita. . . . And the Korean manufacturers, Goldstar and Samsung. The roster reads like a Who's Who of consumer electronics—the amazingly reliable products of the solid-state revolution that, suddenly, no one could do without.

In the mid-1980s, a typical American woke up to his Casio digital alarm clock, turned on his Sony waterproof all-band radio to catch the news while he showered, and watched *Good Morning America* on his portable Panasonic while he dressed. Then he strapped on his Seiko and climbed into his Datsun, where an Aiwa tape player spun TDK and Maxell tapes. At work, he used his Canon copier, Mita fax machine, and Minolta camera. His telephone, calculator, and computer also bore the labels of Asian manufacturing and trading companies. A mere twenty years earlier, virtually all of these items—to the extent they existed—would have been Made in the U.S.A. Today, none of them are. The last surviving American television manufacturing company, Zenith, is now controlled by LG (Goldstar) and does its manufacturing in Mexico.

The military metaphor is not inapt. The arrival of the Asian companies on American shores was marked by their planting, one after another like triumphal flags, their immense, glowing neon logos in Times Square—a major recolonization of the desolate space. Sony, the advance guard, established its beachhead in 1965. It took nearly twenty-five years for the rest to arrive in full force, starting with Canon and Panasonic in 1972, and Suntory—a brand of whisky only scarcely available in the States—shortly thereafter. But the turning point in the campaign can be marked with precision.

In 1979, Douglas Leigh sold his Times Square locations, consisting of fourteen billboards, twelve of which were empty, to Van Wagner, a small but aggressive billboard company on Long Island. In what seemed like no time at all, all the boards were filled. Richard Schaps, the president of Van Wagner, likes to say, "People thought we were geniuses. They thought we saw the Japanese coming. We weren't geniuses. We were just goddamned lucky."

It's always easy in retrospect to attribute foresight to those who later turn out to be pioneers. But one can be right for the wrong reasons. For years, people ascribed almost superhuman precognition and planning to the Japanese advertisers who planted their logos in the landscape of the American imagination long before their products were even available in the States, let alone household words. In 1984 Artkraft Strauss built a major neon-and-message-center display for Hitachi at Columbus Circle, overlooking Central Park. At that time, Hitachi, an industrial manufacturer of things like nuclear plants, was not marketing any consumer products in the United States. Today they sell televisions, computers, and other electronic equipment, as well as industrial products. What planning! What foresight! we marveled, invoking the famous, and perhaps mythical, 500-Year Japanese Corporate Planning Strategies. What a statement! And indeed it was. But perhaps it was a different statement than we thought.

What *were* the Japanese advertisers thinking when they came to Times Square?

"To come to America, to come to New York, was a dream," says Nick Nakahara, vice president of sales for Dentsu Corporation of America, a leading Japanese advertising agency that represents many of these advertisers. "And to have a sign in Times Square was the biggest dream of all."

This was especially true, he says, for those who grew up in Japan immediately after the war. "We were longing to become like America. We watched the TV programs—they all played in Japan. *I Love Lucy. Ozzie and Harriet. The Brady Bunch.* Even *Bonanza,* which is a little bit samurai, when you think about it, only with a lot more freedom and space.

"Those shows represented the dream family. It was beautiful. The standard of living! The freedom! Times Square was an expression of all that." To be in Times Square, says Nick, "was symbolic. It was the ultimate expression of the dream."

Did the early Japanese advertisers know or care, I asked him, that Times Square was physically a neighborhood in decline?

"Not at all," he says. "The image was intact. And it looked fine at night, when the signs were lit."

"Weren't the signs making the corporate statement 'We're here, we're here to stay, we're in your life'?" I asked.

"That's an American view of things. It's more like 'I'm here because I wanted to be here. It's my dream—my symbolic place to be.' It's not a matter of showing off. That wouldn't be...proper. It wouldn't be Japanese. Rather, it's a statement of being proud of having become a company that could have such a sign in the center of the world. An expression of pride in the prestige of just being able to be here."

Even today, he says, Japanese advertisers seek the symbolic statement ahead of the marketing reality. "Of course, there must be a rationale behind it, demographics and so on. We have to please our bean counters, our MBAs with their spreadsheets, the same as you do. But the ultimate motivation is sentiment—the expression of the dream."

In revitalizing the Bright Lights of Broadway, the Japanese reimported the Ginza, a neon aesthetic based on the Times Square of the 1950s. In Times Square—throughout America, in fact—the bright-lights sensibility had been lost to depression and gloom. But it had survived and thrived in Tokyo—as well as in Hong Kong, Singapore, and other points East. This is analogous to the rescue of the French wine industry, decimated by a blight earlier in the century, by the reimportation of rootstock from California—genetic material that had originated in France and been preserved, transplanted, in the Golden West. In short order, the Square was alive again with pulsing, jazzy lights.

And while they were at it, the new Japanese advertisers making their way to Times Square, Toronto, Los Angeles, and other cities during that period helped push new technological advances by demanding the latest in control technology for their displays. Times Square's first all-electronic spectacular, for example, was built by Artkraft for Midori liqueur in 1980. In what turned out to be a pioneering period, the Japanese were the true pioneers.

## Horses Have No Stomach

*In 1975, not long before he died,* Jake confided to me his view of the future of Times Square. It was not a pretty picture.

"Grandpa, now I have a hard question for you," I said.

"Ask me anything."

"Grandpa, what is the future of Times Square?"

"Future? What future? There is no future!"

"What do you mean?"

"The good money is gone. The good people also. One time, a man's word was his bond. Not anymore. Thieves now you see! And not just thieves. Liars. Not only they can't keep their word, they can't even remember their word. No brains they got. Small people.

"It is not just that," he went on. "The empty space you see now in Times Square? The billboards where only pigeons live? It will never be filled."

"Never?" I asked him. "Isn't that kind of harsh? Don't things change?"

"Of course things change! But listen to me, my dear. Real estate is like the ocean. With a very long wave. Fifty, sixty years, maybe. Once the East Side was nothing. Galoots lived there.... Oh, there were mansions, Park Avenue, Fifth Avenue. But Third Avenue was just bars, and over it the El. First Avenue was just slaughterhouses. Second Avenue, nothing but junk stores."

"Today we would call them 'antiquey boutiqueys,'" I observed.

"Never mind," said Jake. "Junk is junk. But look what happened. They tore down the El, built office buildings there. Tore down all those tenements. Doormen now they got. And elevators. With balconies."

"So that's my point," I persisted. "Doesn't this mean Broadway will someday come back again too?"

"Nah! It means the East Side is full up. When they want to build new office buildings, new elevator buildings, where will they come? To Broadway. To Times Square! Here the buildings are old, small, three, maybe four stories. Somebody will notice this. Then they will put money in front of them, and they will build. Do you know what I mean, in front of them?"

"You mean the banks will front them the money?"

"Yes, but no, not exactly. I mean real estate developers are like horses. Do you know what is a horse? Horses have no stomach. So long as there is food in front of them, they will eat. And real estate men, so long as there is money in front of them, they will build. It just comes out the other end. Excuse me, but this is the law of nature. And you cannot put big signs on a fancy office building."

"But, Grandpa, they do it in Japan."

"Don't talk nonsense! Everything is different there. No, no, no. Real estate development is coming. In ten years there will be no more Times Square."

Jake's analysis of urban development trends and his pessimism about their probable impact on Times Square were well founded at the time. Big-time high-rises were lurking just over the horizon, on Sixth Avenue, a block to the east. There was no reason to think that when large-scale development came west to Seventh Avenue and Broadway in the 1980s, it would include the elements of entertainment and glitter that had been the hallmarks of the Theater District for nearly a century.

Neither could Jake foresee the scope of the Asian Invasion that would accelerate through the 1980s and help spark the Square's revival as an internationally respected advertising venue. Or the return of the American advertisers in the 1990s. When Jake died in 1976, most of the early Japanese Times Square spectaculars were still on drawing boards in Tokyo.

Nor could he foresee the modernization of Artkraft Strauss that his grandson Jonathan would bring about, taking the creaky old factory into the computer age—an echo of what Jake had done for Strauss so many years before when he took the sign painter's company into the electric age.

And he could not possibly have foreseen the outpouring of public sympathy and passion for the Theater District that culminated in the Municipal Art Society's successful campaign to "Keep Times Square Alive"—or the role his granddaughter would play in it.

**T**his is a military operation," I told the assembled men, "and that's how seriously I want you to take it. I want to see perfect discipline, perfect concentration, and perfect dedication to win. We are fighting for our livelihood—for our jobs, and for those of our sons and daughters."

I actually spoke these rousing words, and on recalling them I realize how caught up I was in the drama of the moment. I had come to work at Artkraft Strauss full-time in 1982, and was immediately faced with the threat Jake had predicted seven years before. Development was coming to Times Square, and the signs were slated to be a casualty. The evening ahead would be a turning point in the public perception of Times Square and its spectacular images as a glittering but fragile urban treasure, one well worth saving.

Two dozen electricians, members of the Sign Division of Local 3 of the fearsome IBEW, stared at me in disbelief—not only because of my words but also because of who was saying them. Even in the smallest shops, no one took orders directly from an owner, but only from a foreman, a shop steward, or a plant manager. It was almost as if a general—and one from another planet, at that: a gurrl? with a college degree?—were personally leading a guerrilla action.

Perhaps it wasn't quite that strange. Many of them had already taken orders from me on three New Year's Eves. And Mike Dianuzzo, Artkraft Strauss' foreman and the most powerful foreman in the New York sign industry, had introduced me and given them their marching orders: "You all know Tama. She's Mel's daughter. I want you to do exactly what she says. Anyone who doesn't, will answer to me."

These electricians, some from Artkraft Strauss and the rest from other sign shops around the city and on Long Island, had been handpicked for their reliability and union-quality loyalty. It was evening, and the shop was closed. Machinery, trucks, and half-completed sign sections slumbered behind us in the darkened factory. Test equipment, neon samples, and light-bank modules with dangling wires climbed the walls. Outside on Twelfth Avenue, in the shadow of the West Side Highway, the electricians' vans waited like patient steeds, their flanks bearing the logos of the other sign manufacturers with their incandescent names: Silverescent, Spectrum, Universal, Going, County Neon, Midtown Neon, West Side Neon, Manhattan Neon.

We were gathered in a pool of fluorescent light around the electrical bench, a big plywood worktable outside the foreman's office near the downstairs factory door. Everyone was dressed alike: dark pants, dark zipped-up jackets, black watch caps. Part of our job was to stay out of range of the cameras.

It was Saturday, March 24, 1984. On Monday, March 26, the New York State Urban Development Corporation would be starting its public hearings on the massive new 42nd Street Redevelopment Plan.

I explained the importance of the mission. "The politicians have a Plan. Their Plan is to tear down Times Square and give the empty lots to their friends the real estate developers to build big office buildings on them. And the new buildings will have no signs. That's right. The success of this evil Plan will mean the death of signs in Times Square."

There was a grim silence. Even those who didn't work for Artkraft Strauss, and who had never worked in Times Square, understood the emblematic value—the sacred symbolism—of Times Square in the universe of signs and the world of their jobs. Many of them were, like me, second- and third-generation sign people, and several of them had sons (no daughters yet) starting out in the industry.

Everyone was a volunteer that night: nobody was going to get paid. And they were doing this job at some personal risk. Their parent union, the International Brotherhood of Electrical Workers, with more than a million members nationwide, also covers the building trade electricians, and the IBEW supported the Plan, not only because Governor Cuomo was their man but also because of the large number of temporary construction jobs it would generate.

Then I revealed the mission. "Monday is the public hearing, where everyone who is interested will testify about the Plan. The newspapers will have editorials about it, and there will be TV cameras all over the place. People will be watching.

"Tonight, at theater time," I said, "we're going to show the world what Times Square will look like without signs.

"We're going to turn off the lights in Times Square."

What I had explained so simply would be more difficult to execute. For maximum effect, I had decided, the signs would have to turn off one by one.

I handed out watches, forty identical Casios, painstakingly set to within a tenth of a second of one another with the help of the (BONG! BONG!) shortwave radio signal from the National Bureau of

Standards. The watches would be the men's to keep as a souvenir of the job. This was just like New Year's Eve, only more complicated.

Bobby Dianuzzo, Mike's younger brother and our assistant foreman, announced the assignments. There would be one electrician at the switch of each of the big signs. Ordinarily, the signs turn themselves on at dusk and off at around 1 A.M., controlled by timers that are reset every few weeks to accommodate the changing length of the day. But sign timers then were no more accurate than ordinary mechanical kitchen timers—those analog gadgets with a spring inside that go DING! when the roast is done—and this job would require split-second timing.

I had hatched the evening's script with the help of Kent Barwick, president of the Municipal Art Society of New York, and Ted Liebman, president of the New York Chapter of the American Institute of Architects. In a brilliant display of alliance building, Kent and Ted had recruited the presidents of a dozen other major civic organizations. And my Times Square advertising competitors/customers, Van Wagner and Spectacolor, gladly gave me permission to use their displays.

The plan was this: Starting at 7:30:00 P.M., we would turn off all the signs, one by one, from south to north, at two-second intervals. The TV cameras would pan, and it would look like dominoes falling down: off . . . off . . . off . . . off. Then, when the Square was completely dark, Ted, Kent, and the other speakers would talk to the press about the "irreplaceable cultural artifact" that would be lost with the destruction of Times Square as embodied in its great commercial lights.

Then, at 8:00:00, all the lights would simultaneously come ablaze. The dazzled audience would applaud, and the speakers would say, "This is what we want to save!"

We rehearsed around the bench. The lighting effect was to happen as if by magic, from behind the scenes. I had everyone pretend he was at a switch, and shout "Off!" when it was his turn. Then, with fifteen seconds' warning, we all shouted, "On!" We also tried it in case the 7:30:00 cue didn't work for some reason, and the turnoff started at, say, 7:31:42. Everyone had to do the math in his head and still respond in turn, on time. "You are certainly smart enough to do this!" I reminded them, still playing the general.

I was to be down in the street, near the speakers, with a walkie-talkie. I would cue Bobby D., up in the TDK sign, to start the sequence, and the other electricians would follow in turn. The speakers from the civic organizations were also committed to following my cues.

At 6:39 we piled into the vans and set out. We would leave the vans on Eighth Avenue, which was only five minutes away; then Bobby and Frankie Lia, another guerrilla veteran, would quietly lead the electricians into the buildings where the sign switches were located. I kept the timing tight because I didn't want my usually gregarious and affable electricians to get distracted.

## DESTROYING THE VILLAGE IN ORDER TO SAVE IT

*When the 42nd Street Redevelopment* Plan was first announced, in May of 1981, it seemed reasonably benign. It consisted of a set of design guidelines created by Cooper, Eckstut Associates, the prestigious and culturally and aesthetically sensitive architectural design firm. It was issued under the benevolent auspices of the New York State Urban Development Corporation (UDC), later renamed the Empire State Development Corporation (ESDC); the New York City Public Development Corporation (PDC); and the New York City Department of City Planning (DPC). It gave no warning of what was to come.

The Cooper-Eckstut Guidelines were built around the cultural integrity of the street and its historical energy—a call for liveliness, vitality, and variety. Its detail addressed the building exteriors "including facade expression, materials, colors, signage, lighting and roofs," mandated bright lights and big signs, and required setbacks (no sheer building walls) as a way of maintaining the Square's open feeling. In addition, it insisted on the retention of the Times Tower.

Throughout 1981, the Guidelines—two massive volumes, a supplemental volume, and a slide show—were presented to the public and to the twenty-six hopeful bidders on the Project. The UDC, PDC, and DPC patiently explained that the Guidelines were *not* negotiable—that the cocky and commercial spirit of 42nd Street must be kept, in fact enhanced, despite the new element of office buildings. A model was cited: Tokyo's Ginza, which has successfully incorporated large commercial advertising signs into high-prestige, high-rise office buildings ever since its beginnings in the 1960s.

"We do not have to destroy 42nd Street in order to save it," proclaimed the UDC's representatives during their slide shows. "Instead of fighting Times Square," they vowed as bright images of supersigns flashed on the screens, "we're going along with Times Square." They promised that developers "will be given relatively little creative leeway" in the design of the building facades, the configuration of the setbacks, and, especially, the dedication of the sign areas, "since the giant lighted spectaculars are considered one of the area's most striking attractions." Their message was clear: Keep Times Square Times Square.

The Plan was widely praised, not least because it promised "no public subsidies." The state would acquire through condemnation thirteen acres that included the intersection at 42nd Street and Broadway. The state would then turn the properties over to designated developers for what the state had paid for them. At first the developers would pay, as annual rent, the equivalent of the lost property taxes. They would then have the right to construct four office towers, a 560-room hotel, and a mammoth merchandise mart on the six corners—and their rent would rise accordingly. For the developers, it was a terrific deal.

There was a not insignificant quid pro quo. In return for these lucrative concessions, the designated developers would at their own expense restore the nine crumbling historic theaters in the midblocks and provide $70 million in desperately needed improvements to the vast hellhole known as the Times Square subway station. To the local Community Board, the City Council, and other elected and appointed officials, these developer-financed amenities justified the whole proposition.

The 1981 Plan was the culmination of half a century of failed attempts to revive "the Deuce," whose decline from the 42nd Street of Oscar Hammerstein I, Fanny Brice, and W. C. Fields set in with the Depression and accelerated thereafter as though dragged down by gravity. Proposals over the years ranged from the impractical to the absurd, including the "42nd Street Mall," a brainchild of the early

1970s, consisting of a suburban-type pedestrian promenade covered by a geodesic dome and surrounded by armed guards.

Only two years earlier, in 1979, Ed Koch, our irascible but lovable mayor, had vetoed another Plan, "The City at 42nd Street," that featured a fifteen-story-high indoor Ferris wheel that he said reminded him of Disneyland. In an irony that is evident only in retrospect, he said, "This is terrible. New York cannot and should not compete with Disneyland—that's for Florida. We've got to make sure we have seltzer instead of orange juice."

By 1981, people had become royally tired of ambitious Plans to "clean up" 42nd Street that went nowhere. Fred Papert, president of the 42nd Street Development Corp., which successfully converted half a dozen tenement buildings on 42nd Street west of Eighth Avenue into successful off-off-Broadway theaters during the 1970s, commented in 1981: "If I had one dollar for every press conference, and every time a broom was thrust into poor Celeste Holm's hands, I'd have enough money to redevelop the whole city."

Now it appeared that at last there was a Plan in place that everybody could agree to.

The alphabet soup of state and city agencies had said they planned to announce the winner of the development competition in early 1982, with a scheduled completion date for the entire project as early as mid-1988.

Finally, in December of 1983, after two and a half years of drum-rolling and a blizzard of press releases, the winning developer, George Klein of Park Tower Realty, was announced. His winning design, in the form of a light-up model said to cost a quarter of a million dollars, was unveiled at a press conference presided over by Klein, Mayor Koch, Matilda Cuomo (the governor's wife), aging architect Philip Johnson and his then partner, John Burgee. The whole affair was stage-managed for maximum p.r. value and, as it later turned out, to damage-control the criticisms that were bound to ensue.

This event had been eagerly awaited by everyone who fundamentally supported the Plan. At last, we thought, a solution to the perennial problems of 42nd Street was at hand.

But to our collective horror, the Plan was radically different from what had been promised.

Gone were the Cooper-Eckstut Guidelines—along with the city's zoning regulations limiting height and density. Gone was the pledge of "no public subsidies." Gone were the hotel and the merchandise mart, the restoration of the midblock theaters, and the $70 million rebuilding of the subway station. Gone were the lights and signs, gone were the setbacks. And at the center of the model, where the Times Tower stood, was an empty plaza. Poof! The Times Tower had just vanished.

We were confronting a monster, the spawn of misdirected grandiosity and cretin compromise.

The entire Plan—now to start in 1986, with completion slated for 1991—consisted solely of four menacing office towers at the corners of Broadway and 42nd Street. Square-shouldered, identical black glass-and-granite behemoths, blind to the street, they rose straight up to colossal heights without an inch of setback. Three times bulkier than anything that had ever been built in midtown, they would forever block sunlight from entering the Square.

Adding insult, they were topped, in a gratuitous salute to the "old" Times Square, with cute, matching, fake-mansard roofs adorned with little cast-iron gothic spikes visible only from six hundred feet in the air.

Many people thought this was literally for the birds.

Respected urban sociologist William H. Whyte, the father of the study of relationships between people and place, complained, "I haven't seen anything . . . that gives you an idea of what it would look like from where the people are." Architecture critic Ada Louise Huxtable described the buildings as so lacking in aesthetic quality that they would "set back urban design in New York by half a century." More vividly, Barbara Handman, a senior member of Community Board #5, which includes Times Square, told *New York* magazine that the design looked "like Albert Speer's tribute to the Third Reich."

What had happened?

The new design, it turned out, was the climax of what was, according to all participants, an excruciating series of negotiations—including big-time elbowing among politicians and tycoons, deal making and unmaking, alliances and disalliances, repeated threats by the mayor to scuttle the whole thing, and the designation, "de-designation," indictment, and default of various developers along the way, including a couple of "minority-owned" companies who turned out to be so minor as to not exist at all. In the end, politics and greed were the defining forces at work, not any concern for humanism, aesthetics, or public well-being.

I was as shocked as anybody. Interviewed on national TV, I called the buildings "the Darth Vader Quartet," and perhaps intemperately characterized George Klein as "Godzilla on the march" in Times Square. With New Year's Eve approaching, the impending dematerialization of the Times Tower looked ominous.

Our New Year's Eve press release that year implied that, absent the Tower, and Artkraft Strauss' Ball-lowering on the Tower, time itself would end. Now that would be news! In retrospect, I might have approached Mr. Klein, who turned out to be a gentleman as well as an artful negotiator, and asked about a Ball-lowering on one of the new buildings. But at the time, all I could think about was saving the Tower and averting the menace to the Bright Lights of Broadway.

Others had other concerns. Residents of nearby Clinton, west of the Square, feared gentrification pressures on the one hand and displacement of crime and other undesirable activities into their neighborhood on the other. In the Garment District to the south, the Federation of Apparel Manufacturers and the International Ladies' Garment Workers' Union worried that higher rents would put additional pressure on the 200,000 mainly entry-level jobs they provided, and speed up the deterioration of New York's largest manufacturing industry.

Others were troubled by the racism implicit in the destruction of the only regional, low-income entertainment center in the area, especially in view of the closing down of scores of movie theaters in poorer neighborhoods during the previous decade. Crowded together on the two 800-foot blockfronts, easily accessible by subway, were dozens of small fast-food outlets, shops, and arcades—plus fourteen movie theaters that showed an eclectic mix of first-run, action/adventure, kung fu, soft-core, and hard-core films, charging $2 to $4 for double and triple features with as many as eight previews and mini-features thrown in. (Around the corner, in Times Square proper, better-heeled patrons paid $5 to see the same films as single features, without the bonuses.) These theaters served more than 10,000 patrons a day, the overwhelming majority of whom were young, law-abiding, and nonwhite.

And the 500-odd business and property owners and low-rent theatrical agents, costume and set designers, and artists whose businesses were to be condemned ("confiscated," they said) to make way for the Project, all had something to say.

The intellectuals weighed in as well. Thomas Bender, a professor of urban history at New York University, wrote in an Op-Ed, "The plans mean the end, after 80 years, of the public space we know as Times Square. More importantly, they mean the loss of a vital part of our city's history." Tim Prentice, former president of both the Municipal Art Society and the New York Chapter of the American Institute of Architects, wrote: "If the project is built, it's not a matter of changing Times Square. Times Square will disappear. It's the gentrification process that will bring in lots of gray flannel suits and rep ties. It will totally lack spontaneous activity."

Herbert J. Gans, a professor of sociology at Columbia, was skeptical of the whole redevelopment approach: "I've never liked the idea of some people being involuntarily relocated for the benefit of other people." And Brendan Gill, the chairman of the New York Landmarks Conservancy, wrote, "I do strongly feel that of all the things that have taken place since I became involved in these issues 25 years ago, this is the worst.... The office towers would be great, gray ghosts of buildings, shutting out the sun and turning Times Square into the bottom of a well.... It's just going to gut the life out of Times Square, and we will never see it again."

But apparently such reservations were coming too late. A momentum was under way, and the forces of darkness seemed sure to prevail. The Project had been "announced," and, according to a headline in the *Times*, was gaining "wary public approval"—not that any was required, thanks to the condemnatory powers of the state. "We've never been so bypassed," complained Stan Herman, the chairman of Community Board #5's New Construction Committee.

Fans of the Project had a rallying point. Incredible as it seems, they genuinely believed that these buildings would end sin. And for them, boring architecture and a deadened 42nd Street would be a small price to pay.

Father George Moore, the popular pastor of St. Malachy's Church, the Actors' Chapel, on West 49th Street, phrased their argument eloquently: "Some will be concerned about traffic, sky-exposure planes, bulk, pedestrian flow, architectural or configural esthetics. . . . I submit that these considerations are minor when compared to the human need, indeed, the human right to be free from the crime, the depravity, the corruption, the pain and the fear which are rooted on 42nd Street and from there, extend their polluted tentacles to the adjoining streets, to the residents, the tourists, the workers, the theater patrons who use them."

William J. Stern, chairman and president of the UDC, put it less charitably. Likening pornography merchants and other "denizens" to cockroaches, he said, "Scattering them is the first shot. We fire the first cannonball which scatters them and then we hunt them out."

And for those unconcerned with the state of their immortal souls, the $1.6 billion redevelopment plan offered a cornucopia: 25,000 new jobs, it was claimed; and nearly a billion dollars in taxes or "payments in lieu of taxes" over fifteen years. (These immense numbers kept rising and falling like the tide depending on which version one read.)

So the battle lines were drawn—at least among those who cared. (Most Gothamites, in true New York fashion, tended to treat the whole matter with a fatalistic shrug.)

The first and most important opportunity for public comment would be the March 26 hearing on the Draft Environmental Impact Statement. This little study, commissioned three years earlier at a cost of a million and a half dollars from the respected urban design firm Parsons, Brinckerhoff, Quade & Douglas, was an 880-page jargon-filled document in two volumes the size of the Bronx and Brooklyn telephone books.

The timing by the Project's promoters was brilliant. The massive volumes were released to the public only on February 16, so opponents had to assemble their arguments double-quick—in a New York minute, as they say west of the Hudson (sounds slow to me)—or their objections, if any, would expire.

As for "my" issue, the entire 880-page document—I can't believe I read the whole thing—mentioned "signage" only in passing, if at all.

(The document seriously recommended, however, that theater marquees be eliminated, inasmuch as they tend to give shelter to "undesirables.") But as it turned out, the signs, so visible, so symbolic, proved an ideal rallying point for other issues. Just as the bright displays had borne the brunt of the 1970s "energy crisis" for symbolic reasons, now too, for the same reasons, they were to provide a new focus for a new message.

Those who cried "Foul!" or "Bait-and-Switch!" in light of the truncated response time were reviled as soreheads. "Get Out of the Way in Times Square," snarled an editorial in the *Times,* addressing five New York legislators representing the area who claimed that studying the Plan properly and addressing people's concerns about it would require more time. "In effect," said the editorial, "they call for more crime.... Having slept through the first act, they should take their seats for the second. The rest of us are eager for the curtain to go up."

Mayor Koch, never at a loss for words, dismissed the Plan's critics—including anybody who liked anything about Times Square as it was—as "idiots."

# Hey, Mr. Mayor!

*The Saturday night "lights out"* mission was a dramatic turning point in the tide of public opinion. We used the lights and energy of Times Square to raise the specter of their absence. Times Square, its excitement and imagery, helped save itself.

The demonstration grabbed people's emotions in a way no amount of argument or editorializing could. While a jazz quartet in top hats and tails played toe-tapping Broadway melodies, volunteers handed out sailor hats—an invocation of the famous Eisenstaedt photo—imprinted with the neon-pink legend "Save Times Square" and lapel buttons and placards to match. An unforgettable image: eloquent, white-haired Senator Daniel Patrick Moynihan, who grew up in nearby Clinton when it was still called Hell's Kitchen, wearing one of the sailor hats at a rakish angle and reminiscing about the glow of the Square in the 1940s.

Thousands of theatergoers scurrying through the Square to catch their 8 P.M. curtains were stunned when the big lights turned off one by one like clockwork, beginning at 7:30. Only one sign remained lit: the 20-foot-high-by-40-foot-wide Spectacolor display on the Times Tower, which ran two animated messages that alternated for the entire half hour.

The first message, in black and white, showed a cartoon of a glittering city skyline—suddenly smashed to smithereens by a giant, malevolent wrecking ball.

The second message was a rhyming exhortation, in bright, pulsating colors. It said:

HEY, MR. MAYOR, IT'S DARK OUT THERE!
HELP KEEP THE BRIGHT LIGHTS IN TIMES SQUARE!

Meanwhile, representatives of the Architectural League of New York, the New York Chapter of the American Institute of Architects, the Municipal Art Society, the New York Landmarks Conservancy, the City Club, the Regional Plan Association, Save the Theaters, Inc., and a half dozen other civic and planning organizations—as well as historians, artists, merchants, politicians, and ordinary citizens—one by one stood atop a van parked at the traffic island at 43rd Street and Broadway and spoke to the public and to the press, who came out en masse.

The speakers emphasized that the purpose of the visual statement was not to stop the Project, which everyone knew would bring great benefits to the area, but to encourage its sponsors to maintain Times Square's historic glitter, vitality, and people-pleasing glamour.

They echoed the message that had been running all day on all the traveling signs ringing the Square: AT 7:30 TONIGHT THE BIG LIGHTS WILL GO OUT...TO REMIND PEOPLE WHAT IS GOOD ABOUT TIMES SQUARE....AT 8:00 THE LIGHTS WILL COME BACK ON....WE HOPE EVERYBODY WILL ENJOY THE BRIGHT LIGHTS OF BROADWAY FOR MANY YEARS TO COME....

They handed out "Times Square: Crossroads of the World" Fact Sheets, the ones we use to help sell signs. The Fact Sheets are full of statistics that show how Broadway's sparkling images reach far beyond their immediate audience. "More than 10 million people per week pass through Times Square. They come from every state in the

U.S. and every corner of the globe. 23 million visitors per year come to New York, of whom 80% visit Times Square. Why do they come? To see the Bright Lights of Broadway...."

It seemed mighty peculiar that in all the debates about urban focus, architectural values, sin and sex, commercial displacement, quality of life, real estate trends, government intervention in the marketplace, and political cronyism, no one seemed to be giving much thought to the tourists, who comprise one of the city's largest industries. Not only do they distribute currency of all nationalities and denominations in hotels, restaurants, taxis, theaters, and stores, they also add "legs" to our landmarks by sending home postcards and photographs of them. Journalists and filmmakers from around the world do the same thing. What would a black hole at the city's heart do for them?

Times Square spectaculars really do have "legs." They supersede the laws of physics because they're visible even where they aren't. In 1975–76 my brother crossed India and Africa by motorcycle, stopping at out-of-the-way villages miles from cities, public electricity, and TV. When the locals asked him where he was from, he said, "USA, New York, Times Square." People smiled in recognition and said, "Oh yes, Times Square, where the lights are."

The demonstration—which we repeated in November 1984 at a later stage in the hearing process—received national press coverage, which was certainly not lost on the backers of 42nd Street Redevelopment. Even Mayor Koch finally came around and endorsed the brightness and excitement that signs represent.

The demonstrations also attracted the nationwide support we would need through the rest of the decade to help City Planning articulate its vision of the rest of Times Square, north of 43rd Street, as a lively, glittering entertainment district that would delight people into the twenty-first century—and beyond.

The 42nd Street hearing lasted two days. A hundred and thirteen people testified, led off by Governor Cuomo, followed by Anthony Quinn. It too was quite a show.

# The Drama of ZR 81-732

*The events in 1984 were* only the beginning. There was still the matter of the rest of Times Square: the north end, from 43rd to 50th Street, where, in accordance with Jake's prediction, City Planning was encouraging development to help take the pressure off Manhattan's East Side. What would the new buildings look like? Would they have signs?

There was tireless behind-the-scenes work. Endless meetings, conferences, planning sessions, modelings, simulations, demonstrations, and position papers. We solicited and submitted letters from engineers and advertising agencies, advertisers and urban design experts from as near as Madison Avenue and as far away as Sydney.

The forces of brightness—people like Joe Rose, the chairman of Community Board #5 (later chair of the City Planning Commission); Kent Barwick; architect Hugh Hardy; landscape architect Nicholas Quennell; and Philip Howard, the Municipal Art Society's pro bono attorney—demonstrated superhuman dedication and patience. They were committed to maintaining the glow, but nobody knew quite how to go about it. Everybody knew what a spectacular was when they saw one, but nobody had ever tried to define the concept before. And zoning regulations, like other laws, are completely definition-dependent. It was our job to pass them the ammunition.

Mel wrote a three-page document that was widely circulated among the sign allies. In it he defined the qualities of spectacularity. Size and visibility alone, he said, are not enough to make a sign Super. Other conditions have to be met: light quality, animation, color and contrast, and extradimensional effects. If a display possesses any three of these four qualities, he said, it would qualify as a spectacular. This document became the basis not only of 81-732 but also of the sign portion of the DUO—the Design, Use, and Occupancy Guidelines—governing the 42nd Street Redevelopment Project.

Mel was already suffering from heart trouble, but he managed to make it down to the Board of Estimate chamber, in a blinding snowstorm, to testify in one of the final hearings on 81-732. And he lived to see it become a reality. Mel died in 1988, just as the first new buildings that would benefit by the regulation that he helped to define were rising from the ground.

The hearings at City Planning and the Board of Estimate—held in the baroque Board of Estimate chamber down at City Hall—and the debates in the press, were as dramatic as anything that had ever played on Broadway. The testimony was not always verbal. Dancers danced, architectural students displayed models, singers sang songs composed for the occasion. And all of it was Broadway quality. These experiences, and other surprises, made the long hours of waiting in the stuffy chamber for a chance to testify almost bearable.

Professor Eric Sandeen from Wyoming was one interested—and interesting—outsider who showed up to offer support. "The measure of a civilization is how a community chooses to remember its own institutions," he said. The authoritative testimony of this bearded professor in a lumberjack shirt caused the commissioners to lay down their tapping pencils. "We're saving Yellowstone for you," he pointed out. "It is your responsibility to save Times Square for us."

Members of the Sierra Club from as far away as California and Alaska echoed his view. "Times Square is an advertising park," they insisted. "It is an environment with unique characteristics. It's as American as Yosemite."

People often don't recognize the value of something until after it's gone, pointed out landmarks preservationists. New York City didn't even have a landmarks law until after the destruction of the magnificent Pennsylvania Station. And there was no mandate to landmark the antique theaters until after the Helen Hayes and the Morosco were demolished to make way for the Marriott Hotel.

"The Times Square ambience is an integral part of the theater experience," argued the eloquent Jack Goldstein of Actors Equity. "It has a drama all its own that deserves to be part of people's lives, not a mere artifact of nostalgia."

Other articulate thinkers included the dean of the Yale School of Architecture and a city planning commissioner from New Orleans, as well as historians, sociologists, and designers from as far away as Milan.

Some of the most moving testimony was offered by Jack Piuggi, the business manager of Local 230 of the Painters' and Decorators' Union. Lantern-jawed Jack, from one of the toughest neighborhoods in the Bronx, was visibly trembling at the prospect of making a public speech in the presence of so many high-powered politicians and intellectuals. But he made a moving plea, not only for the livelihoods of sign painters and other sign workers but also for those of people in the fields of advertising, art and design, entertainment, transportation, food service, and tourism. The commissioners put down their pencils for him too.

But while from a moral point of view it was clear that these folks were leaving the opposition in the dust, their testimony was essentially evoking lofty values that were historic, aesthetic, and emotional. The opposition, on the other hand, consisting of real estate developers who believed the regulation would hit them in the place it would hurt the most—and their attorneys, bankers, architects, consultants, and paid political and p.r. operatives—represented a force that tends to override such "soft" considerations as historicity, humanism, and ambience: the Big Green. This is New York, pal. Money talks.

Opposition was fierce. But the view of Mr. Klein and other developers that what was wanted was another cool, sanitized Rockefeller Center finally started to give way.

One developer thought he was merely expressing common wisdom when he stated publicly that neon was passé. "People don't want all that nasty glitter," he said in a newspaper interview. "They want civilized little cafés, like in Paris."

"Fern bars!" we hooted. "The man wants fern bars!" (Fern bars, for those who don't remember, were precious little bistros of the 1980s adorned with fluffy ferns in hanging baskets, where Armani-clad yuppies would gather to tipple white wine and discuss their BMWs.) This developer was so mortified by the derision he received that he refused ever to talk to the press again—even though I referred many reporters to him, hoping he would repeat his delicious gaffe.

It's impossible to discern the actual moment when a tide turns. The tide doesn't work that way: it's a series of waves. One day, everybody is accepting a certain set of assumptions. On another day, a different worldview prevails. By January of 1986, even the Gray Lady was saying, with apparent approval, that city planners and private developers were "converging" in their dedication to bringing "new vigor" to the Square "with brighter lights, fancier signs, better theaters, more pleasant streets, and larger crowds."

The result was a law with spectacular implications but an unglamorous name, ZR 81-732, the "Times Square Zoning Amendment" to the New York City Zoning Resolution.

This amendment was greeted with gasps of incredulity through-out the sign community—not to mention among urban planners, land-use historians, and real estate developers and their bankers. It is a law that *requires* signs.

Every new "development or enlargement...between 43rd and 50th Streets with street frontage on Seventh Avenue and/or Broad-way," states 81-732, must comply with hefty minimum "sign require-ments related to surface area, location and number of signs," as well as minimum levels of illumination and animation. Only upon proof of compliance with these requirements does a development receive its all-important Certificate of Occupancy from the Department of Build-ings.

To measure compliance, the amendment established a brand-new unit of luminous intensity: the LUTS, or Light Unit of Times Square. Instead of using any of the traditionally accepted means of measuring light—such as candlepower, wattage, foot-candles, lumens, lux, cande-las, cd/m$^2$ (candelas-per-square-meter), or nits—the brightness of Times Square signs would henceforth be measured in LUTS. (The amendment includes detailed instructions on building and calibrat-ing a LUTS meter, for those who don't happen to have one kicking around in the garage.)

In addition, 81-732 addresses other such people-oriented ameni-ties as building setbacks, street wall heights, curb cuts, retail continu-ity, and pedestrian circulation. Its stated purpose is "to preserve, protect and enhance the scale and character of Times Square, the heart of New York City's entertainment district, and in particular its unique ambiance, lighting and large electric signs."

The masterwork of Loren Otis and Geoff Baker of the Urban De-sign group at the Department of City Planning, the 1987 regulation is a bit tricky to decipher, translating, as it does, the bright configura-tions of the historically liveliest blocks into nearly impenetrable zon-ing jargon. But its results are, indeed, no less than spectacular.

# "The Deuce" Rides Again

*Meanwhile, the 42nd Street* Redevelopment Project was hacking its way through a jungle of lawsuits by local residents, environmentalists, property owners, business owners, scorned developers, displaced denizens, politicians, and others—eventually reaching a total of fifty-nine—that ground the Project to a halt. And the press-released timetable changed constantly. I wish I had a square foot of new office space for every time the mayor (and his successors) and the governor (and his successor) stood on the corner of 42nd Street and Broadway with shovels in their hands, announcing to the flashing cameras that now, really, this time, I mean it this time, the Project was at last under way.

By the time the last lawsuit ran its course (all the challengers lost), the real estate market had changed. Mr. Klein and his financial partner, Prudential Insurance, won the battles but lost the war. The black behemoths—subsequently redesigned, but no matter—were never to be.

At the same time, perceptions were changing. Neon as an art medium was back in style, and a wonderful reunion was under way. American advertisers, long estranged, were coming home to Times Square. Kodak, Camel, AT&T, Maxwell House, Pepsi, and Hertz, among others, were filling the Square with glorious new spectaculars. By 1997, when we staged a commemorative blackout to celebrate Artkraft Strauss' centennial and the tenth anniversary of the passage of ZR 81-732, we discovered, to our amazement, that the job required four dozen workers. The number of spectaculars in Times Square had more than tripled in thirteen years—from fourteen to forty-four!

The renaissance of Times Square starting in the 1980s and early 1990s, including the construction of a half dozen new hotel and office towers, took place at the north end. Ironically, the last part of the Square to come back to life was 42nd Street.

In October of 1994, ten and a half years after our first "Blackout" demonstration, and after the street had stood in lifeless suspended animation for almost a decade, a ten-year "Interim Plan," under which 42nd Street would come alive with a focus on entertainment and signs, went into effect. And the pragmatic George Klein, displaying a graciousness not often seen in the mosh pit that sometimes is Times Square, awarded the contract to market, manage, and build all of his signs to Artkraft Strauss.

Finally, in an irony that was lost on no one, especially the participants, the first office building to go up in the Project area, a mere fifteen years after the Project was announced, was built by one of its most energetic early opponents, developer Douglas Durst. And from the moment of its conception, the building was designed to have plenty of signs.

Perhaps, being an environmentalist, Durst had no problem making the intellectual leap between architecture and the intrinsic nature of a place. Perhaps publicity about the new advertising money rushing into the Square was an influence. Perhaps it's the Square's new look: vividly animated, entertainment-oriented (with Disney as the Project's anchor tenant), tourist-filled. In any case, there is no question about the fact that success breeds more success.

Times Square maintains its mythic place in our commercial culture because of its remarkable power of survival. If any place ever stared down a wrecking ball and lived to tell about it, it is Times Square.

And the secret of this survival is written in the signs.

Today, you can stand on the corner of 42nd Street and Broadway and be dazzled as never before, as "the Deuce" develops into a lively and prosperous entertainment street surpassing even the hopes and visions of Cooper and Eckstut so many years ago.

Lowering the Ball in Times Square on New Year's Eve was my family's job for as long as I can remember—indeed, for as long as anyone can remember. While the rest of the world reveled, our New Year's Eves were quiet, sober, and—as the magic moment approached—intensely serious. It was hard, cold work—harder than it looks, but real magic always looks easy—and, like the audience, we loved every second of it.

For eighty-eight years, from 1907 to 1995, the world's most famous ceremony marking the passage of time was performed in almost exactly the same way.

During the last minute of the year, starting at precisely 11:59:00 and ending at precisely 12:00:00, a crew on top of the Times Tower eased the heavy, bulb-studded sphere down its 77-foot flagpole, using cotton-clad steel cables wound through a pair of pulleys and around the slippery metal railing on the roof. An electrician operated the switches; another worker kept the lines from tangling. The timekeeper, one eye on a stopwatch and the other on the descending electrical cable marked with tape to show fifteen-second intervals, directed the crew to "Speed up," "Slow down," or hold "Steady as she goes"—so that the Ball, viewed from the street, reached the level of the parapet, appearing to turn on the numbers, precisely at midnight.

At that moment, the timekeeper said, "Switch!"—the electrician threw the switches turning off the Ball and turning on the numbers that spelled out the New Year—and the crowd, already aroar for hours like a giant beast or a mighty ocean, flipped its collective lid.

Sometimes, to be fancy, the electrician flashed the numbers on and off while the crowd screamed and the horns tooted. But essentially it was a ceremony, a ritual unchanged that remained unchanged—primarily because it worked, but also because it occupied a place in people's hearts. The audience, both the immense crowd in the street and the millions tuning in via TV and, in earlier years, by radio and Movietone News, delighted in the precision and predictability combined with the human touch—as obvious in the Ball's slight wobble, especially in high winds, as brushstrokes in an oil painting.

We were often asked why, in this age of automation, the actual Ball lowering was still done by hand. We would reply that people are more reliable than computers. "If you had a machine that you used only once a year," Jonathan told a reporter in 1981, "you can be sure it would freeze up, jam up, ice up, or otherwise foul up." And sure enough, in 1995, when we were replaced by a computer, that is exactly what happened.

The atmosphere atop the Tower during the final minutes of the year was like a combination of religious ritual and the Fall of Saigon. Surrounded by hysteria and chaos, the roof was an island of almost unearthly calm. We would look at one another and feel like we were the only silent, sober people within a million miles—and perhaps we were. Time itself took on an entirely different texture.

At 11:45 the timekeeper locked the doors to the roof and quietly began the countdown: "Fourteen minutes to Ball lowering . . . thirteen minutes and forty-five seconds . . . thirteen minutes and thirty seconds . . ." so that by three minutes to, we were all breathing in sync—and, we joked, if a cosmic ray suddenly destroyed all the clocks, we would still be in time.

In those closing minutes of the year, time seemed to slow down—the effect of intense concentration. Time is elastic, as anyone knows who has ever waited for water to boil or a lover to call. The seconds seem to stretch on forever. In that moment of calm, some of us, at any rate, sent wishes for Love, Peace, and Understanding to the world beyond our Tower walls. (Others were no doubt thinking that in only sixteen minutes they would get off work and could go party.)

We did the job in every kind of weather, through bomb threats and kidnap alarms, practical-joke schemes, attacks by drunken revelers and crazed p.r. flacks, landlord scandals and bankruptcies, and political and financial malaise. We did the job whether we got paid or not (most often, not), and we defended the integrity of the Ball and the ceremony from individuals who for commercial or publicity reasons wanted to change it. We were a stabilizing force in a village that sometimes seemed to be running amok. It was the golden thing to do, both for ourselves and for our cynosure neighborhood—and besides, despite the hair-raising stress and tension, it was always major fun.

For nineteen years, from 1976 until 1995, my brother and I shared the timekeeper job. We were never fussy about whose turn it was. Sometimes we would flip a coin, and Jonathan would quip, "The loser gets to be timekeeper."

The assistant timekeeper, the "winner" of the coin toss, had the easier job because it entailed more distraction. After obtaining the time via shortwave radio from the atomic clock at the National Bureau of Standards in Fort Collins, Colorado (more accurate than telephone time), the assistant set everybody's clocks and watches, and then ran around all evening "giving time" to the operators of the other displays, doing telephone and walkie-talkie time checks with the TV and radio networks, and looking after the security and refreshments.

The timekeeper, on the other hand, as befits a modern leader, had to simultaneously remain calm and talk to reporters about what it felt like to be timekeeper.

"How do you feel?"

"How do I *feel?* I feel like I'm going to get *that* Ball from the top of *that* pole to the bottom of it at *exactly* midnight. See? Ball. Pole. Midnight. That's all."

"Would your grandfather be proud of you?" they asked.

"How would I know?" (Ball, pole, midnight. Ball, pole, midnight.) It's like what athletes call focus: a state of essentially empty mind, except for the goal.

Starting in the early 1980s we were joined by Artkraft Strauss project managers—first Roger Mazzuchelli, then Tony Calvano—who kept additional eyes on the clock, the crew, the equipment, and the security—the last of which became increasingly important in later years.

Friends supplemented the work crew, contributing unique expertise in novel ways. Communications guru Jan Bridge could tune in the time signal from the atomic clock in Colorado via ham radio even when entire bands were wiped out by solar flares, electrical storms, or microwaves from MTV. Fred Covan, chief of psychology at Bellevue Hospital, stood parapet duty, using suicide-prevention techniques to keep building owners' guests from walking out on the ledge. Firmly grasping the shoulder of a potential parapet walker, Dr. Covan looked him in the eye. "You don't really want to walk out on that parapet, do you!" he said convincingly. Artist Roberta Rosenthal monitored the ladder to the upper roof, enforcing our ban on alcohol, noisemakers, and high heels, armed only with a pair of mittens embroidered with portraits of Minnie Mouse. "Minnie says, No high heels on the ladder!" said Roberta's friendly fist.

To the audience, the performance always looked smooth and seamless. But behind the scenes, there was often another story.

## BEHIND THE SCENES:
## THE EARLY YEARS

*Ernest Kaufmann, a great-nephew* of Ben Strauss, remembers being invited up to the Tower for New Year's Eve as an eleven-year-old in 1938, soon after arriving with his family from Nazi Germany. Ernest credits my grandfather, along with his uncle Ben, for sending the money and papers that helped them escape.

"My uncle Ben Strauss together with Mr. Starr were the ones who constructed and dropped the first Ball," he writes. "I might point out that they were late in dropping the Ball from the Tower in 1938 because some dumb kid got tangled up in the ropes. That dumb kid was me. I was never again allowed to go up into the Tower with Mr. Starr and my uncle Ben."

And sure enough, youngsters were never again invited up to the Tower on New Year's Eve until Jonathan and I took over the job forty years later and allowed guests to bring their kids—all of whom were invariably better behaved than "Cousin Ernest" apparently was.

When Jonathan and I were growing up, we watched the Ball coming down on TV just like everybody else. The only difference was that we expected it to be perfect because it was "our" job—not because it was a phenomenon of nature. To Jake, Mel, and Gene, it was just another construction job. During Christmas week the electricians checked the wiring and climbed the flagpole to install the cables, the metalworkers built the parapet numbers, the painters painted them, the sign hangers installed them, and on New Year's Eve afternoon, Gene dispatched a crew. Nobody wanted to be on this crew because, they claimed, the job was so boring. I can remember the older guys complaining, "I haven't seen my wife on New Year's Eve in twenty-seven years. Next year she's going to divorce me." Of course, it was cool to be blasé. And with half the world watching and no second chance to get it right, a measure of dispassion was essential.

New Year's Eve starts at 6:00, when the crew hoists the Ball to the top of the flagpole and lights it. Then there is nothing to do but wait. A favorite activity—allowed only to crew members—was to sit on the edge of the parapet, feet dangling down, and watch the glittering crowd 250 feet below.

In the days before glamour, guests, and p.r., the crew spent the evening playing cards around a rickety card table inside the elevator machine room on the roof of the building. The room was cinder block painted yellow and red, and freezing cold. The excited, brightly lit crowd in the Square below was less than a rumor: the roar of a hundred thousand throats and twenty thousand noisemakers was muffled by the twelve-foot-high parapet surrounding the roof, and obliterated entirely inside the room by the elevator machinery's clanking, whirring gears. Sometimes a junior worker, doing the job for the first time, climbed the parapet to gaze down at the crowd. "Hey!" someone would shout before Junior could get himself hypnotized. "C'mon back down here. It's your deal!"

Russ Brown, the red-faced, antediluvian building superintendent, was the timekeeper for many years. He had a big schoolroom clock on the machine room door, a chromium stopwatch in his big, beefy hand, and a Mickey Mouse watch, purchased new in 1949, that he wore for good luck. He would entertain himself during the long evening by serving refreshments in the basement to the police and other folks working the Square that night—hot coffee, rye whiskey, corned beef sandwiches, and chocolate cake.

At twenty to twelve he would appear on the roof, his sense of time unimpaired by the refreshments, and the cardplayers would pack up the game, pocket their winnings, and take their positions around the base of the pole. They would have rehearsed earlier that day and the day before as well; the majority of the crew were veterans of the job; and all wore watches set to within a quarter of a second of Eastern Standard Time, so that anyone could take over if Russ happened to fall down. It was simply unthinkable—impossible—to screw up.

The first Ball lowering took place at 11:59 P.M. on December 31, 1907, replacing the immensely popular fireworks extravaganza that the *New York Times* first presented on New Year's Eve of 1905 to inaugurate its new headquarters. The fireworks display was repeated on the New Year's Eves of 1906 and 1907, but some mishap may have occurred, because thereafter it became illegal to shoot fireworks over crowds, and a bright new focus for the celebration had to be found.

The inspiration was probably the gold-plated "time balls" that were once lowered at noon every day in seaports throughout the world to enable ships' navigators to set their chronometers. Until

1968, one such time ball was still lowered every day for nostalgia's sake on a tower at New York's South Street Seaport.

But the New Year's Eve celebration has its roots in a tradition that is far more ancient, going all the way back to the origins of historical time.

Before literacy, before almanacs, before everyone owned clocks and calendars, celebrants gathered at Stonehenge, at the Pyramids, at Machu Picchu—at every place that was considered a "Crossroads of the World"—to observe the intersecting of a celestial object, such as the sun or other star, with a tall earthly one, such as a mountain or tower, to mark the turning of the year.

The image symbolizes the intersection of the sacred and the profane—the descent of the heavenly element into the human, everyday world. Even the familiar star-topped evergreen, a symbol the Christians adopted from the Celts, embodies this image. Gathering at the winter solstice, when the days would start to once again grow longer, people celebrated the Resurrection of the Light, received prophecies and agricultural guidance, and resolved to be wiser and more virtuous.

All these pagan ideas of transformation survive in our modern New Year's Eve rituals. People use noisemakers, as if to drive away evil spirits. They wear masks and funny hats, as though assuming a different, mysterious identity. They exchange kisses with strangers, as at an orgy. And even the most modern skeptics make resolutions, participating in the belief that the door between the cosmic and mundane worlds is briefly open, so magic, the power of mind over matter, can come through.

All this helps to explain the magnetism of the Ball-lowering ceremony—and why in 1907–8 it was an instant hit that became an instant tradition.

At one time I wondered why people are so drawn to it, not only standing and waiting in the freezing street for hours on what may be the coldest night of the year but also stopping in the middle of their own parties to tune it in on TV, and even watching from other time zones, where it isn't even midnight yet.

Then I realized that it's more than it seems. The vision of a glowing orb descending onto a tower at the "Crossroads of the World" during the minute between the years—a minute that seems to belong neither to the old year nor to the new—meets a primordial need. It speaks to the ancient pagan heart in all of us.

(My theory that the Ball-lowering ceremony is fundamentally a pagan religious ritual was confirmed in 1987 when the Grand Rabbinate of Israel—the body that rules on Halacha, Orthodox Jewish religious law—declared that it would deny a kosher license to any hotel in Israel that conducted an American-style New Year's Eve celebration. When I heard about this, I felt that all my years of going on about Stonehenge to anyone who would listen were vindicated.)

One most unpagan aspect of modern New Year's Eves is the orderly behavior of the crowds. This has been true since the mid-1970s, when Police Chief Mickey Schwartz of Midtown South had the idea of dividing the crowd into blocks behind barricades, so they couldn't surge. This eliminated the biggest peril in a large crowd, and also, by enabling the police and emergency medical crews to get around, it cut petty hazards like pickpocketing and gross inebriation to almost nothing. Today, one of the safest places to be on New Year's Eve is in the middle of Times Square.

In the early days, however, people were unbelievably rowdy. Before New Year's Eve came to Times Square in 1904, raucous crowds and vicious gangs mingled with the genteel public in the streets near Trinity Church, at the end of Wall Street, where the traditional chimes would "ring out the old, ring in the new." Hellions did so much damage, throwing rocks, slashing people's clothing, and tying the tails of cats together and tossing them into stables to stampede the horses, that the Wall Streeters were delighted when the celebration moved uptown.

During the final hours of 1904, the first New Year's Eve at Times Square, it was reported that the roar of the crowd could be heard in Hastings-on-Hudson, some twenty-five miles away. A favorite noise-maker in those days was a large tin can with a brick inside it, used as a rattle. At midnight, having exhausted the noise potential of these devices, people joyously heaved the bricks in all directions.

Another popular plaything was a toy that children still use at birthday parties, consisting of a rolled-up tube of thin paper with a feather glued to one end and a wooden whistle attached to the other.

Blowing on the whistle unrolls the paper, enabling one child to tickle another with the feather. The turn-of-the-century twist on this toy was to conceal a razor blade in the feather. In 1905, when the police attempted to confiscate these gadgets, a riot ensued.

But not all novelties were dangerous. On the occasion of the first electric New Year's Eve celebration—the year of the first Ball lowering—restaurateurs throughout the Square equipped their waiters with electric top hats. When the Ball came down and the parapet numbers spelling "1908" turned on, each waiter reached into his pocket and flipped a switch attached to a battery, turning on the matching parapet numbers on his head.

Apart from the mellowing of the crowd, the Ball lowering remained unchanged through most of the electric century except for 1943 and 1944, when it was suspended for the wartime dimout. The crowd gathered as usual, but they were eerily quiet. In 1943, their mood was hopeful; in 1944, as the war stretched on, somber. A minute of silence marked the end of the year, followed by a carillon of chimes ringing out from an amplifier truck parked at the base of the Tower.

By 1945, the danger of German U-boats offshore was deemed sufficiently abated to allow the Ball to be relighted, "as a measure of confidence," reported the Newspaper of Record, "that it would remain lighted from now on through victory and peace." A subdued crowd the police implausibly estimated at 750,000 gathered in the Square through a night of alternating dank fog and soaking rain to celebrate "hopefully but warily, joyously but not uproariously." At midnight, however, the roar of pent-up emotion that burst from all those throats lasted for nearly twenty minutes, at sufficient intensity to completely drown out the voice of soprano Lucy Monroe, amplified a hundred times, singing "The Star-Spangled Banner" on the stage below the replica of Lady Liberty.

After the war, when new metals became available, the 600-pound wrought-iron Ball was replaced by one of extruded aluminum that weighed a mere 200 pounds. "It looked exactly the same," remembers Mike Dianuzzo, then our electrical foreman, "because we used the old pattern and copied it exactly. But we thought it was light as a feather."

In 1949, a fuse on the roof blew at ten minutes to midnight, and the side of the Ball facing the crowd suddenly went dark. The quick-thinking crew turned off the Ball, lowered it down to the roof, spun it around, and hoisted it back up. Nobody noticed that the back side of the Ball wasn't lit that year.

An oft-repeated legend—believe it if you will—is that a terrible windstorm in the mid-1950s caused the 200-pound Ball to be pushed back *up* the pole while we were trying to bring it down. A brave junior electrician, one of those whose contemplation of the crowd was frustrated by his cardplaying seniors, leaped for a tag line attached to the Ball and held on to it, his additional 120-pound weight ensuring the Ball's descent (and reinforcing the Law of Gravity).

There were exciting New Year's Eves in the early 1960s, when the renovation of the building for Allied Chemical was under way. The entire building was stripped down to its steel structure, and the roof level lacked a floor. Workers lowered the Ball while "walking the plank" on rickety boards that spanned the abyss where the new roof was to be.

For seven years, starting in 1981, the traditional white Ball was transformed into a Big Apple, with red lamps instead of white and the addition of a green leaf and stem. This was ordered by one building owner as a gesture of solidarity with the "I ❤ NY" publicity campaign. When everyone had forgotten the original reason for it and the crew escalated their complaints about the provincialism of the symbol ("The apple stands for New York, but New Year's Eve belongs to everybody," said foreman Eddie Robleski, a twenty-year veteran of the job), we quietly changed it back to the universally recognized white orb.

Jonathan was the first Artkraft Strauss management person in the modern era to work New Year's Eve. In 1976 he was a project manager at Artkraft, and he decided that New Year's Eve would be an interesting project to manage. He faced immediate rebellion. The workers said, "This is a workers' job, not a boss's job," and threatened a boycott. So much for their claim that the job was boring. Jonathan called their bluff, and offered to let everyone stay home on New Year's Eve. From then until 1995, one or both of us were always there.

## LANDLORDS AND CON MEN
## WE'VE KNOWN AND LOVED

*During the 1980s, once the* 42nd Street Redevelopment Plan began to appear imminent, One Times Square changed hands nearly every year right around Christmas, as regularly as clockwork. You could set your calendar by it. The signs represented the only income on the nearly tenantless building, but their revenue wasn't enough to carry a mortgage. Apparently each successive owner hoped to make a killing on the condemnation money George Klein would have to pay to take over the building for his Project—until he surprised them all by deciding he could live without it; and then was himself surprised in turn when, despite his almost superhuman patience, history overtook his grand, dark Plan for 42nd Street.

This pass-the-potato game reminded me of the old joke about the rare bottle of wine that keeps being traded at ever-higher prices. Finally one buyer opens the bottle and tastes the wine. "Hey, this wine is no good!" he exclaims. "It's turned to vinegar!"

"That wine isn't for drinking," the seller informs him. "It's for selling."

Some of the building owners during those years were strange. Others seemed to have recently arrived from another planet. All were unfamiliar with the territory and were glad to have New Year's Eve professionally taken care of. This was especially true for those—not a few—who cultivated anonymity. The secretary to one owner confided to me that he was one of the wealthiest men in the world. "And no one," she said, "has ever seen his name in the newspaper. Not even when he was born."

Jonathan and I moved into this vacuum with aplomb, answering queries from reporters that had hitherto been ignored by our equally antipublicity predecessors, Jake, Mel, and Gene. This led to some disruption in the plant as we struggled to accommodate requests for behind-the-scenes previews of tin-knockers preparing the Ball, electricians climbing the pole, sign hangers installing the numbers, timekeepers keeping the time.

Eventually we hit on the idea of running a dress rehearsal—"Midnight at Noon," we called it—during the slow news week between

Christmas and New Year's. We invited the press to the roof in daylight to see how the Ball-lowering was done and to interview the people behind the Ball, the hands-on workers who actually made it happen. Previously the Ball had been viewed by the general public as a sort of naturally occurring phenomenon, like the moonrise, and we worried that demystification—showing the human side—might spoil the magic. But in the end, it enhanced it. People enjoyed hearing from the actual human beings, folks like themselves, who did this interesting and stressful job flawlessly year after year.

Publicity is an odd commodity. People think one can "get" publicity in the same way one can "get" a haircut or acquire a collection of stamps. But it doesn't work that way. Short of gunning down innocents in a public place in broad daylight—not the sort of thing one generally wants publicity for—the only way an ordinary person without Hollywood grooming or unlimited spin doctor funds can "get" publicity is by having a good story to tell and telling it well. Which we did. So the "Midnight at Noon" dress rehearsal became part of the tradition.

But there were a lot of nifty stories we couldn't tell at the time. The scene behind the scene often seemed like grist for a comic spy novel.

One anonymous building owner was a nameless offshore import-export firm that I called the Caviar People because on the telephone, instead of "Hello," they said, "Caviar!" I tried to buy caviar from them, or, failing that, persuade them to donate some for the troops, but that didn't fly. They did insist, however, that I keep all the reporters locked in the building after the rehearsal until "the owner's representatives" could meet with them.

An hour or two went by, the ineffable champagne generously donated by the Great Western Winery in upstate New York was down to the dregs, and the reporters were growing cranky because they needed to file their stories.

Finally a quartet of lawyers who looked like they came from Central Casting—identically attired in charcoal suits and horn-rim glasses and carrying identical calfskin briefcases—marched in and announced, "Don't ask us about You-Know-What! We have no comment!"

The reporters were baffled. "What? What's You-Know-What? No comment about what?"

"We told you not to ask!" raged the lawyers.

Now intrigued, at least one reporter tracked down a tale of money laundering, death sentences by authoritarian regimes, and embezzlement of public funds in high foreign places.

While we privately found this entertaining, we had no opinion about it. Our job, our only focus, was to get *that* Ball down *that* pole at *exactly* midnight. Both the thrill and the headaches were all ours—and I'm happy to say in retrospect that most of the headaches were more amusing than worrisome. For one thing, most prospective saboteurs showed a remarkable tendency to self-hoist by their own petard.

There was the time the Ballnappers from New Jersey plotted to kidnap the Ball, pretend to hold it for ransom, and then dramatically return it at the last possible moment—in order to get publicity for New Jersey. "Why should New York get all the publicity?" they complained. "We're from New Jersey, New Jersey should get publicity too!" But they courteously called me to find out when the "last possible moment" would be, so they wouldn't seriously screw things up—and thus their scheme was foiled.

There was the Human Fly, posing as an ABC reporter from Los Angeles. He'd made elaborate plans, including bringing an entire crew of assistants to New York with him and putting them up in a hotel in Yonkers. There was something about him and the questions he was asking that didn't ring right, so I called our friends at Dick Clark Productions to check him out. They recognized him right away. "That guy? He's the Human Fly!" ABC had done a TV special on him only a few months before, and they sent me a tape of it.

Why someone who had escaped from Alcatraz, and could climb sheer skyscraper walls with his bare hands and feet, thought he needed my help to get onto the roof of One Times Square on New Year's Eve, I'll never know. But in developing his plan to leap onto the Ball from the rooftop water tank and ride it down while waving a flag and playing the kazoo (very dangerous—he was a big guy, and the Ball would have crashed), the fool was using his real name!

Other risk-takers sought to make political statements. We intercepted one group that planned to protest the 42nd Street Redevelopment Project by transmitting the Morse code message "SOS"–standing for "Save Our Square"–for five minutes at 11:55 with flashlights from unoccupied office windows throughout the building. Anybody seeing this would have thought we were holding them hostage, and sent in the Marines.

Speaking of hostages, in 1979 one building owner's flack man suddenly decided at 11:45 that it would be groovy to turn off the Ball and leave it off for fourteen minutes in honor of the American hostages in Iran. He ordered the Artkraft Strauss workers to turn off the Ball, but they treated him like the Invisible Man. So he made a run for the switch himself. But he had no chance of getting past Jonathan, who played defense on his high school football team and happily assumes the demeanor of a boulder.

Another building owner, who lasted for several years until the bankruptcy court relieved him of his problems, habitually invited five hundred or so of his "closest friends"–mainly people he met in the street that night–up to the roof to lower the Ball. He would auction off the job to all comers for cash (hoping to make the mortgage payment, I guess) and distribute his business card to identify the winners. At five minutes to twelve his "friends" rushed up the stairs to the roof and burst through the doors, shrieking, howling, blowing horns, and waving business cards and champagne bottles–which they occasionally threw at us (reprising the brickbats of earlier years) when we wouldn't let them near the pole. Our friends and co-workers used their own high school football experience to form a defense line. But every year we were pushed farther back, and the precision grew dicier.

The police–even when off duty–couldn't help, since, they told us, police can't restrict the behavior of an owner or his guests within his own building unless someone is actually committing a crime. We tried all kinds of tactics, including, to the dismay of the Fire Marshal, wiring mazes of six-foot ladders across the stairwell. But at best we only slowed them down. Finally we engaged the Guardian Angels, an urban guerrilla parapolice organization, who are less legalistic than the police when it comes to peacekeeping and who did an outstanding, and nonviolent, job of containing the rowdies.

All these shenanigans–as Rebecca Robertson of the Empire State

Development Corporation aptly characterized them the year this legendary building owner decided to threaten not to allow the Ball lowering at all unless the ESDC paid him a large sum of money—led us
to start calling the event "The Battle of New Year's Eve."

One year, that same building owner decided he could make a
buck by agreeing to lower a soft-drink bottle cap down the pole at
midnight instead of a plain old Ball. "Think of all the publicity you'll
get!" he told the soft-drink company. What better example of metaphysical marketing than attaching your product to the Symbol of All
Time?

But the notion of fooling the TV networks into giving away free
advertising is ill-conceived at best. TV networks are in the business
of selling advertising, not giving it away—and they are eminently sophisticated about protecting their turf. They could have blurred the
Ball out, like the face of a crime victim, or not shown it at all. At least
one network kept a simulation rigged up in a studio for just such an
emergency. Someone leaked the scheme to *New York* magazine, who
ran it in their "Intelligencer" column. The snickering this idea engen-
dered could be heard all the way to the soft-drink manufacturer's corporate headquarters, and the owner reluctantly withdrew his plan.

Then he tried to trademark the Ball and charge the networks
large sums of money for a license to show it on TV. When that didn't
work, he demanded that Dick Clark pay him a pile of cash (in un-
marked bills, I heard) for the privilege of broadcasting from the sev-
enteenth-floor roof overlooking the Square, where for nearly two
decades Clark had hosted ABC's "New Year's Rockin' Eve" without
any exchange of lucre. Clark and company said, in effect, "Sayonara,"
and moved the show down to the street.

Over the years, Dick Clark and his ABC team stood in sharp relief to these backstage follies. They were not only a joy to work with—
as professional as can be, and the nicest people besides—they also had
great security, primo communications, and swell eats, all of which
they generously shared. We were sorry to see them go. A subsequent
building owner invited them back, but by then they were enjoying
broadcasting from the street, where the sane people were.

# "Three ... Two ... One ... LEAP ... Zero!"

*If I had to pick* my favorite New Year's Eve, it would have to be 1988—the Year of the Leap Second.

From time to time, at irregular intervals, the world's astronomers agree to add (or occasionally subtract) one second to all the earth's clocks in order to keep them in sync with sidereal time. This compensates for changes in the rate of the earth's rotation caused by atmospheric, tidal, and internal friction (the "sloshing" of the earth's molten core). The earth's rotation is quite irregular—it can vary by as much as one-thousandth of a second per day—while atomic clocks, based on the frequency of oscillation in the cesium atom, are a million times more accurate, measuring time to within a billionth of a second.

"A second is a relatively long amount of time," says Dr. Dennis McCarthy, the astronomer at the U.S. Naval Observatory in charge of the department that measures the earth's rotation. "If you're flying a plane by instruments and you're off by one second, you're going to miss the runway by nearly one-fifth of a mile." Space shuttles and satellites, power companies controlling electric flow over enormous grids, TV networks synchronizing programming and transmission of pure colors—all require accurate time. So coordinating the clocks is crucial. And this year, the second was to be added between the years.

We were intrigued by the possibilities of a midnight countdown that instead of the familiar "... Four-Three-Two-One-Zero!" would go "... Four-Three-Two-One-LEAP-Zero!" Between the LEAP and the Zero there would be a whole extra second that actually belonged, while it existed, neither to "last year" nor to "next year," but to another kind of time altogether.

One second can be immense. It is even larger, in my view, than Dr. McCarthy says. It's enough time to ruin a life, or to save one. It's plenty of time to make a destiny-changing decision. Or experience a revelation. Or utter a prayer that reaches to the ends of the heavens. In a second, the galaxies move billions of miles, and countless creatures are born and die. The world is completely altered. So you can certainly change your life in a second, if you think about it.

And not only that. The Ball lowering is watched by some 300,000,000 people around the world, counting the TV audience. If each one experiences an extra second, the collective total added on to all their lives is *9½ years*. The entire population of the earth, 4,843,000,000 people, would "gain" 153½ years in which to make improvements and cultivate goodwill. So ran our reasoning at the time.

We decided to highlight this singular second by conducting a dazzling one-second light show in the interval between the LEAP and the Zero. It would be a spectacular second: "the shortest-running hit on Broadway," we promised. And it was a terrific show. We rented a bunch of high-powered strobes and multicolor disco lights, wired them to separate switches, and spread them out across the parapet and inside the Ball. When the timekeeper called "LEAP!" the electrician hit the switches, and the strobes and disco lights fired off in all directions, in their preappointed sequence.

It was quite spectacular. Brief, but spectacular. Slowed-down videotapes show the Ball pausing just above the year numbers, strobing like crazy while the parapet did an eye-dazzling, layered "curtain out," and then sinking behind the numbers in the usual way just as they flashed on for the New Year.

Afterward, folks accused us of cheating. (In collusion with all the TV networks?) "That can't have lasted only a second," they claimed. "It seemed like it went on for *minutes.*" Nope. It was just another example of the elasticity of time.

## THE GLITTER BALL

*In 1995, Artkraft Strauss was* relieved of all these responsibilities when the event was taken over by the Times Square Business Improvement District (BID), a recently formed service organization devoted to neighborhood improvement and promotion.

A Business Improvement District is a kind of supergovernment currently flourishing in New York and in many other cities, states, and provinces. A group of local property owners gets together and writes a charter. They may agree to tax themselves and their neighbors to supplement regular municipal services or apply for special grants and privileges as a neighborhood. Unless 51 percent of the district's owners object, the BID becomes a political reality, an overlay on the regular polity beneath it.

With the power to tax, and sometimes to float bonds, to provide security, sanitation, and social services, a BID resembles a municipality in all important respects save one: it isn't accountable to an electorate. Thus liberated from the cumbersome processes of democracy, a BID can be highly efficient. And endowed with both wealth and power, it can be highly persuasive. The Times Square BID—arguably the most aggressive in New York—is exemplary of both these admirable qualities.

Founded in 1993, the Times Square BID immediately placed its stamp on the Square. Armed with a lavish p.r. budget, it started by taking control of all the Square's public events. By 1995, it was ready to "own" New Year's Eve. Declaring that the event was in danger of succumbing to commercialism and losing its media coverage, the BID conceived a bold new plan.

After months of top-secret planning, the BID, with much fanfare, unveiled its grand surprise: the new, rhinestone-encrusted, smoke-emitting Glitter Ball—a modern, computer-driven, high-tech wonder that would at long last, they promised, assure pinpoint accuracy in marking the arrival of the New Year. The old Ball, one BID official sneered to the press, "looked like someone's high school science project."

The Glitter Ball made its debut on the New Year's Eve of 1996. I wasn't watching, but within minutes after midnight, phone calls started flying. "Did you see that?!"

Videotapes reveal what happened. The Glitter Ball lurched down the pole thirteen and a half seconds late, got hung up halfway down, and stayed lit after the numbers 1996, belatedly, turned on. Meanwhile, as Dick Clark was counting down: "...Six...Five...Four," some in the crowd were chanting: "...Four...Three...Two," and the rest: "...Seven...Six...Five," since no one had coordinated the clocks.

Perfectionist Dick Clark takes his longtime identification with the New Year's Eve show from Times Square very seriously—especially its split-second timing. He called me at home the following night, incredulous. He knew that I had always been as concerned with the timing as he was. "I just spent the day watching the tapes from all the other networks," he said. "And they all showed the same thing!"

"That's because it really happened," I assured him. I had seen the videotapes too. It wasn't a glitch in his control room.

"The First Screw-up of 1996—The Balldrop!" exclaimed the front-page headline in the *New York Post* on January 2.

Exercising professional damage control, the BID convened a series of press conferences. First they denied that anything was wrong. (Everyone only thinks they saw what they think they saw, said the BID.) Then, acknowledging two of the nearly fourteen lost seconds, they hung the hang-up on a hapless young spotlight operator, who blasted back in the *Post:* "I'm being blamed for something that wasn't my fault. I was never cued to shut my light off."

Nationwide, stand-up TV comics and irreverent radio personalities enjoyed a weeklong field day. Editorials and letters to the editor urged whoever was in charge to "bring back the guys with the ropes."

Finally, knowing that all this would soon blow over, the BID and their spin doctors explained that there is no "right" or "wrong" spot for the Ball to land at midnight. It's midnight when we say it is, says the BID.

They offered the same explanation the following year, when the Ball landed several seconds early; and the year after that, when it started down the pole twenty seconds late, barely passing the halfway point by midnight.

Nevertheless, the BID has the right idea. Obviously the event needed to be upgraded properly to usher in the new millennium, and technology has to change with its times. And apart from this, the BID does a bang-up job entertaining the midnight crowd with fabulous light shows, twinkling confetti, and cool souvenirs, in a Times Square as clean and safe as Disneyland. Gretchen Dykstra, the president of the BID, deserves credit for all the BID's successes.

Artkraft Strauss isn't the first—and won't be the last—human crew to be replaced by a computer. Looking back, we had Broadway's longest run. Few people have the opportunity to retire from a job after so many years of error-free performance. And it's nice to have a life, like other people, on New Year's Eve.

I'm sure that the reason for our success all those years wasn't the Ball itself—or its image—but the people behind it. The electricians and sign hangers who manned the ropes and switches were all, like my grandfather, skilled workers, individuals of balance and integrity. After all, machines are only as good as the people who operate them.

This idea was best expressed by Loretta Bizzarro, the wife of Artkraft Strauss sheet metal craftsman Michael Bizzarro. Michael does the kind of meticulous metalwork we call "jewelry"—intricate detailing, invisible fastenings, fine historic restorations of canopies and marquees. In the old days, someone like that was said to "have hands." I ran into Loretta one Saturday on the street outside the American Crafts Museum.

"It's a shame about the Ball," she said. "You know, all the high-tech and hype in the world are nothing without hands. The hands are what make a thing come alive."

## The New Times Square

*I can't help thinking* that the sense of brightness and safety that now pervades the Square has a lot to do with its destiny being in the hands of women throughout the 1980s and 1990s. For the first time, women were stepping off the billboards and out of the movie screens into the action. In addition to Gretchen, women of power and ability were suddenly everywhere.

In 1987, ZR 81-732, the zoning resolution mandating bright lights and signs from 43rd to 50th Street, kicked in, under the auspices of Sylvia Deutsch, the stern and fair-minded chair of the City Planning Commission. Half a dozen major new office buildings and hotels were under development then. Today, they are all aglow.

In 1990, the New 42nd Street—a not-for-profit organization dedicated to redeveloping the derelict historic theaters on 42nd Street west of Broadway—came into existence under the directorship of ace theater person Cora Cahan. And one by one, the grand old jewel boxes started to light up again.

In 1994, the 42nd Street Development Project finally lifted off, under the eagle eyes of brightness-loving Rebecca Robertson and her successor, Wendy Leventer, transforming the Deuce, not into a gloomy office canyon, but into a razzle-dazzle entertainment district.

At Times Square Center Associates, the developer-partner of the 42nd Street Development, Elizabeth Counihan of Park Tower Realty and Sharon Barnes of Prudential Insurance managed the project for their respective companies. At Disney, the project's anchor tenant, senior development manager Catharine Cary was the one to see.

Times Square had turned a corner. All the work throughout the 1970s and 1980s by innumerable individuals and organizations who continued to believe in the Square, even during its darkest days, finally started to show results. It was people who made the Square come alive.

And I was thrilled to be a part of it. At Artkraft Strauss, where I became president in 1988, we started to enjoy some of our best years ever.

The signs tell us that the last chapter of the electric century—

like the first—is marked by convergence. Not only in the

ordinary technological sense, describing the short-term

future in which the computer, telephone, fax, and TV, and advertising, shopping, bill paying, and banking are destined all to become one, but also in the paradoxical way apparently incompatible elements—technology and emotion, for example, or the past and the future—are combining to create new forms of expression, promotion, and display.

As we stand, Janus-like, at the threshold of a new era—a new decade-century-millennium—we can't help looking forward and backward at the same time. Nostalgia blends with anticipation to create new, sometimes bittersweet, philosophical flavors.

We are unquestionably experiencing a renewed appreciation of the past. This implies a revival of classical values—a notion that is more than a populist catchphrase. Old-fashioned Modernism—a vision of an ahistorical world dominated by computers and machinery and shiny, high-tech surfaces—looks passé now, almost quaint, like a 1930s science fiction film in black and white. Color and texture and feeling, sensory elements that endlessly recombine to make our world a human one, are flowering again—if indeed they ever stopped. They were not deconstructed out of existence by the 1970s cynicism that called itself Postmodern and was marked by a turning away from the light. The neon revival, which began in Europe, particularly in Germany, in the late 1970s, is only one example of a global rediscovery of the classical.

The same rediscovery is taking place in all the arts. In the theater, revivals are staple fare. In literature, a resurgence of Victoriana—the works of Jane Austen, the Brontës, and Conan Doyle—signify a renewed appreciation of civility, subtlety, and manners, and maybe even of the finer points of traditional sex roles. It's possible that students of tomorrow will recognize the names Sophocles, Shakespeare, Milton, and Dante—not only as Dead White Males but as dynamite storytellers. Yesterday's jalopies are today's classic cars.

In architecture, the stark glass towers of the 1960s and 1970s have yielded to classical and even decorative forms. Landmarking, once considered the province of crackpot elitist preservationists—"little old ladies in tennis shoes," they used to be called—has become commonplace, whereas the verb "to landmark" did not even exist prior to about 1970. Yesterday's debate was about how many city blocks to demolish and how fast; today's debate is between conservation (maintaining aged buildings) and restoration (repairing them to their original state).

Happily, our appreciation of the artifacts of the past now extends to our commercial culture. Organizations like the Chicago-based Society for Commercial Archeology, fighting to preserve everything from historic diners to drive-in movies, add new members every year. And signs, too, have found their champions.

The Hollywood Sign Trust led the way in 1978 by raising the funds to restore and protect the famous HOLLYWOOD sign. Similarly motivated Bostonians succeeded in the mid-1980s in winning landmark status for the great green-and-white Citgo spectacular that overlooks Fenway Park. Baltimore preservationists are seeking the same recognition for their city's beloved vintage Domino Sugar spectacular (which was built in 1951 by Artkraft Strauss). Los Angeles had the nation's first Museum of Neon Art, founded by artist Lili Lakich, whose restored classic neon signs grace the entertainment center, Century City Walk. Philadelphia's popular giant neon frankfurter and other endangered favorites have been lovingly restored by Len Davidson, a former sociology professor called to the cause. And Las Vegas's long-awaited Neon Museum finally opened in 1997.

A classical revival does not mean merely duplicating old forms. Imitation is bad nostalgia. Rather, it means applying classical forms, proportions, and values to new ideas, using new technologies and new insights.

At the cutting edge of the arts, a number of painters, poets, writers, and composers, tired of the political and cultural orthodoxy that has come to define the "avant-garde," have declared themselves liberated. Stefania de Kenessey, founder of a burgeoning movement that she whimsically calls the Derriere Guard, declared in 1997: "What was once revolutionary is now the ruling orthodoxy...the avant-garde has become the status quo. A new generation of artists are actively re-engaging history.... They neither regress to the distant past nor yearn for a now vanished world; instead, they strike out in an altogether different direction. By fusing tradition with innovation... they offer a radically new alternative for the art of the new millennium."

## "It's the Real Thing"

Classical values in form, technology, and emotion have shaped the 1990s and point the way to the future.

In terms of superlative public display, a perfect example of technical innovation in the service of a classic is provided by the Coca-Cola spectacular of 1991. It combines the nearly lost arts of three-dimensionality and mechanical animation with neon, smart computers, and a medium of the future, fiber optics, to create a dazzling icon whose spirit harks back to the first illuminated frosty bottle of Coke that lit up in the Square eighty years before.

When we signed the $3 million contract for the new Coca-Cola sign at Two Times Square in January of 1991, nobody knew exactly what the sign was going to look like. There was a general concept, but no details. No one had built a great three-dimensional display in Times Square in many years. The section of the contract entitled "Scope of Work," which usually says things like "Logo will be 8' H-type Channel Letters per Drawing #A21(b) fabricated of .080 enameled aluminum in preapproved color with 14 mm neo-ruby tubing 4" o.c.," instead said little more than "This will be the most dazzling, eye-popping, inimitable, and memorable outdoor display ever crafted by the hand of Man."

Less intrepid sign makers—or any sensible business folk—might have said, "Wait a minute. Suppose six months from now there's a change in management, and the new people say, 'Gee, I don't think that is the most dazzling, eye-popping,' etc.—and refuse to pay?" But this was Coca-Cola, a truly classy outfit. Everyone who has dealt closely with them over the years knows that their integrity matches the consistency of their product. Like Dick Clark, they are perfectionists with soul. Their old-fashioned business philosophy of "doing well by doing good" serves the public's interests while it serves their own. For example, the price of a Coke is about the same all over the world—as a percentage of the average local hourly wage. The same Coke that costs 75 cents in New York City may cost 3 cents in Senegal, where a civil servant earns $50 per month.

The contract was a "design-build." To save time, construction would start before the design and engineering were finalized—while the new building was still going up. The display, along with the Suntory and Samsung spectaculars "stacked" above it, would be attached directly to the building's steel, and was expected to be completed and lit—and paying rent to the building owner—before the interior of the building was completed and occupied.

Coke conducted a design competition—even the octogenarian Douglas Leigh weighed in, with a proposal to demothball the Epok sign—and came up with nothing that the Coke folk considered sufficiently "dazzling."

Finally, in a stroke of insight, Coke's engineers brought in their packaging team, who work, albeit on a much smaller scale, in three dimensions all the time. And they came up with the concept. My brother, Jonathan, project manager Bob Jackowitz, and the other creative sign men at Artkraft Strauss worked with these engineers and packagers to ultimately create what indeed turned out to be "the most dazzling, eye-popping, inimitable, and memorable outdoor display ever crafted by the hand of Man."

The centerpiece of the 55-ton display is a 42-foot-tall model of the iconic Coca-Cola bottle, nestling in a monumental mound of internally lit ice cubes. A sculptor was engaged to design the ice cubes. I remember him sitting at the conference table along with the rest of the design team for hours at a time, carefully contemplating a bowl of melting ice cubes. If the cubes were too fresh and sharp-edged, they might appear overly aggressive. But if too melted down, they'd seem droopy and flaccid: also the wrong image. Advertising artists take such issues very seriously. Coca-Cola's project managers, Ray Morgan and engineer John Varrieur, were incredibly patient, as if they were planning a cathedral honoring their product. Which, in a way, they were.

The bottle had to be dynamic: not merely an icon but an icon implying action. We promised it would appear to fill and empty, as if quenching a giant's unslakable thirst. But how to accomplish this? Jonathan, Bob, construction foreman Al Miller, and the Coke engineers studied the properties of all kinds of liquids and lighting effects, even considering the possibility of constructing a tank inside the building behind the bottle and pumping Coke-colored water back and forth. But what about below-zero temperatures or a joker with a BB gun?

Finally they decided to create the illusion with fiber optics—

nearly 60 miles of 120-mil tubing embedded in molded fiberglass—the first large-scale display use of this new optical technology. The Coca-Cola–colored bottle, when unlit from the neck down, appears to be full. As the 66,500 points of sparkling bottle-green light twinkle on, sweeping from top to bottom, the bottle lights up and the beverage appears to vanish, as if quaffed through a colossal straw.

So how about a colossal straw? The bottle was equipped with a six-foot bottle cap that slips off by tilting to the right, moved by a concealed robotic arm. A sprinkling of strobe lights suggests liberated effervescence. Then a red-and-white acrylic candy-striped straw emerges eight feet from inside the bottle to meet the lips of an imaginary giant—who then empties the bottle.

Imaginary giants aside, this display ascends into the realm of science fiction with its use of futuristic technology. Besides the fiber optics, which had hitherto been used primarily for communications and in medical applications, the robotics provided a fascinating challenge. Mechanical devices are never completely reliable, and the consequences of a midair collision between, say, the undescended straw and the bottle cap returning to its position, or the turning, neon-covered periactoids ("triads," as we came to call them) that form the sign's background, would be unpleasant, especially 110 feet above Seventh Avenue.

To create the necessary fail-safe mechanisms, we hired a firm that designs robotics for the NASA Space Shuttle. Their task was to make sure that the five separate computers that control the various elements of the display communicate properly with one another.

The sign is extraordinarily intelligent. It has temperature sensors built in, as well as two separate anemometers—one shielded from snow, the other fully exposed to weather—capable of shutting down the mechanical features in high winds. And it has its own (unlisted) telephone number, with special software that prevents hackers from getting into the sign via modem and reprogramming it—or, worse, placing a rival soft drink's advertisement on the message center.

When you call up the sign, a vaguely foreign, digital voice greets you with "Hello. This is telephone number XXX-XXXX. Time is 6:42 P.M. Alert condition: 'Okay.' Temperature is 61 degrees: 'Okay.' Electricity is: 'On.' Sound level: 'Okay.' Listen to sound for ten seconds . . .

[sound is heard]. Have a good day." (This may not be what you'd call a best friend, but at least it's communicating.)

If it shuts down for any reason—as it did, for example, during a recent hurricane when wind speeds reached 82 mph—it calls our service department. If there is no answer, it calls, first, the service electricians at their homes, then the project manager at his home, then Jimmy Manfredi, the chief of operations, and then, as a last resort, me. It keeps calling until it reaches a human. It is a startling experience to receive a phone call from a sign in the middle of the night. "Hello. This is telephone number XXX-XXXX. Time is 2:32 A.M. There is a Max 4 fault. Temperature is 37 degrees. Sign is off. Please call back to acknowledge receipt of this message. Have a good day." And believe me, it keeps right on calling until it receives receipt of this message.

## Things Go Better with Koch

*The New Year's Eve sign* lighting on December 31, 1991, had more than the usual number of surprises. The first surprise was that it took place at all. The completion date we had promised was March 15, 1992, and even then there were caveats for inclement weather and technical problems as yet unresolved. So Jonathan and I were fully floored to open up the newspaper one morning in November and discover that plans had been finalized to inaugurate the new display—which was still in pieces all over the place: the bottle at the fiberglass factory in Pennsylvania, the fiber optics in Florida, the message center components in South Dakota, the half-wired triads at our annex in the Bronx—on ABC network television on New Year's Eve, then only six weeks away. "Impossible!" we agreed. And then we proceeded to do it.

The Coca-Cola people themselves achieved the impossible in mid-December. Despite New York City's regular holiday construction moratorium, they managed to close the George Washington Bridge connecting New York and New Jersey at one o'clock in the morning so we could bring the flatbed truck carrying the monster bottle, with its police escort, across. And incredibly, when the truck reached the

New York side, they turned it around and crossed the bridge again, so the helicopter photographer they'd hired to document the journey could get the shot from the other side. Bemused motorists, lined up in their cars at the approaches to the bridge in both states, watched and wondered what the holdup was. But this was Coca-Cola—a corporation larger (and better liked) than most governments!

For the rest of the night, the bottle was parked in Rockefeller Center near the huge Christmas tree, which was roughly the same size as the bottle: another great photo op. And early in the morning, the immense sculpture on its flatbed was gingerly paraded to the site.

The city was wonderfully cooperative in granting a special dispensation from the crane moratorium—they've seen monumental last-minute Times Square New Year's Eve emergencies before—and we had a permit to lift at 6 A.M., before the early-morning breeze and the traffic build up.

We blocked off the street and rigged the bottle. The harness was ingeniously designed to hold the assembly at a certain angle while it was being lifted into place, and then it would "slip" into position. The lift went as planned—except when the smooth-sided, 7,300-pound bottle, dangling from its steel cable, "slipped" into position sooner than it was supposed to, flipping over like a flapjack in midair. All of us gathered beneath it, holding our breath and watching the lift, scattered like mice.

The bottle was secured, and all of the neon and lamps, and most of the wiring, was completed by New Year's Eve. Granted, a bit of fudging was in order for the TV shot. The mechanical straw and bottle cap, for instance, were not yet operational. So elves (sheet metal workers) inside the bottle operated the long, heavy poles by hand. I imagined electricians holding the ends of the giant feeder cables to complete the circuit and receiving a nice healthy dose of the "cosmic electrical force," à la Tesla.

The New Year's Eve turn-on went perfectly—the first time. I have never been a partisan of Murphy's Law. It seems defeatist to expect the worst. But I do believe in the rule "If it ain't broke, don't fix it." And Coke's advertising agency, risking all for small gain, nearly brought a p.r. disaster down upon its supremely valuable client.

To showcase the sign lighting, Coca-Cola had purchased, at unknown but not insignificant cost, sixty seconds of airtime at 11:53 P.M.

on the ABC network during Dick Clark's "New Year's Rockin' Eve." As spokesmodel they'd hired former mayor and lovable curmudgeon Ed Koch, who since leaving office in 1989 was having a ball as columnist, pundit, and media celebrity. Hizzoner was to stand in front of the ABC cameras on the eighth-floor setback of 1515 Broadway with a great view of the sign, make a brief speech ("Hi! I'm Ed Koch!...") welcoming the renewed Coca-Cola sign to the revived Times Square, and at 11:53:50 fling out his arm and "turn on" the sign.

I was on One Times Square for the lowering of the Ball with New Year's Eve project manager Tony Calvano and his crew, Bob Jackowitz, and Coca-Cola executives and their wives. Bobby Dianuzzo was in charge at the sign at Two Times Square, with a double crew of sign hangers and electricians, and enough walkie-talkies, cellular phones, and flashlights to invade Fredonia. Another Artkraft Strauss team was on the roof of the Bond building on the east side of the Square with the *National Geographic* and Coca-Cola film crews that were documenting the whole thing. And Jonathan, armed with a walkie-talkie, was on the setback at 1515 Broadway with the second ABC crew (the first ABC crew was down on the ground with Dick Clark) and Ed Koch.

The first rehearsal, at 10:15 P.M., went swimmingly. Koch read his speech from the Teleprompter, he flung out his arm, Jonathan signaled Bobby, the sign turned on, and everything was ace. "It's in the can!" announced the ABC people, waving a videocassette. The only thing different from the scene as it would look at nearly midnight was that the crowd was not quite as thick as it would be later.

The second rehearsal, at 11:00, showing a larger street crowd, went just as well. "It's in the can!" said the ABC people. "We have two copies now."

"Play one," Jonathan quietly suggested to the people from Coke's advertising agency, who were with him and the former mayor on the 1515 Broadway roof. "I strongly advise you not to take the chance of doing it live. It works. Don't fix it." Everybody reviewed both versions of the turn-on and agreed that both were perfect.

Then the ad agency people made their fatal interpretation. "We'll ride the winning horse," they said. Meaning that two perfect rehearsals signified that "the real thing" would go even better.

The entrance to the roof was guarded only by one sleepy desk clerk. At 11:52, just as the live turn-on was about to start, an anonymous drunk bulled his way up in the elevator, pushed past the desk clerk and ABC security, staggered onto the set, and kicked over the Teleprompter. Cued by Dick Clark, the live camera turned on. "Hi, I'm—" said Koch, and froze. He forgot his own name! Five or six precious seconds, costly as diamonds, ticked by while the crew scrambled to get the Teleprompter back up.

Koch recovered. "Hi, I'm Ed Koch. How'm I doin'?..." Meanwhile, Jonathan was staring, bug-eyed, at his watch. He knew the sign was supposed to turn on at 11:53:50 and play for ten seconds, but Koch was now running seven seconds late. So he made an instant field decision and signaled Bobby at 11:53:50 to turn on the sign, even though Koch hadn't reached the cue. And it was a good thing he did! Because back at the ABC studios, the technicians, confused, perhaps, by the Koch foul-up, started the following segment, a panty hose commercial, four seconds early. If Jonathan hadn't turned on the sign when he did, its inauguration wouldn't have appeared on TV at all.

"This is Mount Everest," Jonathan said later in an interview in *Sign Business* magazine. "It is the culmination of the sign maker's art, and I doubt we will see its equal in this century." The Coca-Cola display may have been his personal sign Everest. Jonathan left Artkraft soon afterward, seeking comparable challenges in other fields.

## We ... Are ... Information ...

*Throughout this century of invention,* exuberance, and communication, art and technology have allied to create visual wonders. In the 1990s, art and technology seem to have renewed their marriage vows. Improved technology demands more sophisticated art. And modern audiences require better technology, the more readily to process the quantity and quality of information they crave.

Signs learned to talk very early. As soon as there were electric signs, somebody invented message centers—then called "talking signs." The capacity of signs to talk has been greatly improved, but we still use them in much the same way.

Illuminated time-and-temperature displays go back almost to the turn of the twentieth century, as do "counting clocks"—displays that inform the audience how many people have shopped at Macy's, or, counting backward, how many days, hours, and minutes are left until the start of the County Fair. In the mid-1980s, with the advent of personal computers and the consequent appreciation of information as a commodity, counting clocks suddenly proliferated. They counted everything: the number of people worldwide who had seen *Les Misérables,* the number of minutes until the start of the Olympics, the number of seconds until the start of the millennium (incorrectly believed to be January 1, 2000). Sometimes they counted things that had no essential meaning, as with one puzzling display, installed on billboards across the country, that purported to show how many dollars Americans were saving by using the sponsor's telephone service. (As compared with what?)

Sometimes a clock's function was not commercial, but simply to raise awareness. One public-spirited citizen, gadfly Seymour Durst, commissioned us to build a "National Debt Clock" that shows the national debt—a mere $2,000,000,000,000 (that's two trillion dollars) at the time the clock was built—rising at the alarming rate of $13,000 per second. The clock's computer continuously divides the total debt by the current population of the United States to display "Your Family's Share," which of course is also constantly rising—considerably faster than the population is increasing. This graphic dramatization, with the digits on the far right changing faster than the eye can see, enables the public to grasp the enormity of the issue far more clearly than a plain statement of the facts. I was impressed by the way workers in my factory, while the clock was under construction, approached the visiting customer and asked, "Mr. Durst, what's *my* family's share?" They got it—even before the display was hooked up!

Mr. Durst's clock was widely copied, and even parodied. Another man with a cause commissioned a "National Death Clock," which purported to display the number of gun-related deaths in the United States in a given year. This morbid rooftop display not only gave a numerical "count" of gunshot deaths, with associated news stories; it also featured an animation sequence in which marching cartoon citizens were randomly blown away by a menacing, gun-toting hand. This was not our most popular sign.

The effect of these displays is not only to make people smarter and better informed. More important, the displays make us *feel* smarter and better informed. The impact is not merely informational, but emotional as well. And this effect is multiplied exponentially in the case of the reigning granddaddy of information displays, which adorns the world headquarters of the dignified investment banking house Morgan Stanley, at 1585 Broadway.

To me, the most important feature of this display, which Artkraft Strauss built in 1995, is that it is not a sign. It is a manifestation of pure intelligence—and in the form of architecture, no less. By substituting a real-time, computerized data system for the base building's curtain wall, it transforms an entire building into an information device. This represents a completely new way of looking at information, architectural embellishment, and corporate image. And behind the scenes, it employed a number of technological innovations that the sheer massiveness of the project was able to command.

The building, a cool blue prism, was designed in 1987 by the noted architectural firm of Gwathmey Siegel for Solomon Equities, the developers who led the unsuccessful fight in the mid-1980s against the Times Square Zoning. After standing nearly empty for a number of years, it was bought out of bankruptcy by the investment bank, which had originally been slated to be the building's prime tenant. The challenge was to reconcile the new owner's traditionally low-key image—as icy as its new headquarters—with the exuberant, entertainment-oriented Times Square environment and its matching set of zoning requirements mandating brightness, animation, and glitter. Superficially, this presented a dilemma. The two sets of values appeared diametrically opposed. The synthesis—the common meeting ground, as it were—turned out to be information. And more: it is information in motion, signifying the dynamics of an ever-changing world.

Across the front of the building, filling the space between horizontal rows of windows, are three 160-foot-wide traveling messages, made of crisp-looking, amber LEDs. The top one, 10 feet tall, carries the Dow Jones financial news headlines. The middle one, 12 feet tall, is the New York Stock Exchange stock ticker. The bottom one, also 12 feet tall, carries the NASDAQ prices. During the day, while the markets are open, the information is carried in real time as it comes from the exchanges—unlike on TV's financial networks, where it appears after a fifteen-minute delay—and the three amber ribbons, traveling at different, irregular speeds, create an interesting visual syncopation. (At night, when the markets are closed, the tickers rerun the closing prices, and the day's syncopation is preserved.)

Artkraft Strauss' project manager, once again, was creative director Bob Jackowitz, a sorcerer with a slide rule whom we sometimes call Dr. Science. Bob understands that a small detail can make the difference between something that is merely wonderful and something that is great. The three tickers don't travel flat across the face of the building, but emerge perpendicular to the long facade and travel a couple of feet before making a 90-degree turn, and then disappear back into the building the same way. Although it would have been easier to "break" the motographs at the corners, allowing the information to leap the resulting small gaps, Bob managed, after much head scratching and calculation, to configure the LED pixels into a smooth curve, and worked with the supplier's project manager, Jerry Young of Daktronics, to get them manufactured that way. Now the information seems to zoom around the curves, giving continuity to a particular illusion.

"The information is the building, and the building is Morgan Stanley," says Bob. "The idea is that for the information to appear integral to Morgan Stanley, it has to emerge smoothly as if from the heart of the building, travel, and reenter the building smoothly, as if for reprocessing."

On the side walls of the building, a pair of 30-by-60-foot, 256-color LED video-data boards provide animated financial information—world currency exchange rates, precious metal and commodity prices, and the like. The corners of the building, at the base, were turned into cylindrical, internally illuminated world maps, an imposing 44 feet tall, that indicate the time in the time zones around the world where Morgan Stanley has offices.

The name of the sponsor of the 3 million LEDs and all the data they convey barely appears. Its modesty masks a profounder message. "We are information," the building seems to say with quiet pride. And, on a subtler level, "We know you are smart, and we help you become smarter."

Morgan Stanley flatters its viewers, but it doesn't make them grin.

In contrast to dignified, steady-state Morgan Stanley, which almost seems to be entertaining in spite of itself, is Las Vegas's Big-Bang Fremont Street—where the imagery ranges from the hokey to the sublime, but never fails to thrill.

## Viva Las Vegas!

*For technologically induced smiles,* surges of sentiment, and rushes of exhilaration, we must travel to Las Vegas for a visit to the Morgan Stanley display's distant cousin—an equally brainy but much jollier extravaganza that can fill the "sky" over our heads with streaking jet airplanes, place us in the middle of a buffalo stampede, and kiss us a tearful goodbye with "Happy Trails to You."

It is, quite simply, the best show in Vegas. And it's free.

The display, created and built by YESCO, is called the Fremont Street Experience. It isn't on the Strip, that wonderfully grandiose multibillion-dollar architectural hash of pretend Wonders of the World and individual hotel-casino-entertainment complexes the size of small towns—it's downtown, on the main street of old Las Vegas that was once known as Glitter Gulch, a four-block district lined with the city's oldest casinos, and presided over by one of its earliest icons, the giant paint-and-neon cowboy known as Vegas Vic.

The display covers that entire stretch of Fremont Street with an arched canopy, a space frame on which are mounted nearly two million lamps. The lamps, in half a million pixels of four lamps each, comprise a vast concave viewing area that becomes a roof over the street below, now a pedestrian mall between casinos.

Six times a night, the casinos' neon-encrusted walls go dark, and the crowds gathered in the mall are treated to a six-minute animated sky show, orchestrated to a musical medley played over a big, warm, wonderfully clear sound system. Each show is, in effect, an extended music video designed to be shown on an overhead screen the size of four football fields. And each show is themed—among them "Viva Las Vegas!" replete with familiar Vegas denizens, leggy chorus girls, and celebrity caricatures; a country-and-western potpourri of cowboy-gaited standards; and a space age journey through surreal dimensions to a prehistoric planet covered by lush rain forest and populated by fantastic birds.

The quarter-mile-long image area is aptly called a "raceway," a visual fast track for all that marches, dances, prances, gallops, soars, and whooshes. A pair of Vegas kick lines, legs only, pumps in perfect formation across the electric ceiling. Sashaying cowgirls melt into long lines of clapping hands and tapping feet. A giant American flag unfurls the entire length of the arched canopy.

YESCO designed a cap, inspired by the backup light on a 1948 school bus, to place over each pixel that would diffuse the light and make the entire image visible from any vantage point. Each pixel, says YESCO, can produce 65,536 colors. The 121 computers used to control just the video portion of the show produce 3.5 billion lamp transitions each second. The on-line data storage capacity is 96 gigabytes.

The Fremont Street Experience cost $65 million, a price the average American mall would find laughably out of reach. But this is Vegas; ten downtown casinos bankrolled the project. The display was intended to bring new customers to a down-at-the-heels business district left behind long ago by the rapid growth of the Strip. And generate new business it has—so much, in fact, that the casinos paid off the display sooner than expected.

These snappy light-and-sound production numbers—the work of the Jerde Partnership of Venice, California—are futuristically hip and classically cartoon-sweet, and we're keenly aware of both of these forces converging as we allow ourselves to be borne along on their seamless streams of colorful image and music. The immense size and obvious technical complexity of the display is a show, and a statement, in itself. This is America at the millennium, it says. We Do Technology Right! A cartoon image on a flat screen wouldn't wow us. But this extravaganza happens all around us, fills our eyes and ears, washes over us. We're literally inside it. At the same time, the old-fashioned cartoon programming connects us to the past. The songs and the singers are so familiar—Roy and Dale are as recognizable as Mom and Dad—almost anyone in the world, including Vegas's millions of foreign visitors, would know them.

These big little shows are a world away from the standard Vegas hard-sell pitches for gambling and stage extravaganzas that bombard visitors from the minute they step off the plane. There's nary a mention of a specific casino or tourist attraction. And the only references to gambling are glimpses of cartoon dice and slot machines. Instead, the shows are selling pure emotion—laughter, patriotism, wonder, and solidarity with a common culture.

Like the great classic spectaculars of Times Square, the Fremont Street electronic shows are public theater, to be experienced communally. The up-turned faces express the same wonderment people felt when they stood on the street and looked up at the bouncing Floradora girls, the great green Heinz pickle, the playful Corticelli kitten, the placid Wrigley fish, and smart, cheery Little Lulu on her magnificent flying trapeze.

Nightly now, Fremont Street has become Las Vegas's version of a people's park. A feeling of community prevails as the watchers stand together under the electric sky and share these happy minutes. The technology is new but the psychology is timeless.

A final example of 1990s-style high-tech in the service of communal emotion is provided by the 102-foot-long Concorde that was parked on Seventh Avenue for three days in 1996.


## "THE PLANE! THE PLANE!"

*The cold November rain, threatening* for hours, finally came just as we were ready for liftoff. It was 1 A.M. on the Tuesday before Thanksgiving, 1996. The sleek white half-size scale model of the British Airways Concorde sat on the street in its harness, the cables taut, ready to be lifted by the giant crane to its berth on the roof of Hansen's Brewery on 42nd Street between Broadway and Seventh Avenue, the southernmost limit of Times Square.

The small crowd of photographers, British Airways executives, and other exhausted die-hard onlookers who had waited for this moment since Saturday morning dispersed to the perimeter of the staging area. From the shelter of the doorway of the Disney store across the street I watched as the monster crane, towering against the shadowy night sky like a mechanical brontosaurus, growled and stirred slightly. The airplane rose a few inches from the pavement.

The crews manning the tag lines that fanned out in all directions took up the slack.

Tony Calvano, Artkraft Strauss' installation supervisor, stood alone in the center of the rain-slick intersection, soaked to the skin. With a walkie-talkie pressed to his ear, he waved hand signals to the crane operator and the teams on the tag lines with the grace and passion of a maestro. With his leonine shock of silver hair, he reminded me of a construction-sized version of Toscanini conducting "The Ride of the Walkyries."

Inch by laborious inch, the airplane began its stately rise. As if by magic, the police had arrived at just the right moment and stopped the traffic, still crawling steadily through Times Square even at that hour. There were no impatient horns. The people in the cars and trucks watched in hypnotized silence, as did the soggy little throng filling nooks and crannies, in doorways, behind parapets, and under construction bridges, around the intersection. Only the snarl of the crane and the pelting of the rain could be heard as the baby Concorde levitated in majestic slow motion. I wondered how many other watchers heard music in their heads.

*The British Airways display,* with its Concorde replica flying in place above one of the city's busiest intersections, began like so many others—with a customer's vague desire for a big, bold statement in Times Square. Bob Jackowitz, again the project manager, suggested a three-dimensional tableau of an aircraft soaring above the clouds. British Airways and its advertising agency loved the idea and quickly made it their own.

The supersonic Concorde was chosen, though it isn't a new aircraft, because it's still state-of-the-art in air passenger travel. It was a wise choice. The Concorde, which has been streaking back and forth across the Atlantic since 1976, has an aura of romance and exoticism that is undiminished by time. Only the wealthiest air travelers can afford the fare—about ten times the price of an ordinary ticket for a New York–London flight. At the airport, the Concorde gate is out of sight on its own concourse, and Concorde travelers demurely guard their low profile. So a distant glimpse of the futuristic birdlike Concorde taking off or landing, its needle nose pointed toward the ground, is as close as the average person ever gets to this glamorous symbol of the supersonic.

British Airways enthusiastically added to our team Jim Edwards, one of the aeronautical engineers who designed the original Concorde. This was to be an exact scale model, accurate to the smallest detail. Our indefatigable in-house technology detective, research and development director David Ramirez, invited proposals from a number of real aircraft airframe builders. The savviest of these proved to be L&L Tooling, the father-and-son firm of Kevin and Leigh Lorenson of Itasca, Texas. They said they could build a Concorde model so airworthy, it would actually fly if it had half-size engines and a diminutive crew. That wouldn't be necessary. What the model would have to do, however, would be to "fly" in diagonal place, five to seven stories above Times Square, in all kinds of weather for as many years as British Airways wanted it to.

This was the fun part. But it couldn't begin until the plan ran the 42nd Street gauntlet. Besides pleasing the customer, the design had to pass muster by the landlord—our partner, Times Square Center Associates (TSCA), in turn a partnership between Prudential Insurance and Park Tower Realty—who didn't want anything "too" spectacular, lest people fall in love with it and use it to delay construction of the office buildings they were still hoping to build; by various cells and departments within the Departments of Buildings (DOB) and City Planning (DCP); and by the 42nd Street Development Project (42DP)—the new name of the 42nd Street Redevelopment Project—a subsidiary of the Empire State Development Corporation (ESDC), the New York State superagency in charge of the revitalization of the Deuce.

We needed the cooperation of TSCA, DOB, DCP, 42DP, and ESDC to override DUO.

The DUO—the Design, Use, and Occupancy guidelines governing the "look and feel" of the 42nd Street Project area—was created under the aegis of Rebecca Robertson, originally the Project's vice president for design and later its president. Happily, Rebecca was a longtime partisan of bright lights and snazzy signs, so thanks to her vision, the survival of these vital elements is guaranteed. But unhappily, the design for the Concorde was out of compliance.

The irony of DUO is that, like ZR 81-732, the zoning amendment that governs the Square north of 42nd Street, it represents an attempt by government to legislate spontaneity. What an oxymoron! But the sobering fact is that without this government intervention, today's Times Square might not have any signs at all.

So the DUO rules. And like all laws, the DUO is highly specific. But the Concorde wouldn't meet the letter of it. It wouldn't snap, crackle, or pop. It would contain no neon and, apart from the window and wing lights, very little self-contained lighting. Nothing about it would be animated. Yet it would be a spectacular, and a highly innovative one, in every sense of the spirit of spectacularity. It would be grand and imposing, dramatic and luminous. It wouldn't move, but it would embody movement. It would make an imaginative statement. And the workmanship in it would be obviously impeccable.

The ESDC didn't disagree with any of this. But rules are rules, and there were forms to be filled out, drawings to be drawn, charts to be charted, calculations to be amassed. We measured the exact surface area of a Concorde and calculated how much light would reflect off its glossy white fuselage. We charted sight lines and promised floodlights of bold intensity to assure a prominent place in the field of view of every man, woman, and child visiting the fabled intersection. We demonstrated that the Concorde would shortchange neither looks nor LUTS as mandated by the DUO's complex luminosity requirements. The bean counters counted behind us every step of the way.

In the end, we got our variance, as we knew we would.

— O —

*The convoy of eight* flatbed trucks that brought the disassembled Concorde from Texas arrived Friday evening and sat on the New Jersey side of the George Washington Bridge until the early hours of Saturday morning, when loads of that size could be escorted across. Our crew was waiting in Times Square. By the time the first hint of dawn appeared in the cloudy night sky, the first sections of the fuselage were laid out in a three-lane section of Seventh Avenue just south of 42nd Street. This site was to become our home away from home for the next three days.

Early risers in Times Square may well have imagined that the

Seabees were building an airstrip in Times Square in preparation for an invasion. Overnight, a 200-foot crane had materialized from far-off Brooklyn. Trucks were everywhere, all containing identifiable aircraft sections. The area was cordoned off and crawling with workers. Slowly the Concorde began to take shape. Even jaded New Yorkers stopped to take a look.

Tony prowled the work site like a restless bear. He inspected, advised, tested, poked, and probed. He gave orders into his walkie-talkie. He flipped open his cell phone and took endless calls. Tony doesn't suffer fools gladly, whether their folly is intentional or not. A growl from him, and the hammering, drilling, and welding in his immediate vicinity escalated noticeably.

Sign companies all over America routinely lift and install large displays in public places using scaffolding, cranes, and even helicopters. Each job poses its own hazards and challenges. Each job is dramatic, theatrical, and unique. The only common denominator is that the world is watching. And no place is trickier or more visible than Times Square. Hemmed in by walls of concrete and glass, bedeviled by winds that whip through the man-made canyons, pressured by endless impatient traffic, scrutinized by—literally—more than a million passersby each day, the Times Square sign installer's job is as tough as any in the industry.

The city swarms around any job site. Gawking tourists want to stand directly under whatever we're lifting and look up. (City regulations don't allow this, and neither do we.) Angry cabdrivers with impatient passengers and hungry meters cast aspersions on our lineage in a hundred languages. Truck and delivery van operators imagine we live just to frustrate their schedules. Parades of city officials flip badges in our faces and demand to inspect the stacks of permits required for each job.

Tony was at the center of this swirl late Saturday afternoon, when things started to go wrong. The 102-foot-long model was being assembled on a city street with curbs, bumps, and depressions, not a flat factory floor like that on the dry run in Texas, and the pieces didn't go together as smoothly as expected. Sidewalk superintendents were generous with advice that wasn't always graciously received. Hamburgers and coffee weren't enough to revive an exhausted crew. By nightfall, Tony sent everyone home. The airplane sat alone, under the watchful eye of two burly Artkraft Strauss porters.

By then, the word was out: a Concorde had "landed" on Seventh Avenue. WINS Radio carried the news. So did WCBS. Newscopters from WNBC and WABC hovered overhead, beaming the aerial shot of the model airplane parked in Times Square to thousands of homes. It would "take off" again Sunday morning, they told the world, and "land" on the roof of Hansen's Brewery. Film at eleven.

Sunday morning dawned cold, clear, and bright—and a little too soon for Tony. I found him and the men hard at work, like the crew of a Broadway show in the final hours before opening, taking advantage of the last lull before the audience starts to arrive. Will the paint be dry when the curtain goes up? If that trapdoor doesn't open in the second act...?

The British Airways public relations contingent showed up first and established a beachhead in Hansen's second-floor dining room, all the better to see the street through the glass walls. British Airways banners were taped to the windows. Urns of coffee and trays of muffins and bagels appeared. Real Concorde flight attendants on their way to work—stunning young women who looked like, on the whole, they'd rather be in London, and indeed would be, in time for dinner—were on hand to dress up the photo ops that were sure to abound.

Next came the press: newspaper and radio reporters, television crews, and a platoon of still photographers in well-worn ski jackets and Banana Republic vests with dozens of pockets, urban combat-ready lenspersons all. They picked their vantage points, lined the rooftops of surrounding buildings, and waited.

The romance of the Concorde is profound. I didn't know how profound—and I don't think British Airways knew either—until things started to go wrong again.

With photographers lining the staging area like soldiers on the rim of a canyon, the appointed hour for the liftoff came and went. A new hour was set, and it too came and went.

Finally, Tony signaled the crane operator to proceed. Gingerly, the great arm moved and the cables on the harness went taut. The model lifted a foot or so off the pavement—and we heard a loud *snap!*

A single eyebolt in the right wing had sprung. It wasn't a major structural failure, but it was a warning. It advised us to revisit the entire engineering of this massive structure.

While the BA execs and their p.r. folks fretted, we held a coffee-fueled emergency meeting around a table in Hansen's—Tony, Bob Jackowitz, David Ramirez, sheet metal foreman Al Miller, structural engineer Scott Lewis, the Lorensons from Texas. Sketching trusses and calculating loads on paper napkins, we decided to fabricate additional bracing for the entire interior of the aircraft and weld it in place. While we did this, the Concorde was grounded for another thirty-six hours.

In the end, it was bad news that turned out to be not so bad after all.

As the newscopters hovered and the thick Sunday traffic crawled around us, something quite wonderful began to happen. People came in droves to see the Concorde. They came from all the five boroughs, New Yorkers and tourists alike. They came from New Jersey and Long Island and Connecticut and even Pennsylvania. They were amateur photographers who came to make dramatic pictures, airplane buffs who wanted to talk specifications and stats, toy buffs who could only dream of owning something like this, parents looking for something cool and affordable to do with their kids, believers in otherworldly phenomena who suspected there was more going on than the media were reporting.

We set up a pedestrian lane on the sidewalk, and the flow of admiring humanity never stopped. They chatted and laughed. No one was hostile or weird. All the normal New York rules governing eye contact and suspicion of strangers were suspended. Minicams were everywhere, as if this were a wedding reception or a bar mitzvah. They photographed us and traded cameras to photograph one another.

Early on, a homeless man appointed himself traffic coordinator, standing beside the orange ribbon at the street side of the work site, waving vehicles through and loudly admonishing drivers not to dawdle. He was a stocky man with a silver crew cut and tattooed forearms like Popeye's, wearing a tattered army camouflage vest—and even the most cantankerous cabbies obeyed him. He stayed at his chosen post the whole time, asking for nothing—though Tony slipped him a few

dollars and fed him when he fed the crew. Police officers from the local station, who stopped by every few hours to check on our progress,
openly admired his professionalism, and left him alone.

Through it all, the giant baby Concorde—as long as a ten-story
building is tall—was the center of attention. The visitors walked to the
needle nose and sighted along the model's long white body. They
walked to the right wingtip and looked across the swept-back expanse of the wingspread to the left wingtip. They walked to the tail,
peered inside the mock supersonic jet engines, and sighted along the
body from astern.

Everyone wanted to touch the model—but not before looking
furtively around first, like a museumgoer checking to see if the guard
is watching. The Concorde is, indeed, a sensuous object, begging to
be touched. As one young woman observed: "It's so erotic. You just
want to *be* with it."

Everyone wanted to peek inside too, but we couldn't let them. We
didn't want anyone climbing onto the wing, and besides, we were re-
luctant to shatter the illusion. There's nothing inside the plane but
steel ribs and beams, wreaths of wires, and banks of fluorescent
tubes. But an amazing number of people were prepared to believe
that inside the plane was a fully equipped pint-sized cockpit, rows of
small leather seats, and a diminutive crew serving little glasses of
champagne. Many asked where the Concorde had flown from before
landing on Seventh Avenue.

Someone started a rumor—duly reported in at least one newspaper as fact—that the police had issued the plane a ticket for parking
facing the wrong way on a one-way street and had ordered the pilot
to request takeoff clearance from the FAA immediately. Most people
knew better, of course, but joined in the game anyway, so compelling
was the fantasy.

The Concorde had a magnetism no one had anticipated. In the
imaginations of the visitors, it really was from another world—a world
of affluence and jet-set exoticism usually accessible only through television and the movies. Now, here was a symbol of that world reduced
to touchable proportions, like a pet.

The work site continued to be a people's park through two Monday rush hours and the bustling holiday season workday in between.
The traffic police weren't happy; they wanted us to take our big crane

and go home. The British Airways executives and their p.r. contingent weren't happy—despite our reminding them that takeoffs are often delayed due to technical difficulties, and that, in any case, safety supersedes punctuality. Tony and his crew, past exhaustion, weren't happy at all. But the visitors and photographers, and the television news crews reporting in a dozen languages, couldn't get enough of the snappy little Concorde.

— ◯ —

*The music in my* head changed from "The Ride of the Walkyries" to the more appropriate first movement of Dvořák's *New World Symphony*. What we were witnessing was the arrival of a new advertising life into reborn Times Square, not the departure of a slain warrior to Sign Valhalla.

The rain was coming down harder, and Tony and his crews had maneuvered the giant airborne model to a spot above the corner of the building and were about to make the turn. The Concorde was "banked" wildly, frozen in shadowy midair, held steady by lines fanning out in all directions.

The geometry was unbelievable. During the 90-degree turn, the 38,000-pound plane had to do an intricate series of bobs and dips to avoid—with inches to spare—the maze of light poles and construction bridges surrounding the intersection. Photographers' strobes flashed at intervals, filling the entire corner of Times Square with bursts of light that glistened off the white surface of the jet.

I was startled to see personnel from two competing sign installers manning the tag lines alongside our crews. Some had been working in the neighborhood that night; others just happened by to see what their fellow sign hangers were up to. Moved by the sense of mission that drove their counterparts—and by the same desire to touch the project that moved the public—they had volunteered to help, and were welcomed. There is a brotherhood, after all.

So even hardened professionals were susceptible to the romantic power of the model Concorde. We all knew that, fundamentally, all we were lifting that night was a big hunk of outdoor advertising, nineteen tons of steel covered with fiberglass resin, an object with no life or power of its own. And yet, we were all willing to let our imaginations transform it into the embodiment of romantic myth.

No one understood this better than Al Miller, our quietly brilliant sheet metal foreman. Al had designed a much less conspicuous but even more challenging component of the display: the three tall, slim stanchions, each a different height, upon which the model aircraft rests in its perpetual flight. Al devised a combination of hydraulic jacks, adjustable cables with turnbuckles, and tractor-size wrenches that allowed each post to be moved those critical few inches necessary to fit the small "feet" of the aircraft perfectly into their berths. No one could be sure whether Al's invention would work until the plane was poised in place, hanging by its cables, and it was too late to turn back. He had to be worried. But the magic of the moment worked on him too.

Al waited patiently with his crews on the scaffolds around the three stanchions as the liftoff proceeded down below. They heard the snarl of the crane on the otherwise remarkably silent street. They saw the ghostly flash on the sides of buildings every time one of the strobes went off. Then the top of the Concorde slowly rose over the parapet at the edge of the roof.

"I've got to say it was awesome," says Al, who rarely uses words like "awesome." "It just rose slowly, majestically, up in front of us, like a spaceship. It wasn't just another sign. It was like being in a movie."

By then the roof was where the action was. Tony moved his command post up there, still guiding the crane operator by radio. I rushed up the stairs in time to see the airplane hovering above the stanchions. Very...very...slowly...with many minute adjustments... the massive aircraft was lowered into place and bolted in.

To say we were relieved would be like remarking that the neon lights are bright on Broadway.

Thousands of people pass by the display every day now. I doubt that it sells rides on the Concorde to most of them. But the soaring image of the airplane and the airline that flies it touches them anyway. The Concorde will surely fly in their memories of Times Square, and perhaps even in their dreams, long after the model is gone.

*Standing on the roof in* the shimmering rain that night, we felt the elation of a mission accomplished. And as I stood in the shadows of the newly landed aircraft cast by the work lights, I felt something more.

I looked down at 42nd Street. Around the corner to the south, the Corticelli kitten wrestled endlessly with that great lighted spool of thread nearly ninety years ago. A block north, Little Lulu leaped from her trapeze onto the giant box of Kleenex in the 1950s. Across the way, the platoon of World War I-era Wrigley Spearmen went through their calisthenic paces in a block-long electrical profusion of multi-colored peacock tails, lush forests, and Beaux-Arts bric-a-brac. At that moment, I understood Times Square as a time portal. I felt connected to all the sign makers who preceded me. I could feel the electric spirit of their creative work still burning.

At the same time, I could see the signs of the future—a panorama bright with possibility. Blue lasers, forming intense, full-color projections. Audio-animatronic holograms. Electric paint and electric ink. Liquid crystal materials that respond to changes in ambient light, or sound, or weather. Video billboard fabric, cheap, easy to install, and fully programmable. Three-dimensional displays that look different from every angle and even to every viewer. "Virtual" displays that appear and disappear. Interactive displays. Transactional displays. Universally accessible, instant global communications displays. And everything running on wireless power—tapping into the infinite energy fields that pervade the air.

These new display techniques will be costly when first introduced. As with the "old" new technologies, their first patrons will be commercial sponsors—those with the means and motivation to be pioneers. Their needs will force developments that bring down the price, and increase accessibility, for everyone else. Energy-efficient, color-changing liquid-crystal panels, for example, will light up advertising displays well before they illuminate the walls of our homes. But once we see them in the signs, they are on their way into our lives.

The scintillating symbiosis between signs and evolving technology promises to remain constant. As our world becomes larger—full of more information—and smaller—because all of it is connected—fundamentals don't change. The mythic element, Image in the Landscape, remains as important as ever.

What is most amazing to me, as I stand on a rooftop under the soaring Concorde at the corner of 42nd Street and Broadway on a rainy winter night, is the degree to which this ever-changing environment stays the same. The motivation of the advertisers, the attitude of the audience, and the impact of the displays remain constant, whether one looks backward in time or forward.

Old New York hands are fond of telling us that Times Square isn't what it used to be. True enough. The Automat and the Astor Hotel are long gone. But the essence of Times Square remains the same—and that essence is change. The constancy of change, that paradox, is fixed in the environment. It defines the landscape from moment to moment and year to year.

Instantaneously flashing strobes and sequencers, traveling news bulletins refreshed every hour, pictorials transformed overnight, spectaculars rebuilt once in a decade—all combine, like a symphony in light, to express the rhythm, the cadence, the syncopated heartbeat, that animates the Square.

Spectaculars themselves embody change. Their very nature is to express kinetic power. Whether composed of hand-colored lightbulbs and manual switches, neon tubing and electromechanical flashers, or fiber-optic video screens and microcomputers, their purpose remains constant: to bring a corporate image alive with light, motion, and energy.

Change is the essence of life. It's what distinguishes a sequoia from a pyramid, an organic life form from a sterile monument. Times Square, although built by human hands, resists being fixed in time; hence it will never grow old. To adapt and evolve in a changing world, as Times Square and its spectacular art form have done, is the key to the future.